Landmarks of Healing

Landmarks
of
Healing

A Study of *House Made of Dawn*

Susan Scarberry-García

University of New Mexico Press

Albuquerque

The epigraph is from Maud Oakes, ed. with commentary by Joseph Campbell, *Where the Two Came to Their Father: A Navaho War Ceremonial*, given by Jeff King, Bollingen Series 1. Copyright 1943, © 1971 renewed by Princeton University Press and reprinted by permission of Princeton University Press.

Library of Congress Cataloging-in-Publication Data

Scarberry-Garcia, Susan, 1946–
Landmarks of healing: a study of House made of dawn /
Susan Scarberry-García.—1st. ed.
p.   cm.
Includes bibliographical references (p.   ).
ISBN 0-8263-1192-X.—ISBN 0-8263-1193-8 (pbk.)
1. Momaday, N. Scott, 1934–   House made of dawn.   2. Indians
in literature.   I. Title.
PS3563.047H637   1990   89-27559
813'.54—dc20   CIP

For my daughters
Lana and Tania

The unchanging contours of the world of the Navaho few of us have known. Mount Taylor, Black Rock, Black Water Lake, Blanca Peak, San Francisco Peak, and the La Plata Mountains do not confront us, night and day, with their unfathomable silences. We do not hear the yelping of the disreputable coyote. The varieties of lightning, rainbows, and thunder do not come before us as signals from an obscure, all-guiding power: we have explained them mechanically; they are to us no more mysterious now than the universe itself. Furthermore, we have not attended since childhood the elaborate sings of the Navaho, we are not curious to know the sacred origins of the fascinating paraphernalia. Hence the long dwelling of the storyteller on details may serve only to bore us. We should like to hear the narrative move along. It is precisely here, however, that the legend becomes not simply anybody's story, but specifically the Navaho's. The general myth, which in its broadest aspect is known to all mankind, precisely here forcefully applies itself to the local peculiarities of Navaho life.

One cannot but believe that from a thorough study of such a legend as the one here given a rich understanding could be derived of the deep, unconscious attachments that link the Navaho to his world—that is to say, which link Man to the specific phenomena of the American Southwest. For this is a tale built out of a wonderful interaction: an interaction between the cactus-mesas, the great landscapes and colorations of the primeval silences of America, and the human soul.

Spider Woman, Bat Woman, the Cutting Reeds, and the Bear That Tracks are strange to us. That is because America is strange to us. Our fairy world is that of Europe, not of our adopted continent. And yet, it is just possible that the powers of the continent are at work in us, even so. It is possible that the sons of Changing Woman are even now accomplishing within us, slowly and with great pain, the hero task of slaying Enemy Monsters, to establish in a renewed and mighty social image the life potency of the New World.

—Joseph Campbell
Where the Two Came to Their Father:
A Navaho War Ceremonial
1943

Contents

Foreword

Like other contemporary Euroamerican literary traditions, much Native American writing acknowledges alienation and cynicism as the starting point for fiction. Native American writing, however, is attracting more and more readers, precisely because much of it does not accept the brokenness of the present world as an immutable condition of things, but invokes deeper patterns of order and meaning, often rooted in the themes and images of tribal oral traditions, as a means of restoring wholeness. This powerful theme of healing has a long native literary history, in which Momaday's novel, *House Made of Dawn*, holds a special place.

Tribal literatures speak of healing principally as the restoration of harmonious relationships. Assuming the integration of the physical, psychological, and social dimensions of the self, tribal medicine developed ritual therapies that addressed all three. While very little is known of the theory and practice of tribal medicine as it existed prior to European influences, the earliest documents suggest that in addition to physical medicine, healing was also accomplished by psychosocial means. These included rites that reinforced the patient's security in the credibility and importance of those fundamental relationships in the world that were established in the myth time.

The serpent entered the garden in 1492. Christianity undermined the credibility of the myth-sanctioned cognitive and evaluative structures by means of which native peoples ordered the universe. Yet the character of Jesus was not entirely alien, for as Scarberry-García points out in this volume, citing Campbell and Eliade (and, one might add, Otto Rank before them), a globally distributed narrative pattern organizes many hero myths into quests for knowledge, identity, and power that culminate in trial and victory and the transmission of the ritual knowledge acquired at great risk. While Jesus slew no monsters, he certainly could be made to look the part of a culture hero. This was an overt practice among some proselytizing orders who identified Jesus with the Culture Hero and Satan with the Trickster figure. Christian salvation could then be structured as tribal healing was, the conforming of oneself to the pattern of the hero's death and rebirth. For this reason, many Indians, formerly and at present, have had little difficulty in incorporating Jesus into their religious belief and practice alongside their tribal religions.

But if the pattern of healing was familiar at the deepest levels of consciousness, at least in the nineteenth century, it nevertheless had unanticipated and, for many Indians, unwanted consequences. For one thing, the Christian faith was so deeply enculturated in the values and worldview of Euroamerica that indoctrination promoted, often deliberately, the isolation of converts from their tribal communities. The more the pressures of the Anglo world impinged upon Indian people, and manifested themselves in asocial behaviors like alcoholism and violence, the more the Anglo god was proffered as the exclusive recourse. The first Native Americans who wrote in English, men like Samson Occum (1723–92), did so as converts to an alien theology and ideology. Throughout the nineteenth century, many Indians wrote autobiographical narratives of healing based on conversion to Christianity. A few, like William Apes (b. 1798), a Pequot descendant of King Philip and a Methodist minister, could still claim proudly to be both Christian and Indian, but for many healing had required a fateful choice.

The crux of that choice was a radical shift in attitude toward the natural world. Indeed, the very distinction between natural and supernatural, between a created, material, impersonal world and a world of spirits, is alien to Native America, where man not only is in the world, but of it, a person among other kinds of persons. Christianity required the denial of the person-ness of other beings, animate and inanimate, and isolated man as the focus of God's relationship to the world and the fulcrum between the two. At the turn of this century, after Indian reservations had been allocated to different Christian sects for proselytizing, after the final wars and the starvation, after allotment that aimed at transforming Indian tribes into good, Christian homesteaders while expropriating the majority of the land, many Indian people took the measure of Christianity as practiced and found it wanting. Healing took the form of consciously returning to tribal religions or pan-Indian revitalization movements. In 1902 Gertrude Bonnin (Zitkala-Sa), a well-educated Yanktonai Sioux, unashamedly published an essay in *Atlantic* entitled, "Why I Am A Pagan." Later, the Osage writer John Joseph Mathews's novel, *Sundown* (1934), and *The Surrounded* (1936) by the Salishan writer D'Arcy McNickle would tell of the appeal of tribal religion and community tradition to Anglo-educated Indian youth who felt alienated from the land, the community, themselves.

When Momaday's novel, *House Made of Dawn*, appeared in 1968, it signalled the beginning of what Kenneth Lincoln has called a "Native American Renaissance." A modernist exemplar, the novel is rich in contrasts of setting, character, and narrative voice that invites exploration and reflection. But for many readers its virtue lay in its power to elevate the Native American literature of healing, both structurally and thematically, to new levels of complexity and significance. Earlier works, *The Surrounded* for instance, also tried to invoke tribal oral tradition as a matrix for the healing re-formation of the protagonist's character, but did so inadequately. The oral historical narratives that are meant to provide the model for Archilde's restoration are idiosyncratic, bound to historical circumstances, so that one could (though ultimately one doesn't) question their applicability to Archilde's situation. Momaday saw the need to root the history of his protagonist Abel in myth, to invoke the timeless to give significance to a historical moment. Structurally, Momaday wove complex strands of tribal mythic reference as subtext throughout the tapestry of his fiction, rather than blatantly alternate text and pre-text. The result is a more challenging, but also more satisfying experience for the reader, who, as Scarberry-García rightly points out, is, like the novel's protagonist Abel, healed by the recognition of the mythic patterning, the significance, of the apparently mute, idiosyncratic historical moment.

This volume of criticism by Susan Scarberry-García is most welcome as the first, rich booklength analysis of Momaday's use of tribal oral literatures to create a novel of healing. Equally important, this volume not only suggests, but demonstrates the fruitfulness of thinking in new ways about the use of oral traditions as source materials. Two examples come to mind. The first occurs in chapter 2, where the author demonstrates that Momaday depended upon the Washington Matthews text of the Stricken Twins version of the Night Chant origin myth. The fact of this dependence in itself says much about Momaday's interests. Matthews clearly labels it a variant, that is, not the most-often heard version, and indeed, today, few Night Way singers even know of this version, and I doubt if any sing it. But its themes of crippling, inarticulacy, and the power of song, as Scarberry-García points out, were particularly apt for a novel from "The Man Made of Words." Momaday does not adopt the story wholesale, however, and the aesthetic value of Momaday's deviation from his subtext is ably demonstrated in arguing that the novelist "is not restricted to formulaic story patterns" because his protagonist's alienation precludes a neat fit between text and subtext. Again, the third chapter reveals diligent source work in disclosing the bear stories that underlie, even structure the novel. Interesting in themselves, these insights were made even more valuable to me by revising my reading of Angela's role in the novel, especially as they illuminate her growth as a character.

Healing comes to Angela and to Abel as characters, but also to us as readers. Good criticism enables good reading and all good reading makes us whole. This is the best reason to commend Susan Scarberry-García's book to anyone: it provides us, who were somewhat mute like Abel before the novel's intricate power and beauty, with healing words to better articulate our vision.

Andrew Wiget
June 1989   New Mexico State University

Preface

From my home in the southern end of the San Luis Valley, I can see Mount Blanca rising majestically above the cottonwoods, *rios*, and *ranchos* that now glisten with summer rain. Just north of the New Mexico state line, Mount Blanca defines the southern perimeter of the state of Colorado and the eastern border of traditional Navajo hunting territory. This place, where even a hundred-year-old cottonwood is dwarfed by the immense expanse of prairie and irrigated fields in all directions, has been defined and redefined historically by the cluster of stories that tell of the mountain's personal properties and of the human significance of events that have taken place on or near her slopes. For a student of native cultures like myself, to see the Great Sand Dunes that flank Blanca's northwestern side is to remember the adventures of the dual Navajo culture heroes Monster Slayer and Born for Water who appear there in a mythic episode in Enemyway. And to look at the mountain herself, as she ascends 14,000 feet, is to remember the expansive landscapes of *House Made of Dawn* that the character Ben Benally honors in song. When Ben sings "On top of Belted Mountain,/ Beautiful horse— slim like a weasel," he is speaking of Mount Blanca, often snow-capped, banded by dense evergreens. To be in this valley, in all seasons, especially during the spectacular moments of dawn and dusk, is to be "entirely surrounded by beauty," as the Navajo say.

Long passages of this book, *Landmarks of Healing: A Study of*

House Made of Dawn, have been written over the years here in the valley, under the commanding gaze of Blanca. In significant ways the mountain has been the symbolic center of this critical study that was conceived and reworked in Boulder, Colorado Springs, Antonito, Durango, Albuquerque, Los Angeles, and Kauai, Hawaii. My travel, often by train, between family homes in the valley, the Four Corners area, Albuquerque, and Los Angeles, has made the terrain of Momaday's novel ever more vivid and personally meaningful. And it was possible, even when beginning this study on a cliff on the lush north shore of Kauai, for me to imagine the vastness of Navajo sacred space that extends from Blanca to the home of Changing Woman on an island in the Pacific Ocean. Wherever I go within this arc of travel I am reminded of the novel in myriad ways.

My acquaintance with *House Made of Dawn* first began twenty years ago, in the spring of 1969, when the recently published book was required reading for my senior American Literature seminar taught by Professor John Ridland at the University of California at Santa Barbara. My old hard-bound copy of the novel contains detailed notes, gingerly marked in the margin in pencil, so as not to damage the text, so fond was I even initially of Momaday's story. But my paperback copy of the novel is like this old adobe ranch house—colorful, lived-in, and in need of constant repair.

It so happened that N. Scott Momaday was my freshman English teacher at the University of California at Santa Barbara in 1965. As I sat in a small auditorium looking up at Professor Momaday at the podium, it never occurred to me that the formal, impeccably dressed man could be a Kiowa Indian working on a novel that would change the course of my life. Years later when he returned from Berkeley to give a reading on our campus, I was privileged to introduce him and write an article for the student newspaper *El Gaucho* about his talk. The next time I saw him was in the early 1970s at a retreat conference on the D.H. Lawrence ranch. The ranch lies in the Sangre de Cristo mountains above San Cristobal, New Mexico, northwest of Taos, sixty miles as the magpie flies from where I now live near the Conejos River on my husband's ancestral family ranch. What I remember most from the conference was Momaday's disclosure that he had had a conversation with David (D.H.) the night before near one of the cabins that Lawrence had occupied when he had been living there in the 1920s. Much to the audience's surprise, Momaday had evoked the spirit of Lawrence in much the same way that Ko-sahn, the ancient Kiowa woman, had been remanifested in person in Momaday's study when he was finishing *The Way to Rainy Mountain*. Since these intersections with Momaday, I have only encountered him telling stories on two other occasions, far away from the Southwest. Still I can recall at will the cadences of his deep resonant voice intoning "Voice of Thunder," as I imagined him doing this afternoon during a driving hail storm.

Whenever I bind up my old paperback of *House Made of Dawn* with the photograph of Monument Valley on the cover, I think of the need for healing, for fixing things up again. This theme of healing or remaking something in an image of wholeness or beauty is especially crucial, I believe, to our day and age when catastrophic illnesses have plagued us on both a personal level and a planetary level (e.g. AIDS or depletion of the ozone layer), and when the sources of healing, such as the Brazilian rainforest that provides us with a large percentage of our clean oxygen, are being decimated and desecrated in the name of "progress." These imbalances of person and place are, of course, linked, and can be at least symbolically reconstituted through the vital imagery and event structure of indigenous stories that tell of the dynamic symbiotic relationships in a given place over vast stretches of time. These stories from oral tradition (such as the ones incorporated into *House Made of Dawn*) tell one how to behave and how to survive in a particular landscape on the continent, even in adverse circumstances.

House Made of Dawn continues to merit repeat readings because the novel allows the Pueblo stories and the Navajo chantway myths, through a new context, to extend their life-giving values even to recently arrived non-indigenous inhabitants of the Southwest and to reader-listeners elsewhere. Momaday's recognition that myth has the power to continuously transform reality and make reality endure is his gift as a storyteller-teacher to a troubled world that has threatened its own extinction. Even as I write, the Voyager spacecraft launched twelve years ago is carrying a recording of a Night Chant song, along with other world musics, beyond our solar system to unknown beings who may eventually fleetingly contact its healing powers. *House Made of Dawn* is a significant part of this global and intergalactic spinning of songs and stories that restore the taste for living.

Without the careful and brilliant guidance of my teachers Paula Gunn Allen, Kathleen Sands, Davíd Carrasco, and Marianne Stoller, this book could never have been written with the degree of cultural sensitivity and integrity that I hope it possesses. It was Paula Gunn Allen who ten years ago challenged me "to prove how the healing takes place," but little did I know then what a formidable task lay ahead. Paula's critical excellence has continued to prod me to move forward in my thinking. Kathleen Sands's clear, even shrewd, analytical powers pushed me to think more deeply about the relationship of Momaday's novel to other contemporary fiction by Silko and Welch. Davíd Carrasco's penetrating knowledge of Mesoamerican and North American Indian symbolic ceremonial systems helped me establish the comparative basis of my study. And Davíd's vigorous intellectual curiosity, balanced by his fondness for urban street culture, reminded me that you have to pay attention to what the people say, not just to books. Marianne Stoller's influence came late in the project, but her impact on me has been tremendous. She has refined my anthropological sensitivities during conversations on numerous trips over back roads in Colorado, northern New Mexico, and Arizona. Special thanks is also intended for Rose-Marie Oster, a Scandinavian specialist, who cultivated my love of mythology with readings from the Old Icelandic sagas and *The Prose Edda*.

Certain individuals have helped me tremendously by arranging institutional support during the many years of this endeavor. Joe Gordon, Director of the Hulbert Center for Southwest Studies at The Colorado College, has steadfastly provided me with teaching opportunities in an exciting interdisciplinary program, and he has on many occasions sparked me into healthy debate on cultural issues. Red Bird of the Fort Lewis College English

Department has graciously allowed me to develop courses with a Southwest focus, so the students and I can better come to know our place beneath the shadow of Hesperus Peak. Jonathan Batkin, co-director of the Southwest Museum in Los Angeles, has given me hours of stimulating discussion on the subject of the ethics of handling sacred materials, and he has also provided me with unrestricted access to important collections of manuscripts and sandpainting reproductions in watercolor that have been indispensable in furthering my work. Some of these materials I viewed when he was curator at the Fine Arts Center in Colorado Springs. Rodney Dew, head research librarian of the Taylor Museum at the Fine Arts Center, also deserves mention in his willingness to allow me to spend days, even months, with *The Night Chant* manuscript. Grateful acknowledgment is made to all of the research librarians of Braun Library at the Southwest Museum who helped me locate rare texts and conceptualize the project from the perspectives of history, folklore, and the fine arts. These kind librarians are: Richard Buchen, Michael Heisley, Craig Klyver, Daniela Moneta, and Jacquelyn Sunstrand. Additionally, the Anderson Collection at the University of New Mexico's Zimmerman Library proved extremely helpful.

I am indebted to the University of Colorado at Boulder for awarding me a Reynolds Fellowship to begin researching the Ph.D. dissertation that became the core of this book. Kaye Howe, of Comparative Literature, who chaired my dissertation committee, provided direction and a standard of intellectual rigor. Considerable thanks also is due the national literary and cultural organizations whose meetings and publications have provided me with the opportunity to grow through personal contact with other scholars. In particular, I thank the Association for the Study of American Indian Literatures (ASAIL), the Society for the Study of Multi-Ethnic Literature of the United States (MELUS), and the Modern Language Association (MLA).

Throughout the decade of the genesis and completion of this work, my husband Reyes García, a cultural philosopher, has provided consistently insightful criticisms and the "long vision" or large perspective that was necessary sometimes to balance my myopia. I gratefully hope to return the favor by giving him more of myself in the next decade. To the elders in my family, Grandmother Elsie Swoyer and Great Aunt Meta Barthman, approaching one hundred years of age, I send my love and gratitude for the model of endurance they have created by living a long life in beauty. My mother Phyllis Scarberry deserves everlasting thanks for her devotion to my young daughters. Her good will and self-sacrificing care of the children enabled me to stay with the manuscript when it would have been impossible otherwise. Also I wish to give heartfelt thanks to Susan Hodgson, Lucinda Lewis, and Messel McHugh who provided outstanding childcare during key phases of the manuscript's production.

I thank Bill Russ Lee, Navajo artist whose drawing appears on the cover of this book—not only for the exquisite art, but also for taking care over the years, with his wife Carol, to teach me about how things are done "old way." The stories that he tells of his travels have been part of the spiritual backbone of this book. Andrew Wiget also contributed greatly to the quality of this book by kindly consenting to write the Foreword. His far-ranging, perceptive mind and positive attitude about cross-cultural discourse distinguish him as one of the finest scholars of Native American Literature.

The University of New Mexico Press deserves my deepest gratitude for its willingness and enthusiasm for publishing this volume. Special thanks to Elizabeth Hadas, director of the University of New Mexico Press, who has unhesitantly supported my efforts. Barbara Guth, my editor, also receives my sincere thanks for her tenacity and patience during the revisions of the manuscript. My typist, Leslie Donovan, has been remarkable in her concern for perfection.

To the many Indian students and friends who have opened their hearts and homes to me and my family, I offer my greatest appreciation, for they have become my teachers.

Finally, I wish to extend my respect and admiration to N. Scott Momaday who made this book possible and who taught me to see Blanca and other landmarks as sacred spaces.

Antonito, Colorado
August 1, 1989

1

Introduction

Sources of Healing

In the last two decades there has been growing recognition that contemporary Native American Literature is centrally concerned with the process of healing. Speaking in Santa Fe, New Mexico, in the late 1970s, Chicano novelist Rudolfo Anaya said: "The natural end of all art is to make us well, to cure our souls."[1] This statement by an indigenous writer is echoed in Leland Wyman's preface to *Beautyway: A Navaho Ceremonial* where the mythologist Ananda K. Coomaraswamy is quoted as saying that the purpose of the oral art form chant is "to effect . . . a transformation of our being as is the purpose of all ritual acts."[2] Noticing that this connection between oral literature and healing is maintained in written Native American works such as N. Scott Momaday's *House Made of Dawn* (1968), Simon J. Ortiz's *Going For the Rain* (1976), and Leslie Marmon Silko's *Ceremony* (1977), critics have seen that these regenerative stories of personal/cultural transformation have the power to remake individuals spiritually and perhaps physiologically.[3]

Awarded the Pulitzer Prize for fiction in 1969, *House Made of Dawn* is unusual in American Literature in that healing constitutes both the matter and the mode of the novel's being. Whereas many contemporary American novels, such as those by Bellow, Kesey, and Updike, are unfulfilled "narratives of illness" according to critic Richard Ohmann, *House Made of Dawn* is, I believe, both a narrative of illness and a narrative of healing.[4] Critics such as Paula Gunn Allen, Lawrence Evers, Linda Hogan, and Elaine Jahner, among others, have noted that healing takes place both inside and outside of Momaday's novel, that the power of the narrative extends to the reader.[5] Yet previously there has not been a book-length study of the Navajo, Pueblo, and Kiowa oral traditions that provide the symbols, structures, and themes of the healing patterns that Momaday has embedded in this new story cast as a work of imaginative literature.

This study seeks to provide a significant portion of the multitribal mythic context necessary for understanding the development and depth of healing patterns in the novel. Healing is the process of achieving wholeness or a state of physical and spiritual balance, both within a person and between the person and his or her social and natural environment. In *House Made of Dawn* healing occurs when the characters internalize images of the land by means of the symbolic acts of singing and storytelling. The songs are models of the process of composition and reassemblage of inner energies, and the stories from oral tradition are models of redefining or remaking one's place in the natural world. The two narrative patterns that structure the healing process in the novel to make it cohere are stories of twins and stories of bears. When these stories intersect the protagonist Abel's life, and he becomes incorporated into them, he begins to heal.

House Made of Dawn has received widespread acclaim, largely due to the eloquence with which Momaday, a Kiowa/Cherokee, conveys the dilemma of a young Indian man struggling to survive between his traditional tribal world and modern industrialized society. This extraordinarily complex novel tells the story of a returning World War II veteran, Abel, trying to find his place in relation to the land and his home community, Jemez Pueblo, New Mexico. Much criticism of the work has been directed toward analyzing the clash of cultural values and identity problems that Abel experiences.[6] Previous critical interpretations have centered on the sociological and psychological dimensions of the work, barely touching on the hermeneutically puzzling mythological traditions that unify the novel.

The first full-length study of Momaday's writings—*N. Scott Momaday: The Cultural and Literary Background* by Matthias

Schubnell—is quite comprehensive in its assessment of certain historical materials necessary for contextualizing *House Made of Dawn*.[7] But the study focuses primarily on Momaday's Euro-American literary influences, such as Faulkner, Dinesen, D. H. Lawrence, Melville, and Thoreau, almost to the exclusion of Momaday's native literary sources.[8] Nevertheless, Schubnell's work provides a solid synthesis of other critical studies and points up Momaday's linkages to the mainstream literary tradition.[9] My own study, however, seeks to present another dimension of the "cultural and literary background" to Momaday's novel through an interdisciplinary discussion of the multitiered mythic structures of healing that form the native vertebrae of the work. These scholarly studies taken together contribute to a fuller, more complete analysis of the complex origins and mechanisms of Momaday's literary artistry.

In the Introduction to *N. Scott Momaday: The Cultural and Literary Background*, Schubnell makes a bold statement. Charging that "literary critics have directed their attention largely to his [Momaday's] American Indian background and the ethnic elements in his work," and that "this narrow critical perspective has failed to reveal the more complex literary and cultural influences which have shaped his writing," Schubnell reevaluates Momaday's writings from the perspective of the larger American literary tradition.[10] The real issue here, but misstated by Schubnell, is that critical studies of the "Indian elements" in *House Made of Dawn* have often been incomplete or misinformed, not that they are ethnocentric or valueless if done well.[11] Furthermore, these two critical emphases on the Euro-American and the Native American literary influences on Momaday's work are not mutually exclusive, as even Schubnell acknowledges in his chapter on *House Made of Dawn*, where he recognizes: "Momaday's preoccupation with Navajo culture . . . reflected not only in the novel's title and the symbolic healing act, the Night Chant, but also in the figure of Benally."[12] In order to achieve balance and perspective then in this critical debate, Momaday's text must be looked at squarely within both the contexts of the larger Euro-American literary tradition and the vast Native American oral traditions out of which it arises. My aim in this study is to provide a significant missing piece in the scholarly interpretation of this densely textured novel by focusing on the thematic structure of healing, which reveals that native language acts can dissolve fragmentation and discord as they create wholeness.

There are some problems in trying to determine the contours of the healing processes in the novel, since healing, a largely "invisible" dimension of the narrative, takes place as a result of the spiritual exertion of language on place. In order to be able to read the difficult religious levels of the text, which voice in symbolic language the relationship between person, place, and healing powers, it is necessary to comprehend the culturally distinct Native American belief systems that underlie the composition of the novel. Navajo, Pueblo, and Kiowa mythic texts that form the warp of the novel reveal native aesthetics, cosmogony, metaphysics, and epistemology, the symbolic structures of world view that generate deep meanings in the novel. When Ben Benally, for instance, sings the "With beauty" chant from Mountainway to heal Abel, or reharmonize him, the totality of power from the time of creation of the Navajo universe is invoked.[13] But without knowing this mythic context for Ben's act, the "With beauty" song might appear shallow, repetitious, and ineffectual. In a recent essay Laguna Pueblo writer Paula Gunn Allen makes precisely this point about knowing the mythic subtexts in the novel:

> As familiarity with the Bible makes Western culture accessible to the understanding, the basic texts of the Pueblo or the Navajo make their cultures, especially their literature, accessible to scholarly interpretation. It is a nearly hopeless task to explicate *House Made of Dawn* without such a familiarity . . . The basic meanings important to these American Indian systems are carried over into the book. To be unaware of the meanings of these symbols and their accompanying structures is to miss the greater part of the significance of the novel.[14]

And these symbols, structures, and themes from oral tradition can often be flushed out of the centering stories of the creation and re-creation (healing) of the world recorded in the ethnographic data.

This study attempts to interpret the dialectical relationship between the text and the cultural worlds that engendered the text by examining the ethnographic record as it pertains to Navajo, Pueblo, and Kiowa events in the novel. My approach to this task is based on the realization that the systems of symbol formation in Native American Literature are continuous with the living cultures that originated them, and the realization that literature is the world itself, not just a "window" on the world. Another way of looking at this issue is to say that all texts exist in a mass of texts and that studying their relationship or intertextuality reveals aspects of the way the world works. Ethnographies may provide part of the cultural context for situating the details of written Native American Literature, such as *House Made of Dawn,* concretely in an oral mytho-ritualistic tradition. And by examining research from the fields of anthropology, literature, medicine, music, and religion, a fuller picture of the relationship of the healing arts to native spiritual traditions may be gained. By using an interdisciplinary approach to research and critique the novel, it is possible to reconstruct the wholeness of the cultural lifeways whose coherence promotes healing.

My approach to uncovering the healing patterns in the novel consists in comparing symbolic event structure in the novel to stories and descriptions of cultural rituals in the relevant ethnography. By examining the mythic traditions that inform the novel, it is possible to recognize the replication of portions of them in Momaday's text. And by seeing how the myths are instrumental in the healing process in culture, it is possible to recognize the role that the songs and stories play in facilitating Abel's healing.

One version of the Jemez emergence story, which establishes the cosmo-symbolic patterns of the culture, was recorded, along with other ethnographic information, by Elsie Clews Parsons in 1925.[15] Her extensive monograph, *The Pueblo of Jemez,* contains data about Jemez history, language, customs, and ritual, as well as exhaustive genealogical records. While potentially useful in

establishing a cultural context for interpreting the novel, however, this information is not altogether accurate and trustworthy.
And it contains no interpretative apparatus that helps us see the
data as descriptions of related symbolic processes instead of as
mere descriptions of material artifacts or isolated facts.[16] Jemez
historian Joe Sando mentions that Parsons's culturally insensi-
tive publication has outraged many Jemez people, because it
reveals religious secrets and represents a breech of hospitality.[17]
Thus the use of ethnographic materials, while revealing potentially valuable resources about ethnic cultures, can be offensive
to the tribe or misleading to scholars.

In conversation with San Juan Pueblo anthropologist Alfonso
Ortiz in 1981, Ortiz told me that Momaday was a great reader
of the ethnographic record, in particular the Bureau of American
Ethnology reports. Momaday consulted some ethnographic
sources, such as the Parsons material, to expand his knowledge
of Jemez culture in the process of writing the novel. Although
Momaday is a Kiowa from Oklahoma, he lived on the Navajo
reservation in Arizona and at Jemez Pueblo in New Mexico during his childhood and witnessed some ceremonies first hand.[18]
Some of the sources for the novel were the author's personal
experiences and some were the written record. The imaginative
piece of literature that resulted is a compilation of portions of
old stories from oral tradition, which I call "storysherds," and
new stories that situate Abel fully in the modern world. Momaday gives the old stories new life by recontextualizing them
meaningfully in his new narrative.

This matter of learning the old stories is a serious undertaking
for anyone, because the stories themselves are intrinsically powerful and may contain ritual knowledge. Acquiring ritual knowledge always carries both risk and responsibility. Dr. Washington
Matthews, whose text *The Night Chant, A Navaho Ceremony* Momaday consulted in crafting his novel, suffered in old age from
deafness and paralysis, two of the afflictions the Navajo Night
Chant is said to heal.[19] Some Navajos say that the power of the
chant was too strong, that Matthews needed more ceremonial
protection against the Holy People involved.[20] After over twenty
years of diligently studying the Night Chant, Matthews confessed

to knowing it imperfectly, and added: "I merely claim to have done my best to search carefully for the truth."[21] Just as story-tellers and ethnographers have taken their own risks for the sake of acquiring knowledge, so too must scholars who follow them risk spiritual imbalance if sacred materials are not treated properly.[22] A study such as this must be undertaken cautiously and carefully, with readers cognizant of the ethical issues raised by approaching highly specialized cultural knowledge too closely.

Sacred stories from oral tradition, especially origin and creation myths, have a healing dimension because they symbolically internalize images of the land within the listeners. Through participating in the story, the listeners learn about their own relationship to the cultural/geographic history of their homeland. And it is this knowledge of one's place in relationship to all else in the natural world that reintegrates an individual and fosters survival. Momaday has shaped his narrative as a modern expression of oral tradition by drawing on the conventions and content of old sacred stories, especially the orally recited origin myths that generate the complex healing ceremonials known as the Navajo Chantways. Although *House Made of Dawn* is a written work of fiction, it retains the oral ability to reorder existence and personal lives by naming sacred places. Within the narrative, Black Mesa at Jemez and Tségihi Canyon in Navajo country are landmarks where a reconstitution of life takes place.[23]

House Made of Dawn takes its name from a prayer for restoration sung during the Night Chant.[24] The prayer opens with the word *"Tségihi,"* the name of a canyon north of the San Juan River in Navajo Country, and proceeds to describe this place in relation to the play of light and rain upon the land. As the land is renewed by moisture, abundant blessings also fall upon the person who speaks and walks in beauty there. The novel establishes place, the sacred space of its action, by voicing these words at the beginning of the story and at crucial points in the narrative afterwards. Jemez Pueblo, New Mexico, further to the east, where the central events of the story occur, is also described as a powerful ancient place. As the words of the ritualistic "House Made of Dawn" prayer are uttered, the world that is imagined comes wholly into being.[25] When language touches land, place is created.

In *House Made of Dawn* Momaday has used the precise sacred language of Navajo and Jemez traditions in order to establish the truth of his text. Because the Navajo chantways, such as Nightway, Mountainway, and Beautyway, are immeasurably old and trustworthy, their myths establish "the foundation of truth for the culture."[26] Momaday's use of portions of songs and stories from the Night Chant then give authority and credence to his work. When Momaday opens the novel with *"Dypaloh"* and ends with the word *"Qtsedaba,"* conventional formulaic words used at Jemez Pueblo to frame a story, he is placing his story solidly within oral tradition. Through this device, Momaday stresses the importance of language acts as he establishes the bond between narrator and audience or writer and reader.

The heart of the methodology of this study is to look at the symbolic processes of ritual and storytelling in *House Made of Dawn* and to see these working to achieve healing. Momaday draws upon Pueblo and Kiowa traditions for the novel's design, but he primarily structures the novel around Navajo healing patterns; therefore a comprehension of the Navajo model of reality is indispensable to understanding the function of healing in the story. Momaday uses structures from Navajo ritual and oral tradition, as well as symbols of transformation to achieve unity, order, healing, and *hózhǫ́* in the narrative.[27] Chapters 2, 3, and 4 of this study derive from inquiry into the healing patterns of the Navajo chantways Nightway, Mountainway, and Beautyway and from inquiry into the patterns of purification and remaking contained within the Navajo rites Blessingway and Enemyway.[28] A brief discussion about Navajo land concepts, storytelling, and healing practices is intended to contextualize these inquiries. Subsequently, I will highlight the other concerns and discoveries of these chapters.

A significant overview of Navajo culture, *Between Sacred Mountains: Navajo Stories and Lessons from the Land*, begins by linking place and knowledge:

A piece of land is like a book. A wise person can look at
stones and mountains and read stories older than the first
living thing that crawled on the earth . . . The earth is old.
No book can tell all that is written on the land.[29]

Story emerges from the land. For the Navajos, each landform
contains an inner form. This concept of inner forms is very specific and originates at the time of the creation of the world. First
Man placed the inner forms of the earth, an experience recounted
in Blessingway.[30] The inner life forms are the humanlike forms
that are the in-standing ones that animate all of creation.[31] In
Holy Wind in Navajo Philosophy James McNeley refers to an inner
form as "the Wind within one," *niłch'i.*[32] These forms possess the
"power of life and movement," shape the character of the outer
forms (physical appearance), and bring strength.[33] Although the
inner and outer forms of plants, animals, and mountains are
inseparable, the inner forms or spirit essences remain the same,
while the outer forms may change or transform.[34]

During Chantway performances, the sources of healing are
the inner forms of the Holy People who are the inner forms of
the elements of nature and natural phenomena. These performances or "sings" are complex symbolic healing ceremonials last-
ing as long as nine days. The ritual elements that concentrate
power on the ill person include purification baths, administra-
tion of emetics, setting out of *kethawns* or prayersticks, blessings
with pollen, recitation of lengthy prayers and songs, and the
construction of elaborate sandpaintings on the floor of the *hogan*
or Navajo home. These sandpaintings depict key episodes in the
myths that explain how a particular ceremonial originated.[35] When
a singer (medicine man) identifies one-sung-over (patient) through
a sandpainting with the Holy Person whom he or she had offended, the strength of that Holy Person is internalized. At such
epiphanal moments the Holy Person's ill will is transformed into
benevolence and healing takes place. Inner form of the Holy
Person merges with inner form of the ill person, as the one-sung-
over is brought toward a whole reintegration with the land,

through association with specific places and phenomena such as Mt. Blanca, who is the embodiment of the Holy People White Shell Woman and Talking God.[36] The rupture between inner and outer landscapes is closed and illness recedes. The *niłch'i*, or inner wind, within the one-sung-over is reanimated. As John Farella says in *The Main Stalk: A Synthesis of Navajo Philosophy*: "By means of *niłch'i* we are connected to all beings around us, and by this means our feelings and thought are aspects of connectedness, rather than attributes of an illusory self."[37] Although there are no actual sandpaintings depicted in the novel, the verbal blessings that Ben ("singer") bestows on Abel ("one-sung-over") associate him with a means of reconnection with the Bird People and the rest of the natural world.

In the novel Ben Benally sings a version of the "House Made of Dawn" prayer from the fourth day of the Night Chant.[38] This prayer, which attracts holiness and repulses evil, appeals to "the dark bird who is the chief of pollen" (Thunderbird—a Holy Person) to remake the speaker in an image of beauty and vitality.[39] During an actual sing or healing ceremony, the one-sung-over repeats this prayer after the medicine man or singer. But in the novel, Abel sings this prayer at "the end" of the story as he runs in the dawn, a delayed response to Ben for sure but still a gesture of completion and fulfilled obligation. "He could see the dark hills at dawn. He was running, and under his breath he began to sing . . . *House made of pollen, house made of dawn*."[40] Abel's *niłch'i* (signified by breath here) has been reanimated through direct contact with the inner form of Thunderbird. Happily he runs in beauty in the land.

Naturalist writer Barry Lopez draws a helpful distinction between interior and exterior landscapes that further explains the primacy of man/land relationships. The interior landscape within a person, which includes the contours of thought, the place where the spirit lives, is shaped considerably by the "character and subtlety of the exterior one. . . ."[41] A skillful storyteller from a culture of oral tradition produces a "profound sense of well-being" in the listeners by "bringing the two landscapes together."[42] When the land is internalized, the listener experiences "a pervasive sense of congruence within himself and also with the world."[43] This "sense of congruence" promotes healing or rebalancing of the inner self. Lopez further describes the qualities inherent in sacred landscapes that become at once manifest in story and transformers of the "interior landscape."

> The exterior landscape is organized according to principles or laws or tendencies beyond human control. It is understood to contain an integrity that is beyond human analysis and unimpeachable . . . Among the Navaho . . . the land is thought to exhibit a sacred order. That order is the basis of ritual. Rituals themselves reveal the power in that order.[44]

Lopez mentions that the native arts also spring from this sacred order of the universe. The land has an inviolate sacredness that is ordered according to the prominent landmarks or land and water forms of a given region. For the Navajo the four sacred mountains of the cardinal directions, Mount Blanca to the East (*Sis Naajiní*), Mount Taylor to the South (*Tsoodził*), the San Francisco Peaks to the West (*Dook'o'oosłííd*) and Hesperus Peak to the North (*Dibé Nitsaa*), demarcate the perimeters of *Diné Bikéyah*, Navajo Country, and are the homes of *Diyin dine'é*, the Holy People.[45] Through the rituals of Navajo chantways, the resplendent sacred order of these mountains reorders the "interior landscape" of the one-sung-over by bringing *hózhǫ́* within.[46]

The sacred order in the land, reflected in story, ritual, and healing is communicated by means of natural or "organic" symbols. A symbolic process such as singing or running may be a means of making a seemingly remote reality present or of conveying a concept.[47] It is a means of traversing worlds and distance, and of identifying people with landforms and the Holy People. A song of a sacred mountain, such as a Blanca Peak Song from Blessingway, brings the mountain within the singer and listeners, so they can experience its character directly.[48] When Ben Benally in the novel sings: "I am the Turquoise Woman's son./ On top of Belted Mountain,/ Beautiful horse—slim like a weasel," Ben actually becomes one of the Twin War Gods as he chants his horse prayer.[49] The strength and beauty of this horse infuses the narrative with exuberance and a sense of peace that may contribute to healing. The specific imagery of the prayer dramatically connects horse and rider to sky and earth:

His mane is made of short rainbows,
My horse's ears are made of round corn.
My horse's eyes are made of big stars.
My horse's head is made of mixed waters—
From the holy waters—he never knows thirst.
My horse's teeth are made of white shell. . . .[50]

This horse is formed of sacred substances, reflecting a kinship of celestial phenomena, water, food, and flesh. The singer's knowledge of these relationships empowers him toward wholeness. Songs and stories that contain ancient symbols of place, of time and space, put the listeners or readers in "contact with the pervasive truth of those relationships we call 'the land.'"[51] For those who are fully aware that the land is composed of significant relationships among all who live in it, a harmony is achieved "between the two landscapes" and "a state of psychological confusion" is reordered.[52]

In his essay, "Story at Anaktuvuk Pass," Barry Lopez speaks further about the relationship between storytelling and healing:

The power of narrative to nurture and heal, to repair a spirit in disarray, rests on two things: the skillful invocation of unimpeachable sources and the listener's knowledge that no hypocrisy or subterfuge is involved.[53]

In the context of *House Made of Dawn* then, Momaday invokes the Holy People who are "unimpeachable sources" of truth embedded in landforms or the elements of nature. The Holy People (*Diyin dine'é*) are the inner forms of animals, plants, and sacred places whom Navajo medicine men invoke through sandpainting, a sister process to storytelling, in order to effect cures. Although Momaday seldom mentions the Holy People by name, lie does summon their blessings by incorporating their songs and stories into the narrative. In *The Sacred Hoop: Recovering the Feminine in American Indian Traditions*, Paula Gunn Allen comments on this point:

> The Holy People do not appear directly as characters in the novel until the final episode, but they are present throughout in a number of indirect ways. . . . They are most present in the superb descriptions of the land, in which Momaday expresses the reverence for the land and its creatures that is the hallmark of American Indian consciousness and of tribal literature.[54]

In *House Made of Dawn*, Momaday invokes the Holy People in order to stimulate healing. The reader of *House Made of Dawn* learns of the healing powers of the Navajo Night Chant or Nightway through a long complicated chain of transmission. The Holy People, Navajo deities some of whom inhabit specific places in Canyon de Chelly such as Broad Rock, White House, and Red Rock House, gave the healing songs of the Night Chant orally to the Stricken Twins, Navajo mythical culture heroes, who in turn taught the ceremony and its oral literature to the Earth Surface People (humans).[55] Countless generations of singers or medicine men then passed on the chantway through performing it for one-sung-over or a patient.[56] At the turn of the century the singer Hatáli Natlói [Laughing Chanter] told the surgeon/ethnographer Washington Matthews a version of the crucial songs and stories to the chantway.[57] Then in 1902 Dr. Matthews's *The Night Chant, A Navaho Ceremony* appeared. As the first comprehensive written manuscript of the chantway, this text became years later one of Momaday's sources for the novel. Momaday subsequently voiced the Nightway songs through the chanter Ben Benally who sings for Abel. Momaday's narrative has become a small but integral part of this long continuous chain of transmission. When we read *House Made of Dawn*, we are experiencing, first hand, the transformation of oral tradition into written literature. The heart of the text has come slowly, but directly, from the Holy People who are ultimate sources of truth and knowledge and the means to restoring health. Momaday's story is an outgrowth of events that he has imagined taking place in and near the homelands of the Holy People.[58]

Chapter 2 contains a discussion of the character-brothers Vidal and Abel who, as symbolic twins, represent a model of wholeness or completeness. The Navajo Twin War Gods Monster Slayer (*Nayénĕzgani*) and Born for Water (*To'badzĭstsíni*), masked figures of the Night Chant who appear pervasively in the ceremonial literature, represent a paradigmatic model for the Stricken Twins, heroic boys of the Night Chant, who, in turn, become a literary archetype for Vidal and Abel.[59] Like the War Gods, Vidal and Abel could be conceived of as "the follower pair" because younger brother always follows older brother.[60] Momaday makes use of the Navajo ritual principles of pairing, sequence, multiplication, and numerology in defining the ordering characteristics of the brothers' relationship. The distinctly Navajo principles of multiple selves, change of names, and role reversals refer to the ability of Holy People or spirit beings to be transformed into plural physical manifestations of their complementary opposite. According to Gladys Reichard, Monster Slayer may become Holy Man or Reared-in-the-Earth, depending upon circumstances.[61] In *House Made of Dawn* younger brother Abel appears to take on the attributes of his older brother after Vidal dies. When Abel kills the albino Juan Reyes Fragua who has been threatening the village cornfields, Abel uses a knife reminiscent of the black flint knife that Monster Slayer used to kill monsters in Diné Bikéyah. The suggestion being made here, that is presented more fully in chapter 2, is that due to the recurring cyclical nature of myth, Abel is a recent manifestation of Born for Water, Younger Brother of the Twin War Gods and of the lame Younger Brother of the Stricken Twins, and that for much of the novel Abel also assumes the identity of Elder Brother, thereby still completing the wholeness and unity of the pair.

Insofar as Abel becomes identified with Younger Brother, hero twin of the origin myth to the Stricken Twins variant of the Night Chant, Abel undertakes a parallel spiritual journey that separates him from his people so he can acquire knowledge of the supernaturals, only to return home reintegrated within his culture. According to Joseph Campbell, this archetypal pattern of separation-initiation-return is one that holds considerable healing power for the initiate.[62] The fact that Abel is able to move toward wholeness testifies to the strength of his traditions, which recognize that humans acquire power from ceremonially being put in touch with the natural healing forces of the universe. Momaday's partial replication of the structure of the Night Chant shows how the oral tradition infuses the written tradition with ritual power and how a recreation of prototypical events in sacred time still suffuses the characters with positive, transformative energy. Human and supernatural events may keep reappearing in slightly different form due to the cyclical nature of reality.[63] In the case of the twins, not only does the brothers' relationship create a healing pattern (two become one or a whole self), but also the twins' kinship with the Holy People reconstitutes wholeness for them.

Chapter 3 demonstrates how certain animals in the novel, most notably the bear, provide symbolic models of transformation for the characters. Bear can be both enemy and healer, and in his role as healer he is a model of regeneration or reemergence into new life. Traditional bear stories from Navajo, Pueblo, and Kiowa cultures embedded in the novel tell of illness, transformation, and renewed health. They provide Abel with access to power, strength, and endurance, as they connect him to wilderness.

Bear's powers range from deadly to protective and curative.[64] Bear shifts back and forth in his manifestations as a Holy Person. In the Stricken Twins story in the Night Chant, the Bear People are at times guides, advisors, and protectors and at times enemies.[65] In *House Made of Dawn* Abel is Bear Man and Angela is Bear Maiden, for a time. Angela's negative and positive selves are both represented by female bear figures. This study looks at symbolic models of bear behavior to see how Momaday has generated bear energy in the novel as a source of healing. Like the Stricken Twins, Bear becomes a model of integration for Abel in the novel.

Chapter 4 explores the relationship of the process of Abel's healing to the composition of the novel as a whole. Abel's illness and healing proceeds according to the Navajo theory of disease called "fragmentation and reassemblage."[66] The narrative mythic pattern that corresponds to this symbolic healing is: being stricken, acquiring vision, knowledge, and identity. Momaday's method of text-building is parallel to the healing experience. The novelist creates a powerful unified story by overlapping multiple, seemingly fragmented, narratives. Using the techniques of parallelism, circularity, and repetition from oral tradition, Momaday presents sacred songs and stories as models of the process of composition and reassemblage of inner energies.

Whereas the Twins and the bears are the central images in the novel that make the healing process cohere, the dense complicated storysherd structure of the novel forces the reader to think imaginatively and to associate parts of the story holistically. This act of consciously seeking relationships in order to create a whole meaningful story is parallel to, or even contiguous with, the healing process. To recognize that the powers of the natural world and of Native American Literature are inseparable is to unite the sources of healing in the land with the intrinsic healing power in *House Made of Dawn*.

2

The Twins

"Abelito, Vidalito"

In *House Made of Dawn* the protagonist Abel has a brother, Vidal, who dies of a mysterious illness at a young age.[1] The two brothers are depicted as being close, virtually inseparable, in their childhood activities, and it is clear from the story that when Vidal dies, Abel has lost his older brother.

These brothers, born of a Jemez mother (who also dies of Vidal's disease) and an unknown father, possibly a Navajo, are symbolically twins because they are interdependent and appear to compose a unity. As Claude Leví-Strauss has pointed out, it is conceivable that two children may be considered morally and psychologically twin if they are in close relationship, even if they had different fathers.[2] Leví-Strauss views a pair such as this as "equivalents to twins," and twins as "two individuals which are exactly similar or identical because they are both part of a whole."[3] And Victor Turner points out that while birth order is important in determining individual characteristics of each twin, "twinship presents the paradoxes that what is physically double is structurally single and what is mystically one is empirically two."[4]

There are fewer than half a dozen scenes in the novel where Vidal and Abel appear together, and they have been largely ignored as brothers in the critical literature, except for a few critics' statements about them. Paula Gunn Allen, LaVonne Ruoff, Joseph DeFlyer, and Lawrence Evers have all noticed that the brothers' relationship is important to understanding the composition of the story and the origin of Abel's pain and illness.[5]

I would like to suggest that the brothers' relationship also creates a dynamic healing pattern within the novel.

In both Pueblo and Navajo cultures there are mythic prototypes for the creation of Vidal and Abel. It seems probable that Momaday consciously used these mythic twin models, since the novel's title comes from a prayer of the Night Chant that was sung by two boys, the Stricken Twins, as they wandered into Tségihi, Canyon de Chelly.[6] Furthermore, the Stricken Twins are mythic reflections of the Navajo Twin War Gods, Monster Slayer (*Nayénězgani*) and Born for Water (*To'badzĭstsíni*), widely thought to have evolved in oral tradition from the neighboring stories of the Pueblo War Twins.[7] In this paradigm, the Pueblo War Gods, known at Jemez Pueblo as *Masewi* and *Uyuyewe*, have an unknown father who turns out to be the sun.[8] Similarly, the Navajo Twins or War Gods, Monster Slayer and Born for Water, born of Changing Woman, search as young boys for their father the sun, or their fathers the sun and water.[9] Other twin culture heroes, appearing to the Navajo after the first pair have rid the world of monsters, include the Stricken Twins of the Night Chant and the Twins of Male Shootingway, this latter pair said to represent Monster Slayer and Born for Water in the form of Holy Man and Holy Boy.[10] All of these Navajo twins are the heroes in the origin myths of their respective chantways. These origin myths explain the occasion for the first performance of the ceremonial and reveal detailed knowledge about the ritual to be used in each subsequent performance.[11] Just as all of these heroes undertake life-jeopardizing adventures in order to receive power and knowledge, so too do Vidal and Abel risk their lives journeying into unfamiliar country in order to experience the secrets and beauty of remote places.

The general hero pattern for the origin myths to the Navajo chantways is a culture-specific variant of what Mircea Eliade and Joseph Campbell recognize as the "monomyth" or the world-wide hero pattern.[12] Navajo story patterns reveal a hero or heroes (or occasionally heroines as in Mountainway and Beautyway), often "outsiders" from birth, forced by circumstances to leave home and combat numerous terrifying obstacles that confront them for reasons unknown. After undergoing a symbolic death experience and being reborn through the aid of the Holy People or spirit helpers, the heroes return home to their people to teach the healing ceremonial that remade them. This basic mythic pattern can be interpreted on many different levels. One way to look at these stories is to view them as fundamental tales of spiritual growth, wherein heroes are separated from their people in order to be initiated into esoteric knowledge that they eventually share when they return home. This pattern of separation-initiation-return accumulates power for the heroes, as it expresses deeply held cultural values, such as the riskiness of violating taboo or the strength and obligation of kinship.

House Made of Dawn partakes of this hero pattern, as is evident from the onset of the novel when Abel is described as a person on the fringes of his culture from birth, a person "somehow foreign and strange."[13] He is forcibly removed from Jemez when he is drafted into the army and sent overseas. Later, after returning to Jemez and killing the albino, Abel is once again forced to leave, this time for prison and relocation in Los Angeles. Seven years after he first left Jemez, Abel returns home just before his grandfather dies. This double cyclic or spiral pattern of separation and return, separation and return, is not altogether typical of the Navajo hero patterns in the chantways and is an example of Momaday's imaginative adaptation of oral traditions. This complex spiral pattern also echoes the theme of twinning or duality in the novel. Unlike the chantway heroes who are privileged to have a healing ceremony performed over them, Abel has no extensive cure performed for him, even though he could use a full-fledged ceremony.

Symbolically, however, Ben's singing of the "House Made of Dawn" prayer spreads profuse blessings from Nightway in all directions, as if the whole ceremony radiated outward from that one ritual act. The Navajo singer Jeff King said before telling *Where the Two Came to Their Father: A Navajo War Ceremonial:*

This story is the beginning of people. East, south, west, and north, it goes everywhere, because it is full of power—good power. My story has no evil in it. It is straight. It is to save and protect people. It is to save and protect men going to war, or in enemy country.[14]

So too does the beauty of the "House Made of Dawn" prayer extend into the world, effectively influencing Abel's recovery. And although Abel fails to teach ceremonial knowledge or even tell his story at the "end of the cycle," there are mythic precedents for this break with the hero pattern.[15]

At times Abel's personal story sounds like a contemporary version of the suffering heroes' encounters with tests, obstacles, and monsters of all kinds. His story seems to closely fit the old pattern, especially when he slays the albino, a monstrous threatening being. Abel appears to be in his warrior manifestation, akin to the Twins when they kill Big Ye' ii in Enemyway.[16] And at other times Abel's story seems to break with the broadest contours of the Navajo heroic journey. For example, Abel meets no spirit helpers or Holy People who reveal to him the intricacies of the universe or the means of overcoming his dilemmas, in contrast to the way that Water Sprinkler (*To'nenili*) gives words of advice or directions to the Stricken Twins.[17] Yet Momaday spawns a symbolic image that helps to fill this gap or anticipated stage in the process of Abel's spiritual journey. When Abel nearly dies after being beaten up on the beach in Los Angeles, the narrator tells of the death-rebirth journey of the grunion "a small silversided fish," thus creating a parallel image to Abel's at the moment, and possibly providing the impetus for Abel's recovery.[18] And, as previously mentioned, Abel does not repeatedly tell his story, as the Stricken Twins do, nor does he become a teacher in his home community.[19]

Disjunctures such as these between Navajo chantway origin myths and the novel tell another kind of story. Not only do they indicate the extent to which Abel is prevented from following the course of cultural healing patterns, but these disjunctures also allow Momaday the creative leeway that he needs to tell a contemporary story that is imaginatively both within and outside of oral tradition. The novel maintains the integrity of oral tradition and is bound to truthful telling, but it is not restricted to exactly repeating formulaic story patterns. In fact, one of the points that Momaday makes is that a person's separation from the natural world, such as Abel's, precludes living in the beautyway of the chantway patterns.[20]

The only previous extensive attempt to work out the twin pattern in *House Made of Dawn* occurred more than a decade ago when Joseph DeFlyer analyzed dual structures of consciousness.[21] DeFlyer maintains that Abel resembles older brother, Monster Slayer (Navajo) or Masewi (Jemez), and that Ben resembles younger brother Born for Water (Navajo) or Uyuyewe (Jemez).[22] The basis of his identification is that Abel takes on Monster Slayer's aggressive, active qualities when he kills the albino. And Ben, according to DeFlyer, is "in Navajo terms, the Twin 'Born for Water,' the peaceful, integrative Twin who provides a balance to Monster Slayer, the analytic and more violent Twin."[23] DeFlyer also says: "Abel is Benally's brother in a profoundly Indian sense, and Benally knows this."[24] Abel in DeFlyer's reading is associated with adventurous, destructive tendencies and Ben with intuitive, peaceful ones, based on his kindnesses to Abel.[25] The other basis for identification of these two is DeFlyer's observation that "The ritual tone of their leavetaking suggests that these two are indeed the archetypal Twins, who will have a last reunion before leaving the world."[26] Although DeFlyer also touches upon the relationship of Ben and Abel in regard to Mountainway and Beautyway, he stops short of developing these parallels beyond a speculative level. The DeFlyer critique opens up areas of inquiry about the nature of duality and the relationship of Abel to other male characters in the novel, but DeFlyer's bases of identification are not complete enough, and, thus, only partially accurate.

The fact that Vidal is always the leader when he appears with Abel, in the box canyon scene and in the geese hunting scene in particular, indicates that Abel is indeed Younger Brother of the Follower Pair.[27] Moreover, considering the Navajo ritual principles of pairing, and multiple selves, it is possible for Abel to occasionally appear to take on Elder Brother's aggressive qualities. If Ben is a surrogate twin at all, he seems more likely to be another representation of Younger Brother. As Ben says:

We were kind of alike, though, him and me. After a while he told me where he was from, and right away I knew we were going to be friends. We're related somehow, I think. The Navajos have a clan they call by the name of that place. I was there once, too. That was eight or ten years ago, I guess, and I was going to the Santa Fe Indian School, and some of us went over there for the big dance they have in November. It was cold that winter, and there was a lot of snow all around. It's a pretty good place; there are mountains and canyons around there, and there's a lot of red in the rocks. Except for the mountains, it's like the land south of Wide Ruins, where I come from, full of gullies and brush and red rocks. And he didn't have any family, either, just his grandfather. He said his grandfather used to have a bunch of sheep. I herded sheep from the time I could walk.[28]

In this passage Ben recognizes his kinship with Abel based on common ties to places. Jemez has strong associations for Ben because he has been there on Feast Day, and because the Navajos have named one of their own clans after Jemez.[29] Yet perhaps the strongest tie between Ben and Abel is the revelation that their home landscapes are similar and they were both raised by grandfathers, two more images of twinning.

Ben's ability to vividly remember the details of place is one reason why his singing of the "House Made of Dawn" prayer is so compelling for Abel.[30] The Four Corners landscape is reimagined in California in Ben's song. In *Navaho Symbols of Healing*, Donald Sandner describes how landscape can become internalized through repetition of "identifiable place names." Concerning this symbolic language of place, Sandner says:

All this symbolism has a definite purpose: to link the mythic events to physical reality, just as the prayers do when they begin with familiar places and proceed to mythic ones. This allows the psyche to fix on well-known images such as familiar mountains, rivers, canyons, etc., and then gradually move beyond them into an inner mythic landscape.[31]

Speaking about the way that humans absorb landscape, Barry
Lopez says: "One learns a landscape finally not by knowing the
name or identity of everything in it, but by perceiving the relationships in it. . . ."[32] For Ben then, as for Lopez, one learns
about a place by walking through it. This activity may bring to
mind mythic places or power spots such as Canyon de Chelly,
where healing has taken place, because the relationships among
the Holy People and the Earth Surface People were in balance
there.

In *House Made of Dawn* the stories about Vidal and Abel's childhood experiences together are briefly told, but replete with
meaning. The first mention of their relationship occurs just after
the passage describing Abel's drunken homecoming and his ensuing attempt to gain perspective in his life by climbing a hill at
dawn. The narrator tells, as if a flashback in Abel's memory, how
Vidal and Abel go out into the land, doing ordinary things like
riding horses and throwing stones at birds.[33] Then Vidal leads
Abel on foot into a red rock canyon. It is clear from the story
that Vidal is Elder Brother and Abel, Younger Brother. "He [Abel]
climbed up on the horse *behind Vidal.* . . ."[34] Later "*Vidal took him*
to the face of the red mesa and into a narrow box canyon which
he had never seen before."[35] Abel follows Vidal like Younger
Brother of the Follower Pair. Once they are in the canyon, five-
year-old Abel is frightened by walls that "seemed to close over
him," and cries.[36] No mention is made of Vidal's reaction to the
experience, and one can only assume that he was brave and
fearless as older brothers are expected to be.

Initially this experience may seem like a minor incident in the
novel but it relates to other childhood fears of Abel's, especially
the moaning wind that is associated with evil.[37] Most impor-
tantly, the occasion for the brothers' walk that day was to accompany their grandfather and the other planters out into the
fields to open the ditches. There is a parallel established here
between the motion of new life in the soil and the swaying
canyon walls. Abel as a little boy is moved by a reality vaster
than he has ever known, the power of the natural world. He is
transformed into a person aware of the ability of the "exterior

landscape" to affect a psyche or "interior landscape." And this awareness is a prerequisite to being healed.

There are two other accounts of Vidal and Abel spending time with their grandfather. In one instance he teaches them about the journey of the sun in relation to the village, and in the other story, the grandfather asks Abel to accompany him to see "the race of the dead."[38] The narrator says: *"He would go soon to the fields, but first there was something he must do, and he sent Vidal ahead in the wagon. He put his younger grandson in front of him on the horse. . . ."*[39] Even while Vidal is still alive, Francisco the grandfather seems to favor Abel, preparing him to inherit the tribal traditions. When Vidal dies, Abel is still very young, and it is difficult to discern his response to his older brother's death.[40]

Besides the canyon scene, Vidal and Abel only appear at length together in one other scene, presumably shortly before Vidal's death. In the geese hunting scene, Abel "crept along behind his brother, bending low and weaving after him through the brush-covered dunes, going silently on the cold ripples of sand."[41] When Vidal motioned, "Abel followed."[42] Years later when Abel is a grown man with broken hands, his pain triggers this memory of the time he had held a dying goose. And the memory of the beautiful flying geese prompts Abel to tell his story of this experience to Milly—one of the rare moments in the novel when Abel talks. It is as if Abel's suffering, parallel to the goose's, has prompted a story. As Isak Dinesen has said, "All sorrows can be borne if they are put into a story." And Momaday himself has said: "We tell stories in order to understand our experience."[43] Without consciously realizing it, Abel transforms his suffering into a return to health by verbalizing the origins of his pain. Or to state the process differently, Abel permits the beauty of the natural world to penetrate his "interior landscape." The goose is a source of beauty, and sources of beauty are sources of healing.

Now that the basic outline of Vidal and Abel's relationship has been discussed, it is appropriate to compare their family history and literary development to that of the Stricken Twins. As previously stated, the Stricken Twins in the variant origin myth to The Night Chant present the mythic prototype for the Jemez brothers' lives.[44] More reasons for this identification will become apparent as the details of the two sets of brothers' adventures are more extensively compared.

The Stricken Twins' primary names are Elder Brother and Younger Brother, and it seems that the first born is considered the more dominant of the pair, even though they were born so closely together.[45] Born of a poor Navajo woman and fathered secretly by Talking God (*Hastséyalti*), a Holy Person, the Twins grow up in a four-generation family that can neither support nor accept them. When the boys are nine they wander away from home only to take refuge in a rock shelter that collapses on them, maiming them severely. Elder Brother is blinded and Younger Brother is paralyzed or lamed by the accident. There are indications that they may have been cursed by Squeaking Yéi (*Hastsédíltsosi*), another Holy Person who frees them.[46] The Twins devise a clever way of traveling, with the crippled, but sighted, Younger Brother riding on the strong, but blinded, Elder Brother's back. This posture is a physical representation of their complementarity and interdependency, of two operating as one.

Upon returning home, they are cast out to fend for themselves. No longer a burden to their family, the boys wander about searching for a cure to their ailments. Talking God, who shelters and feeds them, sends them to the Holy People of *Tsé'íntyel*. The Twins retell the story of their accident to "the holy ones" who promptly deny that they have the power to cure them.[47] Eventually, the Twins are sent on to other Holy People who might cure them, but no one does, because of lack of precious offerings. All together the twins experience fourteen refusals of help. After a test (choosing Talking God's poor bow and arrow), the Twins' kinship with Talking God is proven, and the Holy People decide to hold a curing ceremony in a sweathouse for the boys. But the Twins happily cry out as they are being healed, and this breach of taboo stops the ceremony. After this mistake, the only way to be cured is through a gift of the proper offerings. As the Twins depart the Holy People's beautiful home, sadder than ever, their cry turns to song.

The Holy People are so moved by the beauty of the song that they equip the boys with magical weapons (wind, a worm, a kangaroo rat, and grasshoppers) to provoke the Mokis (Hopis) into giving over their valuables. These offerings please the Holy People who then proceed to give a full-fledged ceremony to restore the Twins' vision and mobility. One ritual of the ceremony is the shaping or massaging of the Twins' bodies by the daughters of *Hastséhogan,* in order to make the boys stunningly beautiful once again. Then the Twins depart to teach the ceremony to the "People on the Earth." Afterwards they disappear to control the thunderstorms and animals for the people's benefit.[48]

The Stricken Twins' story adheres to the "monomyth" hero pattern. Just before their final cure this conversation takes place:

> "What, O father, were your thoughts about us while we were gone? We have suffered much and escaped many dangers in getting these things for you. . . ." "Tis well," said the old man [Talking God]; "now you shall have your eyes cured and your limbs cured, and you shall walk as well and see as well as you did before the evil spell was cast upon you."[49]

And upon the Twins' third rejection from home,

> One of the boys . . . said to the other: "I am sorry we came back . . ." But the other replied: . . . "It was the holy ones who sent us, and we did right to listen to them. Our mother and her people do not want us to be of the People on the Earth. Let us go back to the holy ones and remain with them forever."[50]

This cycle of rejection, suffering, enduring tests, receiving aid from the Holy People, and finally disappearing to join them is typical of chantway origin myth patterns. But the Stricken Twins story has its own distinct narrative colorations, as Donald Sandner points out:

> The Warrior Twins strike a bold, dominant theme and bring

a larger boon to mankind; but the Stricken Twins, echoing the same mythic pattern, transpose it to another key—a gentler, softer tone that is closer to ordinary humanity. They mollify the gods not by bravery or endurance or even clever trickery, but by the longing of their hearts expressed in song. The gods cannot refuse.[51]

So it seems that the Stricken Twins' human mother grounds them in ordinary reality, and their imploring pleas for help liken their vulnerability to that of "People on the Earth."

Returning to the Vidal/Abel scenes, it is possible to expand the basis of identification between the Jemez boys and the Stricken Twins. It has already been established that Vidal is a representation of Elder Brother of the Follower Pair and that Abel is Younger Brother. There are numerous motifs and images that appear in the Stricken Twins myth that are replicated in *House Made of Dawn*, suggesting that Abel is projected into a specific healing pattern. Apparently Vidal and Abel are both illegitimate children whose paternity is a secret. In the Stricken Twins story this same situation likely drives them away from home, as they aimlessly look for their absent father. (And in the case of the Twin War Gods, they leave home to seek their father, the sun.)[52] When Vidal and Abel go off into the box canyon, they may or may not be seeking their father, but the effect of the journey is similar—they wander into strange alien territory. The box canyon is reminiscent of the dark confining rock shelter that attracted the Stricken Twins.

Both sets of twins have almost no family. Abel and Vidal have a mother and grandfather and the Stricken Twins have five human relatives and Talking God.[53] Yet kinship ties are strong—in the novel between the grandfather and Abel and in the Stricken Twins story between the father and his offspring. The violation of kinship ties that occurs when the Stricken Twins' family rejects them is faintly akin to the old priest Fray Nicholas' rejection of his illegitimate son, Francisco, when he (Francisco) performs native ritual:

He is evil & desires to do me some injury & this after I
befriended him all his life. Preserve this I write to you that
you may make him responsible if I die. He is one of them
& goes often in the kiva & puts on their horns & hides &
does worship that Serpent which even is the One our most
ancient enemy.[54]

One of the close connections here between the two sets of twins'
circumstances is that they have little help or family support in
their sufferings. Consequently, the boys become helpers to one
another, solidifying their ties even further. In the Stricken Twins
story, the discovery of the Twins' kinship with the gods is a
matter of great ceremonial importance, because this factor makes
them eligible for a cure.[55] In *House Made of Dawn*, the marked
lack of recognition of kinship, that occurs when Abel drunkenly
stumbles off the bus ("He was drunk, and he fell against his
grandfather and did not know him."), is shocking in a culture
where elders are highly valued.[56]

   Still, this loneliness that the twins experience can eventually
lead to power and knowledge, as well as suffering.[57] For the
Stricken Twins, the fact that they are unable to determine the
causes of their despair (grieving over sudden lost health) leads
to a series of misadventures or "wild goose chase" journeys as
they look for a cure. When they wander about the landscape,
however, they gain power through acquiring personal knowledge of sacred spots and the Holy People who inhabit them.
Furthermore, wandering around, running into "new" Holy People here and there, forces the Stricken Twins to retell their story
as more gods inquire about their misfortunes. When *Hastséhogan*
asks about their identity, the following conversation takes place:

   "If you wish to have your diseases cured why do you come
   to us? The People on the Earth understand how to treat
   disease. Whence do you come, and who told you there was
   a house here?" One of the boys replied that their home was
   at Ĭndestsíhonia', and he went on to tell the whole of their
   sad story, all over again.[58]

Repeating the story is a means of understanding the experience
or of integrating their adventures toward a whole, complete
comprehension of what happened. And, as they come to know
more about their heritage, they become stronger.

When they originally returned home in a weakened state, after
their accident, "the children told this story":

> They had not wandered far from the lodge on the day of
> their departure when they came to a rock-shelter where
> they sat down to rest. While they were seated the roof of
> the shelter closed over and entrapped them. In the cave
> thus formed they remained (as they now found) four days
> and four nights in utter darkness. On the fifth day the rocks
> were opened by the god Hastsédiltsosi and they were al-
> lowed to come out. Then they found that one was lame and
> the other was blind, and they thought of the way of trav-
> eling by which they came home, that the one who could
> walk should carry on his back the one who could see. They
> thought it was Hastsédiltsosi who had imprisoned them in
> the rocks and cast the evil spell upon them.[59]

Afterwards their family tried to cure them through herbal treat-
ments, but with no success.

In the Stricken Twins story, Elder Brother is blind and Younger
Brother is lame or crippled. At first it may be difficult to see how
either Vidal or Abel could be said to have similar physical ailments. However, it is possible to construct a case for Vidal's
blindness and Abel's lameness based on a strong symbolic identification with these infirmities in the narrative. In the geese
hunting scene, although Vidal is the leader as Elder Brother, he
appears not to notice the beauty of the water birds arising from
the moonlit river. Intent upon hunting, Vidal concentrates on
the wounded bird. But Abel, speaking, as he rarely does, says:
*"Did you see? Oh, they were beautiful! Oh Vidal, oh my brother, did
you see?"*[60] Years later, as Abel tells this story to Milly, he breath-
lessly recalls the aesthetic dimension to this scene:

> *Oh Milly the water birds were beautiful I wish you could have
> seen them I wanted my brother to see them they were flying high
> and far away in the night sky and there was a full white moon
> and a ring around the moon and the clouds were long and bright
> and moving fast and my brother was alive and the water birds
> were so far away in the south and I wanted him to see them they
> were beautiful and please I said please did you see them how they
> pointed with their heads to the moon and flew through the ring of
> the moon. . . .*[61]

Abel had desperately wanted to share the beauty of the place
with Vidal. It is as if that perfect moment would only have been
complete if "the twin" had seen it too. As it was, Abel seemed
to see for Vidal. Vidal's utter lack of response to Abel's question:
"Oh Vidal, oh my brother, did you see?" indicates that these
passages from the text could be discussed in terms of sight imagery. Oddly enough, a curious reversal of roles occurs when
Abel remembers this childhood incident years later, after being
beaten up.

> *Oh Milly oh God the pain my hands my hands are broken.* He
> tried to open the other eye, both eyes wide, but he could
> not. He stared into the blackness that pressed upon and
> within him. The backs of his eyelids were black and murky
> like the fog; microscopic shapes, motes and bits of living
> thread floated obliquely down, were buoyed up again, and
> vanished in the great gulf of his blindness. He did not know
> how to tell of his pain; it was beyond his power to name
> and assimilate.[62]

As an adult, Abel takes on Elder Brother's blindness. He is at
once the younger crippled twin and the elder sightless twin (with
broken hands, and "blackness . . . within"). After Vidal dies Abel
takes on some of his attributes. In the "present time" scene literal
and metaphorical afflictions or physical and spiritual afflictions
merge. Abel appears blind and severely limited in terms of self-
knowledge—black within. His outer condition mirrors his inner

state. In terms of health, the "exterior landscape" of the river had once been beautiful, but when the world turned ugly in Los Angeles, Abel's inner self sickened.[63]

Scholars have noted a host of associations for both Elder and Younger Brother. George Mills has observed about characteristics of the Navajo hero pattern: "In the plot outline older brother is identified with courage and heroism while younger brother, the stay-at-home, receives and domesticates the new power."[64] John Farella adds that Monster Slayer functions in the role of male in the pair, while Born for Water protects his brother, functioning in the role of the female twin.[65] Clyde Benally adds that "Elder Brother is concerned with game animals and the power of death. Younger Brother . . . is concerned with agriculture and the power of life."[66] The Pueblo War Gods share similar attributes.[67] In a monograph published in 1916, H. K. Haeberlin points out about the Pueblo Twin War Gods: "They are war gods par excellence but are at the same time intrinsically associated with fertilization."[68] This point may explain why Vidal and Abel, in the novel, appear in the newly irrigated fields together, and why Abel, as Younger Brother (Born for Water), is attracted to but confused by sources of water. "Why should Abel think of the fishes? He could not understand the sea; it was not of his world. It was an enchanted thing, too, for it lay under the spell of the moon."[69] Abel as Younger Brother was sired by water or by the moon in some accounts.[70] Abel is of water, close to the source of life, but in his lack of introspection and lack of knowledge about his father, he fails to know who he is.

The twins' complementarity reveals the paradox of the interdependency of the forces of creation and destruction. Possessing both the powers of war and fertility, the twins can decide life or death. And since the twins are also a representation of the female and male sides of existence, their presence represents a dynamic balancing of gender relationships.

Gladys Reichard says that in the "Navajo conception . . . nothing exists of and for itself, or absolutely at a particular time, or at a given point. . . ."[71] Navajo world view is based on a recognition of transformation as the primary process that relates all aspects of nature to one another. Reichard also says that:

One condition frequently referred to in the myths, and by implication in the chants, is the possibility that any god may be duplicated. The Stricken Twins, seeking help, wander from one god to another having the same name but living in different places.[72]

What Reichard calls the principle or "notion of multiple selves" is a "supernatural device" that functions aesthetically and ritually to achieve balance in oral and visual art.[73] According to Reichard, ". . . Navajo design . . . ignoring time and space, allows each spiritual being as many selves as it needs."[74] These other selves are but "a representative of themselves in a different role."[75] Monster Slayer can become Holy Man or Reared-Within-the-Earth in different chantway contexts. Reichard further illustrates this "principle of multiple selves" by stating:

> The Twelve Brothers of the Endurance Chant are almost certainly duplicates of The Twins in their idealized domestic form. RM [Red Mustache], who told the story, said explicitly that the Youngest Brother, the little one with power, was Monster Slayer.[76]

Bearing in mind then that this mythic identification of Monster Slayer with Younger Brother is possible, Abel can be seen to temporarily become one of Monster Slayer's multiple selves when he (Abel) kills the albino.

Repulsed by the gruesome albino who had been threatening the village corn fields, Abel struck out at the "alien presence."[77] At this time, Abel is a combination of both Elder and Younger Brothers. He is the pair. This violent act of striking out at the albino is a way of maintaining contact with Vidal's reality. Soon, however, Abel reverts to his essentially meek, passive self. According to Enemyway, a Navajo rite, a warrior needs to reconstitute the other half of himself to be whole after having been tainted by an alien ghost. When a warrior is in the aggressive mode of being, he is said to be "*sǫ'a nagháí*," associated with a state of maleness and long life. This state of being is a "state of incompleteness," however, and must be joined ceremonially with the state of femaleness and happiness: *"bik'e hózhǫ."*[78] Again the Navajo principles of pairing, duality, and alternation operate to produce a unified state of harmony within an individual. Farella says: *"Anaa'jii* [Enemyway] in this sense, then, is a re-entry process, a bringing back of the dangerous one to society."[79] Abel resumes his role as Younger Brother, here associated with the state of bik'e hózhǫ, although by this time the white judicial system has sent him to prison for acting out Elder Brother's murderous impulses.[80] Subdued in prison and lonely, Abel is once again merely Younger Brother, without Elder Brother. This theme of loss of a twin continues throughout the novel until the end when the grandfather's memories of the children together reconstitute the pair. A symbolic twin reunification takes place as Vidal is restored to Abel through story.[81]

This "twin reunification" is a form of healing, and may signal a temporary state of well-being that might be disrupted once again for Abel, outside the scope of the novel. The motif of the interrupted ceremony occurs in the Stricken Twins myth when the twins who are partially cured violate taboo and must wait to be cured until they have procured guarded valuables from the enemy Mokis. A parallel interrupted ceremony exists in the novel. Ben, like a medicine man, sings the "House Made of Dawn" prayer, but Abel does not repeat it until dawn, after nine nights, back home at Jemez.[82] A delayed response between singer and the one-sung-over is not customary during an actual ceremony, but the fact that Abel repeats the song when he does means that he has symbolically endured a nine-night ceremony, the correct length for the full version of the Night Chant. The ceremony always concludes at dawn. Consequently, there is a pervasive sense of completion, healing, and symmetry at the end of the novel.

Healing is necessary in both *House Made of Dawn* and the Stricken Twins story because of the presence of evil. In *House Made of Dawn* the origins of evil are obscure and complex. Not only are Abel's bloodlines tainted with evil (". . . for evil had long since found him [grandfather Francisco] out and knew who he was."), but he has personally experienced evil since he was a child.[83]

Something frightened him. There was an old woman. They called her Nicolás *teah-whau* because she had a white mustache and a hunched back and she would beg for whiskey on the side of the road. She was a Bahkyush woman, they said, and a witch. She was old the first time he had seen her, and drunk. She had screamed at him some unintelligible curse, appearing out of a cornfield when as a child he had herded the sheep nearby. And he had run away, hard. . . .[84]

Even Abel's dog sensed the evil in the air. It "quivered and laid back its ears."[85] Abel was aware of the intensity of the witch presence.

Then he heard it, the thing itself. He knew even then that it was only the wind, but it was a stranger sound than any he had ever known. And at the same time he saw the hole in the rock where the wind dipped, struck, and rose. It was larger than a rabbit hole and partly concealed by the chokecherry which grew beside it. The moan of the wind grew loud, and it filled him with dread. For the rest of his life it would be for him the particular sound of anguish.[86]

The Stricken Twins story contains parallel images of fear. The Holy People have a watchdog. When the Twins approach one side of a canyon, he barks on the other side. Hastséyalti says: "Our dog never barks unless he sees something strange."[87] This image of the Twins as aliens is sustained throughout the text. When Abel returned to Jemez for the first time in the novel, dogs barked as he walked through the streets on his way to climb a hill at dawn. The dogs did not recognize him, just as he had not recognized his grandfather the day before. Even the dogs knew that Abel was out of place. In the passage from the novel about the witch presence, the wind blows obliquely through the hole in the rock, ominously suggesting the witch's evil spirit on the loose. When the Stricken Twins sit by the edge of a hole at the top of a mountain, two gods appear out of a turbulent wind. Associated with Squeaking Yéi who imprisoned the Twins in the rock shelter, these gods threaten to whip the boys and never release them.[88]

When the Yéi (Holy People) decide to cure the Twins, Talking God says: ". . . now you shall have your eyes cured and your limbs cured, and you shall walk as well and see as well as you did before the evil spell was cast upon you."[89] The cure takes place at Tsé íntyel "where the two creeks join."[90] This image is a natural or organic symbol of twinness, suggesting that when two separate entities come together a healing wholeness is achieved. To put it otherwise, the rivers flowing into one another parallel the image of Navajo human twins being treated as one in ceremony.[91]

The Stricken Twins offer the gods gifts of beads, turquoise baskets, and unwounded buckskins in exchange for a cure.[92] Abel may not receive his full ceremonial blessing until he prepares offerings for his grandfather on his death-bed, nine nights after hearing Ben's song. Abel dresses Francisco in his beautiful ceremonial clothes and blesses him with pollen, cornmeal, and sacred eagle and turkey feathers.[93] In both the Stricken Twins story and the novel one must consciously create beauty and offer love in exchange for the reciprocal gift of health. When Fat Josie, a great bear of a woman, hugged Abel to realign his body after his fall from a horse, Abel was healed.[94] The daughters of Hastséhogan similarly remake the Stricken Twins through holy massage.[95]

Ultimately the key to the durability of the healing process is the continued renewal of the world through song, for song celebrates the lifeforce. But Abel was *"inarticulate."*

. . . he wanted to make a song out of the colored canyon, the way the women of Torreón made songs upon their looms out of colored yarn, but he had not got the right words together. It would have been a creation song; he would have sung lowly of the first world, of fire and flood, and of the emergence of dawn from the hills.[96]

Abel spontaneously wants to sing an emergence/creation song telling of the sacred history of the Jemez on their journey from the underworlds onto the present earth surface. This song would be reminiscent of the Navajo origin songs and stories told visually in intricate rug designs at Torreón, west of Jemez Springs.[97] Abel's urge to sing is an impulse toward performing a meaningful symbolic act. By recalling the character and order of the world, such an act would bring the power of origins to his "interior landscape" to spark his integration with his homeland and tribal tradition. But his stifled voice does not allow him to fully express his heritage in the hills above the Valle Grande. Because he cannot name the sacred places surrounding him, nor tell of the sacred epochs of life in the underworlds, he remains physically abstracted from his environment and in a dangerous spiritual state. The song Abel wants to make would transform the energy he receives from walking along the radiant canyon into a useable form for healing, for singing charges the atmosphere where it takes place.

As the Stricken Twins wander through canyon country, they are coaxed into verbal expression by the Holy People who secretly seem to have the boys' best interests at heart. The narrator of the *To' Nastsihégo Hatál* myth says that the Holy People ". . . asked the boys all the questions that had been asked at the other holy places, for they wished to hear how the boys would tell the tale themselves."[98] This repetition of the story of the boys' misfortunes interests the gods less than the manner of the telling, which always emphasizes the clever way of traveling that the Twins devised. By remembering that the two of them depended on their own resourcefulness to form a whole "healthy" person (blind brother walking, sighted brother riding), the Twins begin to develop faith in the ability of their own organisms to regenerate or be reassembled. The plaintive vocal quality of their song moves the gods' "interior landscapes" toward compassion. Perhaps the boys' singing is even more compelling to the Holy People than the boys' perseverance in seeking a cure. The Follower Pair of Stricken Twins, "the pair who traveled," epitomize motion in their use of mythic space in a vast landscape as they walk and sing.[99] The Twins, then, are a living visualization of *nitch'i*, as they wander about, their breath turning into song.

Through overcoming their afflictions, the Twins learn what it means to be *Diné*.[100] When robbed of their sight and power of locomotion, the Stricken Twins learn through deprivation what it is like to live outside of the Navajo way, for the Navajo know themselves through freedom of movement to be beautiful.[101] Sight and motion are essential to the way that the Navajo define themselves. As the singer Grey Mustache says:

> And so it is that when one doesn't know the traditions one has nothing to light one's way. It is as though one lived with a covering on one's eyes, as if one lived being deaf and blind. Yet when one knows the traditions, one has vision to see . . . all the way to where the land meets the ocean. It's as though one's vision becomes as good as that.[102]

Grey Mustache's metaphor of sight representing inner knowledge aptly describes the Stricken Twins' predicament. The Stricken Twins' story provides a pattern of resolution for their identity problems. When they are children, not yet extensively educated in their people's ways, they have limited knowledge. The blinding of Elder Brother and crippling of Younger Brother forces them to seek a means of survival. This hardship propels both brothers out into the world and into intimate contact with the Holy People. Once the Twins live the myth and learn the ceremonial procedures to Nightway (in Grey Mustache's language "the traditions"), the Twins are completely restored by life-sustaining knowledge. Once again they are ready to set forth, to go.[103] The gift of motion is the gift of life.

The final scene of *House Made of Dawn* depicts Abel running into the dawn, running for himself and running for Vidal, seeing for himself and seeing for Vidal. Elder Brother and Younger Brother have been spiritually reunited in Abel since the morning before, on the last dawn of their grandfather's life, when the old medicine man murmured their names together: "Abelito, Vidalito."[104] As Abel runs, he becomes repossessed by the land:

". . . he could see at last without having to think. He could
see the canyon and the mountains and the sky. He could
see the rain and the river and the fields beyond. He could
see the dark hills at dawn."[105]

The run is a perfect expression of the beauty of vision and motion, of the gift of life passed down to the boys through grandfather, who long before them had run on the snowy wagon road
at dawn. Francisco had marked his own 1889 sunrise race by
drawing an image in his ledger book of himself as a sooty black
runner in the snow.[106] Half a century later Abel recreates this
dark image when he smears his body with ashes and runs over
the encrusted snow as it begins to rain. This act occurs perhaps
an hour or so after he had taken the ledger book, prayer feathers,
pollen, and corn meal down from the rafters of Francisco's house,
only to place these personal effects and offerings alongside the
elder's body.[107] As his grandfather's spirit begins traveling to the
world beyond, Abel becomes an embodiment of Francisco, as
well as Vidal. These multiple male selves fuse into the image of
an enduring ashen runner who runs home into the house made
of pollen.

3

Bears and Sweet Smoke

Animal Transformers

There is a story that the Cochiti people tell about their neighbors over the western mountains, the Jemez:

> At Jemez they had a deer dance (*heemishikia*). The dancers turned into deer and ran up into the mountains. They never came back any more. For four days they made ceremonies in Jemez to bring them back, but they could not.[1]

In her notes to this story, Ruth Benedict, collector of the tale, says:

> There are supernatural dangers associated with the dances. At a certain deer dance the deer dancers were permanently metamorphosed into deer and ran into the mountains. They tried to recover them through the curing society ceremonies but they could not.[2]

This story provides a helpful perspective to begin this discussion of symbolism and the animal world because the story focuses on an image of human beings so powerfully transformed by ceremony that they become part of the natural world in a compelling new way. When a sick native person is healed communally through ritual symbolic means, he finds new life as if he, too, had gained the strength to run like a deer at an exhilarating pace into the mountains.

Abel's personal transformation from illness to returning health in *House Made of Dawn* can be understood only within the context of the larger cultural/religious transformations of the story and these traditions' inherent linkages to the yet larger patterns of reality in nature. In the novel, Momaday has regenerated time-less, archetypal literary symbols, embedded in myth, to produce living images of events in nature and human responses to them. Because the novel has a "high degree of internal reference" to such esoteric events as eagle-catching, ritual running, bear hunt-ing, and plaza dancing, it becomes difficult but necessary for the reader to unravel their complex interrelationships and signifi-cances, thereby making the text intelligible.[3] My approach to uncovering these symbolic networks is to draw upon ethno-graphic documents, some of which Momaday appropriated for his work, and upon other works of scholarship in an effort to better comprehend the primary holistic relationships in the nat-ural world that the storysherds or traditional stories in the novel voice, and to see how mythic reality is continuous with present-day reality.

In this chapter I explore both animal stories and ritual events in *House Made of Dawn* in an effort to understand how certain animals—eagle, snake, and bear—and particular ritual events— the rooster race, the race for good hunting and harvests, and the squash clan dance—become models of transformation for the characters in the story, as well as for the tribal community. The primary model of transformation is the bear, for Bear is the living embodiment of the continuously generating healing pow-ers of nature. Although both domesticated and wild animals may be models of transformation, the novel makes the point that the spirits of wild animals are still intact, whereas domesticated ani-mals are largely alienated from the land.[4] Thus, certain wild animals, in particular the bear, are appropriate to summon and identify with in story and ritual. Abel learns about the process of alienation, transformation, and healing through contact with six significant animals: rooster and horse, bull and snake, eagle and bear.

Rooster and Horse

Father Olguin, the Mexican priest serving Walatowa (Jemez Pueblo) in the 1940s and 1950s in the novel, relates the story of the origin of the feast of Santiago.[5] Olguin tells how the hero/saint Santiago destroyed enemies and subsequently brought about the creation of domestic animals and plants for the Pueblo people. Aided by a kind old couple and a regurgitated rooster, Santiago survived to provide great benefits for the Pueblos. The story is full of transformations. The rooster's spur becomes a "magic sword." Both horse and rooster plead with Santiago to sacrifice them "for the good of the people." Santiago kills his enemies and the horse by stabbing. Afterward he "tore the bird apart with his bare hands and scattered the remains all around on the ground." The blood and feathers mix with the soil and the horse's blood to multiply into "a great herd of horses" and "cultivated plants and domestic animals."[6] The horse and the rooster are sacred victims whose gift of their own lives enriches the lives of the people.

In the novel this sacred history is reenacted on Santiago's feast day, July 25, as it is at Jemez annually. By recreating the dismemberment of the original rooster, through ritually sacrificing a rooster each year, agricultural and animal life for the village are renewed for another cycle. Reenacting or performing the myth expresses gratitude to the powers of fertility and transforms Walatowa into a blessed plentiful community. The dying rooster's blood, like water, becomes the sacred substance that engenders more life.[7] The people celebrate after the "chicken pull" by feasting, an activity that has been made possible by the rooster myth.[8]

Startlingly, Abel, who has just returned home from war less than a week before, chooses to participate with the other riders in the rooster race in The Middle, the village's dance plaza. Back in his old clothes, an outward sign of return, Abel is unable to pluck the buried rooster out of the ground as he rushes past on horseback. The albino Juan Reyes Fragua, though, grabs up the bird and flails Abel with it, apparently an appropriate act for the victor.[9] Angela, the white visitor to Jemez Springs who soon afterwards becomes Abel's lover, notices "something out of place, some flaw in proportion or design, some unnatural thing" when the albino appears.[10] A week later after the town has celebrated the Fiesta of Porcingula, which features the dancing Pecos horse and bull, the latter animal a figure of evil, Abel and the albino meet in Paco's Bar up the road for a scene of final reckoning.

Bull and Snake

It is as if the Fiesta of Porcingula, which honors Pecos relatives and the growth of corn and mocks the Spaniard's historical presence as personified by the bull, rouses Abel's emotions to bait the albino, as the clowns had taunted the bull.[11] Abel's deadened, alienated attitude changes when he participates in the rooster pull by throwing up his hands to protect his face from the bloody rooster. He becomes engaged in the sacrifice. If "sacrifice is primarily an act of violence without risk of vengeance," then oddly, the albino's chicken pull sacrifice has escalated violence, instead of diminished it, presumably because Abel has partially misunderstood the nature of the pueblo's ritual and taken the affront of the rooster slap personally.[12] When Abel kills the albino the murder appears, at least partially, to be an act of retaliation for the humiliation of being struck during the rooster race.

Clearly, the albino is associated with evil. He looks hideous and is said to give "a strange, inhuman cry—as of pain. It was an old woman's laugh, thin and weak as water. It issued only from the tongue and teeth of the great evil mouth. . . ."[13] The origins of Abel's illness as a little boy are related to his negative transformations by the sources of evil in the novel. As mentioned previously in chapter 2, the old woman witch (here symbolically related to the albino through a similar cry), the sound of the moaning wind, and the tainted family heritage all contribute to trapping Abel in a state of fear and, depending on mood, either passivity or violence. He remembers the whine of the tank on the battlefield as reminiscent of the moaning wind that he had heard as a child and that he will hear again when he kills the albino during a rainstorm.[14] The narrator comments:

He had always been afraid. Forever at the margin of his mind there was something to be afraid of, something to fear. He did not know what it was, but it was always there, real, imminent, unimaginable.[15]

Grandfather Francisco had confronted evil in the person of the albino whose presence in the cornfield threatened to harm the town's main food source. It seems that Francisco's "blessing upon the corn" was spiritually strong enough to temporarily ward off the witch's evil influence, a few days before Abel killed him.[16]

When the albino is dying near Jemez, he transforms into a fishsnake figure, confirming his psychic-spiritual connection with *culebra* (snake), the brutal Los Angeles cop, Martinez, who beat Abel.[17] Abel "felt the blue shivering lips upon him, felt even the scales of the lips and the hot slippery point of the tongue, writhing. . . . The white, hairless arm shone like the underside of a fish. . . ."[18] The albino is one of the gliding ones who may be killed with a knife but who has supernatural power to be re-manifested as culebra later in Los Angeles. These evil figures are ones whom the pueblo "runners after evil" pursue relentlessly. "Evil was. Evil was abroad in the night; they [Runners After Evil] must venture out to the confrontation; they must reckon dues and divide the world."[19] When Abel was tried for murder of the albino, he said he had killed "an evil spirit," something according to Father Olguin that only "the psychology of witchcraft" could explain.[20] Abel thought: "A man kills such an enemy if he can."[21] Tosamah, Kiowa Priest of the Sun, says that Abel "killed a goddam *snake*."[22] Abel killed his enemy, the witchsnake.

Snakes are slippery and essentially mysterious, because of their ability to appear and disappear rapidly. Mircea Eliade points out that the image of a snake sloughing off its skin makes it appear changeable. He says: "it is immortal because it is continually reborn."[23] This image of a snake as transformer of its own self is a crucial one to the consideration of healing in the novel. Discussing snake in the context of pueblo deities, Hamilton Tyler remarks:

Since the snake can kill, it can also cure. In its role as com-
municator between the upper and the lower world, it knows
of seeds and fertility, and the tilling of the soil.[24]

This rather positive view of snake, as maintainer of life as well
as death, is offset by Marc Simmons' comment:

Regarding snakes and their relation to witchcraft, some
ambivalence exists among the Indians. . . In fact the eastern
[Rio Grande] villages seem to have been won over, at least
partially, to the Spanish view that snakes were loathsome
creatures, the servants of evil, and the accomplices of
witches.[25]

Since pueblo witches can change into snakes, Abel's violence in
killing the witchsnake, a predator, may be viewed as more beneficial than harmful to the village.[26]

Lawrence Evers, in a provocative article, recalls a conversation
with Momaday wherein the author stated:

portions of the plot of his novel *House Made of Dawn* were
loosely based on an actual case history. He recalls reading
of a young Indian who when brought to trial for murdering
a man testified that he killed the man because he was a
witch.[27]

Evers describes an event in which two young Acoma Pueblo
brothers acted on the basis of "witch perception."[28] In detailing
the psychiatric evaluation of the younger brother, Gabriel Felipe,
Evers mentions that ". . . a normal Acoma would have called in
a medicine society. . . ." Yet Gabriel Felipe did not. His examining physician, Devereux, stated: "The normal Acoma considers
witchcraft a public matter. This inmate [Gabriel] considered it a
private grievance."[29] It seems that Abel, like Gabriel Felipe, violated
similar established procedures of his own culture for dealing with

an evil witch presence, and that in doing so Abel becomes a rule-breaker, a transgressor of cultural restrictions.

Paula Gunn Allen calls the albino that Abel kills "the alien other." She describes the albino symbolism operating in the novel: "Certainly, the albino in his death resembles the white man, the Church, and the unseen, nameless evil which Abel seeks to destroy or evade . . ."[30] Previously Allen had explained:

> He [Abel] seems to be haunted, and the deaths of his mother and brother intensify his preoccupation with the terrors of the unseen evil that seems to stalk him. His grandfather, Francisco, no stranger to evil, has made an uneasy peace with it, but perhaps he has been cursed; his crippled leg, the deaths of all those he loved with the exception of Abel whose crippling is less visible but more complete, indicate that he is a victim of some supernatural ill will.[31]

The "unseen evil" that haunts Abel is ever present whether manifested in the albino or the snake. Although snake has the positive potential to transform itself, in the context of the novel, snake consistently reveals only its death-giving self, thus preventing it from becoming a positive transformative model for healing.

Eagle and Snake

As a young man, Abel had been privileged to accompany the Bahkyush Eagle Watchers on their annual hunt, because he had seen the "holy sight" of a pair of golden eagles playing in flight with a snake. After catching a beautiful eagle himself, he became repulsed by its inert form and suffocated it, disregarding a cultural restriction.[32] Surely this act of desecration brought an additional curse on his life. As Paula Gunn Allen says: "he strangles her [the eagle], thus violating the ceremony and separating himself further from the religious/ceremonial life of the tribe."[33] Abel's multiple transgressions keep him suspended in a state of disharmony or illness on the periphery of Walatowa. He has violated the proper sacrificial patterns of his culture. Whereas Abel's relationships with Snake and Eagle harm him, his association with Bear heals him.

Bear

Bear emerges prominently in *House Made of Dawn*. Momaday utilizes ideas from the Navajo creation story and passages from Mountainway, as well as hunting stories from Jemez Pueblo tradition, to create a pervasive bear presence in the novel, a presence so strongly delineated that it envelops even one of the non-Indian characters, Angela. Essentially Momaday uses bear stories in the novel to present an image of physical and spiritual renewal through contact with the wilderness. In both Pueblo and Navajo traditions, Bear is both enemy and healer, a powerful transformer of self and of other persons. Paul Shepard speaks of Bear as "elder brother" who though his sacredness "is freed to be almost wholly symbolic, to *convey* in the richest sense, to mediate between the world of humans and the world of spirits."[34] Bear's life cycle, moving into a death-like hibernation in winter and reemerging into full life in the spring, represents a pattern of transformation that is symbolically parallel to the healing process. Bear is said to have knowledge of other worlds, those that he visits when he "disappears" during his winter journeys, and the underworld that he digs into in his search for medicinal roots.[35] This power of medicine is expressed in Bear's life cycle. *House Made of Dawn* contains four bear stories that connect Abel in a kinship way to Bear, to the wilderness, to oral tradition, and to the principle of transformation inherent in life.

An image of Bear and Badger appears early in the novel in Angela's imagination, as she makes love with Abel. Four bear stories are developed later in the text, although critics have generally paid attention to only two, and Nora Baker Barry only finds three.[36] The four bear stories are: Tosamah's Kiowa legend of the bear brother, Angela's story of the bear boy, Ben's related stories of Changing Bear Maiden ["Esdzá shash nadle"] and bear father/bear maiden/bear boy from Navajo tradition, and Francisco's own Jemez bear hunting story. These four stories appearing together, although structurally distinct in the narrative, indicate a completeness of bear knowledge in that "four" signifies wholeness and truth in Jemez tradition.[37] The fact that these stories derive from Jemez, Navajo, Kiowa, and Anglo-American sources suggests that confronting Bear and internalizing the experience may be an important need for humans living in bear country on the North American continent. As Paul Shepard says, each animal has an "inner twin" counterpart in humans.[38] People then need to know the imaginary bear within or their own bear-like reservoirs of strength, endurance, and healing energy. Hearing stories about bears interacting with human beings helps dramatize this relationship.

By examining each bear story in the novel, and previous critical comments about each appearance of bear, it is possible to determine the key structural, symbolic, and thematic roles of Bear. Although Snake and Eagle have been extensively commented on in the critical literature as the embodiment of the powers of earth and sky, and the dualities of evil and good, little work has been done on the importance of Bear. This may have been the case because the cultural sources and details of Ben's bear story, for instance, are obscure. Providing a multicultural mythic context that can assist in interpreting this part of the novel, and citing sources that Momaday used in constructing this aspect of the book, makes it possible to see the relationship of the text to the larger cultural milieu and, at the same time, to assess Momaday's artistry in adapting old stories to his new one. Lastly, I will illustrate how Bear in *House Made of Dawn* primarily serves to establish a complex model of transformation that can be emulated by those in need of healing.

Tosamah's Bear Story

Tosamah, Priest of the Sun, called both "orator" and "physician," possesses the healing power of words when, in Los Angeles, he tells the story of his people's journey from the headwaters of the Yellowstone to the land around Rainy Mountain, Oklahoma.[39] A story within his story is the legend that the Kiowa made when they encountered Devil's Tower on their migration.

Eight children were there at play, seven sisters and their brother. Suddenly the boy was struck dumb; he trembled and began to run upon his hands and feet. His fingers became claws, and his body was covered with fur. There was a bear where the boy had been. The sisters were terrified; they ran, and the bear after them. They came to the stump of a great tree, and the tree spoke to them. It bade them climb upon it, and as they did so it began to rise into the air. The bear came to kill them, but they were just beyond its reach. It reared against the tree and scored the bark all around with its claws. The seven sisters were borne into the sky, and they became the stars of the Big Dipper.[40]

This story, for Tosamah, explains the Kiowa's relationship with the physical landscape. "Man," according to Tosamah, "must never fail to explain such a thing to himself, or else he is estranged forever from the universe."[41] This story, an imaginative projection of the Kiowa ancestors, accounts for the scored monolith and the guiding stars of the Big Dipper. Thinking of Bear as the active agent who brought about these transformations in earth and sky is a means of accounting for the massive energy that created this upheaval. Bear makes possible the creation of the Kiowa's "kinsmen in the night sky."[42] And once the Kiowa could see this night light they could redefine themselves as people no longer hampered by the confines of dark mountain wilderness.[43] This historic redefinition of tribal identity is transformative and renewing. Symbolically, the people were "healed" through their new self-created sense of place.

The details of the tale all point toward transformation as a central theme. The motif of the brother "suddenly" being "struck dumb" is reminiscent of the Navajo Stricken Twins' unaccountable transformation into blind and crippled boys. Here the mute Kiowa boy's loss of the power of speech (contrasted to the tree's acquisition of speech) is both a sign of transformation and a terrifying element, preceding as it does the growth of claws and fur and the loss of human behavior. Since the seven sisters, who manage to escape the bear, become supernaturals when they are transformed into stars, the potentially destructive confrontation with Bear actually provides the girls with access to power. And since the Kiowa are symbolically identified through kinship with the seven star sisters, it is as if the tribe is finally freed of its long association with mountain wilderness, as Bear retreats. The scored bark around the huge tree—a vertical image of the Kiowa's emergence log—is the incised mark of the bear's story.[44] And the rising stump, a striking image of regenerative growth, like the old log, signifies passage into another life.[45]

Writing of this sacred site to Matthias Schubnell, Momaday discloses that he believes that the bear is still guarding *Tsoai* (Devil's Tower) and even guarding Momaday himself. Reflecting on his ability as an outsider to survive his early education on the Navajo and Jemez reservations, Momaday writes:

> How did I survive that? How did I come through that experience with my tongue in one piece? It was of course medicine. The bear was watching close by. The bear is always there.[46]

Momaday here is emphasizing the bear's power of protection, called bear "medicine" or a force for good. The bear, Momaday's "guardian spirit" has protected Momaday's gift of language.[47] Since language used carefully and appropriately can control the universe and insure survival, Bear functions as "medicine person" by perpetuating the life of a storyteller.

Concerning the significance of Bear in Kiowa culture, Alice Marriott in *The Ten Grandmothers,* a collection of stories revolving around the ten medicine bundles of the Kiowa, says:

> Sitting Bear and Heap of Bears were related in a medicine sort of way. They were both named for the bear, the most powerful animal there was in a medicine way. Unless you were named for the bear, or were speaking to somebody that was, you mustn't even say the word *bear.* It was that powerful. Bears could drive you crazy, just for saying their name, and to look at them could almost kill a man. Nobody

knew what would happen if you killed or ate a bear. People were too afraid to try.[48]

This passage binds together the dual images of Bear as enemy and healer, a seeming paradox which will be discussed more fully later. In *House Made of Dawn*, the full range of Bear's powers—from deadly to protective and curative—is represented.

The Kiowa bear story, positioned midway through the novel, alerts the reader to the bear themes in the latter part of the book. These themes include fleeing from evil, accumulation of spiritual power, and transformation. And the Kiowa's journey to their new home is a distant parallel to Abel's long journey home.

Angela's Bear Story

The second bear story in the novel is told by Angela to Abel and Ben in a hospital (a place of curing) in Los Angeles where Abel lies bedridden after a severe beating by Martinez, the culebra cop. Summoned by Ben, Angela walks into the room talking, prefacing a favorite story. Ben recalls:

> She said she was sorry he was sick, and she was sure he would be well again soon. She went on talking kind of fast, like she knew just what she wanted to say . . . she started telling him about her son, Peter. . . .

and saying that "he [Abel] would always be her friend."[49] When Peter asked her about Indians "she used to tell him a story about a young Indian brave."

> He was born of a bear and a maiden, she said, and he was noble and wise. He had many adventures, and he became a great leader and saved his people.[50]

Ben comments that "she always thought of *him*, Abel, when she told it . . . I could tell that story was kind of secret and important to her. . . ."[51]

Angela appears in the room with the self-assurance of a healer. She uses language in this scene in a positive commanding way. To a Navajo, such as Ben, Angela's statement that Abel would soon be well helps to make it so, for language creates reality.[52] Ben reacts to Angela's story in much the same way that he acts a couple of weeks later as he prepares to sing the prayer from the Night Chant for Abel on the hilltop. After Angela's story, Ben felt "kind of ashamed to be there listening."[53] Before singing "House Made of Dawn," Ben had thought:

> The others were singing, too, but it was the wrong kind of thing [social songs], and I wanted to pray. I didn't want them to hear me, because they were having a good time, and I was ashamed, I guess. I kept it down because I didn't want anybody but him to hear.[54]

Ben may feel "ashamed" in both instances because he is embarrassed by the intimacy and impropriety of the situation. It is unusual that a white woman should tell such a biculturally meaningful archetypal story, and it is extraordinary that an ordinary "49" should be the social context for an eruption of sacred power.[55] Angela's story prompts Ben to tell his. Benally's story will be discussed shortly.

Angela's story conforms to the widespread formula of the bear's son tale, which appears in Indo-European as well as Native American cultures. A young hero, born of a bear father and a human mother, acquires bear characteristics and supernatural strength. He undergoes many adventures before returning home.[56] This story may at first seem superficial or only suitable for children, but it carries an abiding reality as a fundamental sketch of a pervasive multicultural pattern. Some versions of the tale emphasize the bear boy's parentage, particularly the mother's experience of abduction by Bear, whereas other versions tend to emphasize the bear son's adventures.[57] The fact that Angela's story is "true" in the sense of verisimilitude to other stories of

its type suggests that she as teller is presenting a reliable por-
trayal of relationships in the natural world. Lawrence Evers contrasts Angela's story to Tosamah's and Ben's and concludes that
"unlike the Navajo legend and the Kiowa bear legend . . . both
etiological legends tied firmly to cultural landscapes, Angela's
story is as rootless as a Disney cartoon."[58] Whereas it is apparent
that Angela has failed to imagine a specific landscape for her
story, she has imagined herself into the story, thereby symbolically connecting herself to Abel and Peter and to native tradition.
Since she had years before imagined that she was making love
to a badger or a bear when she made love to Abel, she has
identified with the "maiden" of her story who "marries" Bear.[59]
Her son Peter then is identified with the young hero, bear boy.

Already pregnant with this child fathered by her doctor husband, Angela had touched her belly, remembering something as
she listened to Abel chop wood:[60]

> Once she had seen an animal slap at the water, a badger
> or a bear. She would have liked to touch the soft muzzle of
> a bear, the thin black lips, the great flat head. She would
> have liked to cup her hand to the wet black snout, to hold
> for a moment the hot blowing of the bear's life.[61]

Four days later she makes love for the first time to Abel.

> He was dark and massive above her, posed and tinged with
> pale blue light. And in that split second she thought again
> of the badger at the water, and the great bear, blue-black
> and blowing.[62]

This sensual image which depicts Abel's bear-like physique and
presence has been dismissed in the criticism as a forlorn white
woman's fantasy about having a dark elemental man as her ideal
lover. Peter Beidler in his article "Animals and Human Development in the Contemporary American Indian Novel" comments about these scenes:

Her identification of Abel with bear is, of course, part sexual fantasy . . . Analysis of Angela's sexual fantasies is beyond the scope of this study. The point here is that her association of Abel with bear triggers in Abel much later an awareness of his own bear nature.[63]

We will return to Beidler's last point later, bearing in mind that it may be short-sighted to assume that Angela has merely projected her "fantasies" onto Abel. Matthias Schubnell recounts Angela's memory of Badger and Bear, and then says:

In the ensuing love scene Abel is portrayed as a Pan figure who revitalizes Angela. In this sexual communion the young woman again has the vision of the bear and the badger, the symbols of animal life.[64]

Schubnell is essentially on the right track here because he sees that Angela is genuinely renewed, but a more appropriate interpretation requires a shift in perspective. There is no textual reason for introducing a classical allusion to a Greek god of nature, and there is every reason to specify precisely what kind of "symbols of animal life" Bear and Badger are.

In Jemez culture, Badger and Bear are the primary animals that possess healing power. There is a badger clan and a bear curing society at Jemez.[65] Badger is little brother to Bear; Bear is elder brother to Badger.[66] They are considered in close relationship to one another, echoing the twin paradigm discussed in chapter 2. Their powers are complementary and constitute a strong force when taken together. Abel, then, is symbolically identified with Bear or the elder brother, as, on occasion, he has been before Angela's story. Of course, Angela does not consciously make all of these connections between the animals or between the animals and her lover, but as Beidler points out, she has remarkable instinct.[67] And she does choose a lover who revitalizes her by putting her back in touch with her own physicality through exposure to the natural world.

Bear is dangerous, and Abel as Bear is both fearsome and

sexually exciting to Angela. Schubnell charts the change in Angela's attitude toward her own body as she moves from a state of "neurotic shame" to "a new state of balance."[68] Although Schubnell acknowledges that Abel had a strong part in bringing Angela into a "new awareness of human nature and the nature of her environment," a good therapeutic change, Schubnell ultimately claims that Angela is "restored, if only temporarily, by the natural healing powers of the sun and the magnetism of the desert landscape."[69] This description of her restoration is vague and incomplete. The bear of Angela's dream vision or memory is associated with water, actually "slap[s] at the water" drawing his sustenance or life from it.[70] The "slap at the water" she reexperiences when she makes love to Abel may be the force of a gesture of transformation that links the healing powers of water to Bear, and through Abel, to Angela. Thus, Abel's bear powers, which were initially frightening to Angela, become the means of activating her transformation toward renewal of self. Her physical sensation with Abel, like the bear "slap at the water," is a sign of contact with wilderness. And her soaking hot mineral bath just before they make love indicates that Angela has been purified to undergo a personal ritual.[71] Contact with water, one of the sources of life, is the source of Angela's "symbolic baptism" into new life.[72] The Jemez Springs medicinal waters have the curative effect that Angela sought when she came to the region.

Momaday presents a web of symbolic associations between humans and the natural world that shows that subconsciously even a cultural outsider like Angela can be partially incorporated into Jemez reality, so powerful is that world view. The more that she becomes psychically immersed in both physical and cultural landscapes, the clearer she becomes about the order of her own life. Angela changes and survives because she imagines the linkages between Badger and Bear, terrain and water, in a way that is consistent with relationships in the natural world, and she survives because she imagines herself into the heart of this pattern of events. In creating a character such as Angela who seems to intuitively sense the patterning of Jemez knowledge of animal kinship and storytelling, Momaday has imagined an astute Anglo woman who to some degree transcends her own cultural background. Referring to Angela's remarkable bear story, Beidler says: "Whether through Angela's instinct or by chance, this story is similar to a Navajo legend which Benally recalls. . . ."[73] It appears that Angela creates her story out of her own personal experience and imagination, not by chance. Since she perceives Badger and Bear from a native-like perspective and even winds up in the role of a young Indian woman in her own story, she is something of a cultural anomaly. But fiction allows for this transcultural leap of the imagination. When Momaday puts Angela into a mythic role, he is being true to a reality where transformations occur suddenly with profound effect. Angela may not expect to be pursued by Bear Man, but she appears no more surprised than her mythological sisters Mother Moon of Jemez and *Bispáli* of Navajo Mountainway, or the seven Kiowa girls whose brother became Bear.[74]

Nora Baker Barry analyzes Angela's bear's son tale from the point of view that Abel is, of course, the heroic bear son who encounters monsters on his adventures before he returns home.[75] Yet Barry has difficulty making a positive identification of Abel with the hero "raised by bears." She has less trouble describing Abel's "strengths and adventures" and "struggles with supernatural foes," and relating the structure of these incidents to a generalized worldwide heroic pattern noted by Panzer.[76] My reading of Angela's story in the context of the novel continues to identify Abel with the bear "husband," Angela with the human "wife" or mother, and Peter, her son, with the bear boy whose adventures are yet to unfold. Barry's conclusions, like her methodology, are too restrictive. She thinks that Momaday has used the bear's son tale to express "the heroic conflict of cultures" and Abel's "inner struggles."[77] All of Barry's efforts to locate and interpret mythic motifs in the novel that resemble those of the general bear son pattern (i.e., hero as wanderer, tracking the enemy, presence of water and an abyss) point in this direction. She believes that ". . . Abel becomes not simply a Native North American hero, but, as a Bear's Son type, he becomes a universal hero . . ."[78] Yet Barry has used no native story patterns as a basis of comparison with *House Made of Dawn;* she uses only European stories such as *Beowulf* as models in framing her article. And, most significantly, she fails to ask: "Why Bear?" There is no penetration of the nature of bearness in her analysis. It is important to look at symbolic models of bear behavior in Pueblo and Navajo stories in an effort to see how contact with Bear can generate supernatural power that can be used for healing humans. These models also show how Momaday has generated bear energy in the novel as a source of healing.

A traditional Jemez bear story helps to clarify the pertinent narrative patterns. In 1914 Albert Reagan collected the Jemez "Myth of the Mother Moon and the Great Bear."[79] This story tells of a great bear who abducts the pregnant moon mother when she goes to get water for her husband the sun. In the bear's cave she gives birth to a son (stepson to bear) who emerges with great powers. He "put his mother on his back, and ran all day toward the place where the sun goes to rest at night." Eventually he reached "the palace of the sun" and drove the bear off. The sun rewarded the boy and his brother with places in the sky as morning star and evening star. The story ends here. It is noteworthy that the image of the son with his mother on his back is an image of closeness and complementarity, parallel to the twins' mode of traveling in the Stricken Twins story discussed in chapter 2.

This Jemez myth contains several of the motifs that *House Made of Dawn* develops in the Angela-Abel sequences. There are two stories in *House Made of Dawn* that parallel this "great bear story." First, in Angela's bear story, a woman is abducted by Bear and afterwards bears a heroic son with supernatural powers. Her "made up" story is consistent, in its broadest outlines, with this traditional Jemez story. Second, in the larger story of the novel, Angela is already pregnant when she is abducted by "bear man" Abel. She, as woman, is associated with water and water with the moon, all sources of fertility and life. Angela and her son Peter, in utero, return to her husband, leaving Abel to fend for himself. Abel as Bear had acquired a family when he "possessed" Angela and her unborn son. When he loses them, he loses his family once again. His wholeness dissolves into incompleteness or illness. This bear-woman theme then is a means of dramatizing the dynamics of family. Tragically, Francisco is Abel's only blood relation during Abel's mature years.

Momaday may have consciously constructed his text to echo this Jemez origin story, since the mythic parallels are so strongly sustained. These parallels suggest that the motif of abduction functions to transform the heroines through fear. Bear is enemy in the Jemez story:

> Ever since the rescue, the bear and his descendants have been enemies of the moon, our mother-god, and we, her children, and ever since then it has been . . . the woman's duty to destroy the bear every chance she can. . . .[80]

Angela, although not conscious of this mythical history, behaves through the early part of the novel in a way consistent with the woman's role in this old story. Having acquired power from contact with Bear, Angela herself is manipulative like Changing Bear Maiden of Navajo mythology. Later she is transformed into a more peaceful person, capable of using her power for healing. We will return in greater detail to the Jemez significances of Bear for healing in the discussion of Francisco's bear hunting memory.

Ben's Bear Story

In the hospital Angela amazes Ben. In this scene they appear to work together as storytelling healers to help Abel who is very withdrawn. Angela's bear story triggers a longer, more involved Navajo story from Mountainway in Ben's mind. Ben says:

> Ei yei! A bear! A bear and a maiden. And she was a white woman and she thought it up, you know, made it up out of her own mind, and it was like that old grandfather talking to me, telling me about *Esdzá shash nadle,* or *Dzil quigi,* yes, just like that.[81]

These words preface the complicated origin myth to the Mountain

Chant that Ben remembers carefully, taking his time to fill in detail of landscape and event. Angela's story, as undeveloped as it may appear, contains the rudiments of a narrative familiar to Ben. He supplies the graphic description of specific landforms that are a part of Navajo sacred geography in a way that Angela could not. Ben remembers these stories, of course, through oral tradition, and can retell portions of them as his grandfather had. Memories of his grandfather's voice are life-sustaining to Ben as are memories of Francisco's early teachings to Abel.[82]

Momaday has modeled Ben's telling of Mountainway on a version of the story given by Sam Ahkeah to Aileen O'Bryan in the winter of 1928 at Mesa Verde, Colorado.[83] Other versions of the Mountain Chant have been collected as part of the ethnographic record by Matthews, the Coolidges, Newcomb and Wheelwright, and Haile, this latter version published by Wyman.[84] Mountainway has both male and female branches and the origin legend to each differs accordingly. Ahkeah tells the story of the female branch which emphasizes the adventures of the heroine Elder Sister Bispáli. Wyman says of the female branch:

> The first Mountain chant(s) was held to finally and completely cure Older Sister of the infirmities, swollen joints, pain, and debility, incurred during her various travels or to remove the evil alien influences from the captives of the Utes.[85]

Briefly, Mountainway relates the extended episode of Elder Sister's seduction by Bear Man and her flight away from him.[86]

I will first analyze the elements of Ben's story in relationship to the parallel stories of Abel and Angela, then analyze the resemblance of Ben's Mountainway to O'Bryan's recording of it, and, lastly, discuss Momaday's use of Ahkeah's story as a new retelling that transforms the fruits of ethnography into literature.

As Ben remembers it, the story begins: "And after those things happened, the people came down from the mesas. And they were afraid of *Esdzá shash nadle.*"[87] The story is already underway when Ben picks it up, for storytellers in oral tradition tell longer or shorter versions of their tales depending on storytelling circumstances.[88] It is a long story that is not yet over even when Ben intones the prayer: "With beauty all around me . . ."[89] The story speaks of the dramatic displacement of a people who flee their home out of fear of Esdzá shash nadle, Changing Bear Maiden.[90] Changing Bear Maiden is "a ruthless female power" who embodies evil.[91] The people bury the Calendar Stone, wrap their dead, and abandon their possessions. But before departing in haste, they make a strong image: "And there on the rock where they lived, they left the likeness of a bear."[92] Making this petroglyph is a symbolic act of controlling the powers of the bear that threaten them, and of recording their history in relationship to that particular spot. It seems that the cliff people described here in mythic time are either the Anasazi, the ancestors of the Pueblos who abandoned their villages during the thirteenth century, or else the Navajos who intermarried with them.[93]

This condensed story about the cliff dwellers is grafted by Momaday onto the beginning of the Mountain Chant myth that has emerged out of Enemyway.[94] The bear links the two stories. The Mountain Chant story is introduced by Ben's grandfather saying: "Grandson, it was here, here at Kin tqel that they killed two of the cave people."[95] The emphasis upon "here" and not "there" brings the listener imaginatively close to the storyteller and to the site where these events took place. The story moves into the lives of two warrior brothers' sisters who are seduced by the two old men, Bear and Snake, who transformed themselves into attractive young men. The men's sweet smoke so entrances the young women that they swoon into sleep shortly after asking the men: "Where do you come from?"[96] When the sisters awake, they realize that the elder one has slept with Bear from the mountain and the younger one with Snake from the plain. The sisters run away. Ben's story focuses on the adventures of Elder Sister who is blessed and ritually purified by a group of the Holy People, the Yéi, before she gives birth to a bear girl. As the Yéi direct the people to sing the Mountain Chant, Elder Sister receives the name of Bear Maiden.

Sometime afterwards, Bear Maiden bears a son whom she abandons. Owl raises the boy, teaching him hunting skills, until he becomes so expert that frightened Owl plots to kill him, causing him to run away fearing for his own life.[97] Later he marries "the elder daughter of a great chief, and he was then a medicine man."[98] Through deception, he also sleeps with his wife's sister who bears him a child who is "found by the Bear," presumably grandfather bear. As this segment of the story concludes, Ben's grandfather blesses his words by singing the "With beauty" chant.

The latter episode of this story about bear boy coincides perfectly with Angela's story except that Angela's story is briefer and she adds that the hero "saved his people." Harold McAllister goes as far as to say that: "In Angela's mythmaking, her son becomes the savior Christ."[99] These closely parallel stories suggest, rather, that there may be other significant native thematic and symbolic parallels in the bear-related sequences in the novel.

The story about Changing Bear Maiden, and the stories about Bear Maiden and her son Owl Boy, all develop the theme of running away from evil or flight from death. The people run from Changing Bear Maiden, Elder Sister runs from Old Bear Man, and Owl Boy runs from Owl. Both bears and owls are associated with the power of death in Navajo culture.[100] LaVerne Harrell Clark says that bears are capable of "turning into anything," that Bear can travel invisibly, and that Bear and Big Snake, partners in Navajo myths, "frequently represent evil."[101] In *Navaho Religion*, Reichard remarks that: "The Navaho have what amounts almost to a phobia about bears, so that, despite the mythological references as elements of good, they are to be reckoned with primarily as evils."[102] This mutability makes Bear "a major power" in the Mountain Chant.[103] Bear's role has changed among the people:

> After doing much good by protecting people from their enemies, Bear started to cause coughs, fever, and bad luck. The leader of the Navaho performed a ceremony over him and Bear allied himself with evil.[104]

Bear's powers are sought after by warriors and medicine people alike. There are bear songs for strength and protection, "used against anything that bothers the people, whether enemies or disease."[105] It is said that Bear and Big Snake possessed two medicines that could make "men invulnerable" and "could restore life."[106] The bear medicine is known as "life feather."[107] If Bear's violent evil powers can be turned around, or brought under ritual control, then his/her powerful energies can be channeled for healing. Bear's life at once provides a model of transformation into wholeness, and a warning that the healing process, realized through bear ritual, is very dangerous.

The flight from evil, then, is really an affirmation of life. Not only does this run save life, but it also leads to adventures that bring knowledge and power.[108] Noting that Owl Boy listens to the wind and runs away to escape Owl's deadly powers, later to become a medicine man, Beidler says:

> It cannot be a coincidence that, as soon as he gets out of the hospital, Abel, like the son of the Bear Maiden, runs away from the evil which would destroy him in the city and heads east to the reservation. He has come, like Angela, to see the applicability of the bear story to his own situation.[109]

Beidler suggests here that the flight motif in the Mountainway story is repeated in parallel fashion in Abel's life. Furthermore, Abel seems to identify with Owl Boy and internalize his story so he can also learn to choose life by recentering himself in his homeland. Although Abel does not become a medicine man, like Owl Boy, he does return home to make contact with the medicine powers of his grandfather.

Beidler, like Barry, has identified Abel with Bear Boy, also known as Owl Boy in this case. I would like to suggest that the parallel Beidler finds is there in the text, but that Abel can also be imaginatively linked to the bear father, as pointed out earlier in this chapter. Since characteristics of fathers are often remanifested in their sons, and in *House Made of Dawn* aspects of Ben and Abel's grandfathers' experiences are transmitted to their grandsons, then it should be possible to identify Abel at times with either old Bear Man or young Bear Boy (Owl Boy). The principle of multiple selves delineated in chapter 2 may be appropriate here, for a generational pairing occurs. Abel as Bear Man embodies both age and youth, and manifests Bear's powers for aggression, beauty, and regeneration as he makes contact with Angela.

In a subtle reversal of the motif of seduction by Bear, Angela seems to pursue Abel almost relentlessly before she flees from him back to Los Angeles. Her contact with him gives her both pain and knowledge of the natural world.[110] After she returns home to California her power builds accordingly. For, in the hero/ heroine pattern, returning home galvanizes power. She changes from a person in need of rebalancing her own life into a protective healer for Abel.

Various critics have viewed Angela as relentlessly manipulative of Abel and Father Olguin. Oleson, Hylton, and McAllister, for instance, have widely differing views of her ranging from saint to an instigator of misery.[111] Evers claims that she is an "obstacle in Abel's re-emergence journey" or growth into wholeness.[112] One of the most stinging comments that Evers makes about Angela's nature is that: "Her attitude toward the land is of a piece with her attitude toward her own body. . . ."[113] She continually denies the flesh, and, according to Evers, delights in projecting her negativity on the landscape. For the most part his assessment is accurate, but it is important to note that she changes significantly through the course of the seven years of the novel. The early scenes portray her as alternately cold and vicious in her designs on Abel. When he refuses to bargain for his labor, she wants to exact a "vengeance," and when he will not reply to her questions she is "full of irritation" . . . "that [makes] her seethe."[114] Yet the later scenes portray her as compassionate and understanding.

This investigation of the role of bear imagery in the novel has yielded some insights into the complexities of Angela's character and may explain why, as Schubnell says, some critics appear to loathe her while others adore her.[115] I have already treated Angela's identification with Bear. In the same way that Momaday grafts the story of Changing Bear Maiden onto the Mountainway legend, he merges images of her as Changing Bear Maiden with images of her as Bear Maiden or Bear Mother. Whereas, she is initially deceptive and cunning in her relationship with Abel, she begins changing as they make love. As she experiences the symbolic slap on the water, by Badger or Bear, she begins her transformation into a fuller life that recognizes the power of love and the responsibilities of motherhood.[116]

Donald Sandner states that: "The negative or evil side of bear power is associated with Changing Bear Maiden, who is the dark counterpart of the chant heroine."[117] Sheila Moon in a psychological study of female deities in Navajo Mythology, states that: "Changing-Bear-Maiden also is a sorceress, power-driven, autonomous, plotting."[118] Moon continues: "In the story of Changing-Bear-Maiden the balance between Feminine and Masculine— so basic in Navajo thought—is dangerously disturbed. (Things are evil, out of order.)"[119] Moon sees Changing Bear Maiden as a representation of "incompleteness" and "the negative and life-denying aspect of the Feminine . . . in us."[120] But she also sees her as "a model for ways needing change."[121] In the Navajo Creation Story, Changing Bear Maiden is transformed into a good, useful figure when her youngest brother kills her, and her nipples become the sacred food piñon nuts as they are tossed into the air. Her severed head, when thrown against a tree trunk, "changed instantly into a real bear such as those we see roaming in the mountain forests today."[122] This figure's death and rebirth, expressed in terms of a change of state from monster to ordinary creature with beneficent powers, suggests that the process of transformation is always at work to reorder an imbalanced world. Angela, like Changing Bear Maiden, experiences a personal death and rebirth. She changes during the course of the narrative from being manipulative to nurturing.

If Changing Bear Maiden is the negative side of Angela's character, then, Bear Maiden is her positive side. As John Farella says about Navajo culture: "Wholes seem to be composed of two parts which are in a sense complementary and in another sense opposed."[123] The shifting balance between Angela's selves, then, defines her whole complex character. Sandner says that:

the chant heroes . . . meet powerful women. . . . Many of
the chant heroes and heroines marry sons or daughters of
the Holy People, and thus not only obtain chant knowledge
but become part of the family.[124]

In the case of Bispáli, Elder Sister of Mountainway, after her
baby was born "she started on a journey for power, during which
she met many holy personages and learned from them the ceremonies of Mountaintop Way."[125] She is "identified closely with
bears and bear power."[126] Bears "are said to carry powerful medicine and are associated with the mountains, healing herbs, and
fire."[127]

The Mountain Chant story in *House Made of Dawn* says that
"elder sister came at last to the great kiva of the Yeí bichai," after
she had run away to the mountains from her bear husband.[128]
Meanwhile younger sister had run away from Snake to the plains.
The sisters' choice of places to take refuge is associated with the
homes of their respective "husbands" and reinforces the pro-
fundity of their transformation into animal people, the transformation that began with the whiff of sacred smoke. The phrase
"elder sister came at last to . . ." refers to her solo journey, after
separating from her sister, to the home of the Holy People. The
text describes the blessing of Elder Sister before she gives birth.
She is welcomed by "four holy men and four holy women."[129]
Four is the most sacred number in Navajo culture.[130] She is given
a corn meal bath and blessed with pollen, "and she was beautiful."[131] Her daughter is a bear child resembling both parents.[132]
The Mountain Chant is sung to heal Bear Maiden's (Bear Mother's) anguish from being separated from her family and her aches
from journeying so far.[133] The story says: "and from that time
on the elder sister was called the Bear Maiden. Afterward a male
child was born. . . ."[134]

Between the event of being named "Bear Maiden" and bearing
a son, Elder Sister went on many adventures. The tale of her
guided travels with the Gods constitutes a lengthy story in and
of itself. For this reason, Momaday may have chosen not to
include it in Ben's story. But a brief summary of Elder Sister's

adventures is necessary because they illuminate her acquisition of knowledge and her transmission of medicine power to her son, and, in a parallel sense, they illuminate Angela's life. In the origin myth to the Mountain Chant, as told in Mary C. Wheelwright's *Myth of Mountain Chant and Beauty Chant*, Elder Sister was privileged to learn of many extraordinary things. "Then the Gods took the older sister who married the Bear on a journey beginning at Taos, and they saw many ceremonies."[135] Eventually Elder Sister returns from her circular journey to her old home among the bears. On the way south they meet animals such as the Bluebird people, the Deer people, the Mountain Sheep people, and the Jemez Beavers. They also encounter Rock Man and Water Monster, two threatening figures. This second monster teaches his medicine to them. And they visit a "garden of the lightning full of squash and beans."[136] As they go, Elder Sister not only learns of the powers of the natural world—the animal and plant people—but also attends ceremonies and hears stories in hogans near the Chuska Mountains. When Bear Maiden and the gods attend a "very holy ceremony" at Rainbow Mountain, they witness "Changing Bear maiden Shikinh-nah-tlehay (Sickness), and Etsan hothgani (Hunger), the Thin Old Woman" in the guise of corn grinders.[137] These women trick two men into marrying them. Changing Bear Maiden's man develops boils and sores, and the other man becomes ill, too.

> The Thin Old Woman (Etsan Hothgani) took a man and he starved to death, for these two women always hurt their lovers, and after the travellers *understood this* they passed on to the big ceremony nearby. [138]

Elder Sister's journey for knowledge and power places her among the most formidable of the heroines of the Navajo story cycles. Like Elder Sister the Bear Maiden, who sees the deadly harm that Changing Bear Maiden inflicts on her man, Angela apparently comes to realize that her own former viciousness to Abel was inhumane. In her journey for knowledge, Angela has learned to control her aggressive, manipulative impulses, although this change must have primarily occurred during the seven years that Angela was back home in California. During this time Angela passes on her love of Indian tradition to her son Peter and presumably passes on a personal sense of the wholeness of native culture that may center him as he grows older, perhaps to become a doctor like his father. Bear Maiden does not become a full medicine woman in the sense that her sister Glispah of Beautyway does, but she does gain medicine knowledge and give birth to a son who becomes a medicine man.[139]

The last part of Ben's Mountain Chant story in *House Made of Dawn* tells of the Bear Maiden's son who develops strong powers in the hunt and in curing. This story prefigures the fourth bear story of the novel that tells of Abel's grandfather's growth in hunting and medicine knowledge. This Mountain Chant story also develops the incest/adultery theme that is played out in the novel in relationship to Fray Nicholas's affair with the witch Nicholás *teah-whau* and Nicholas's illegitimate son Francisco's parallel affair with Porcingula, his sister or half sister.[140] The suggestion of witchcraft is introduced in the figure of Owl who may have influenced Owl Boy to covet his wife's sister. In Francisco's case it is clear that his father's affair with the witch has tainted the family line and cursed Abel's life, as discussed in chapter 2. In any case the family lineage continues, and the model of an ordinary human mating with a person of supernatural powers (either Bear or a witch) is a means of introducing extraordinary contact with the powers of nature into the family.

Perhaps it was fear of strong evil powers in the universe against them that caused the mesa people in the first part of Ben's story to bury the Calendar Stone before leaving home. It is said that "the story of the sun and the moon and the 12 months were upon it," that it was guarded by a medicine woman of Blue House in Chaco Canyon.[141] "Having this rock gave her the knowledge of what is beyond the blue sky, what is under the earth, and what is in the air and the water."[142] The power of the stone enabled this woman to foretell events. When the people made mistakes, the "medicine woman saw in the Calendar Stone that the lives of all the people were threatened from above."[143] All of those who did not listen to the warning were destroyed, but those who had paid attention to the story were saved. The Calendar Stone may have been buried in an effort to stabilize or restore a disordered universe. Surely the Calendar Stone story tells of shifting balances in the universe and suggests that survival comes from remembering the story. Hearing this story from Ben may have helped Abel find his own place in his own story. When he returns home a week later, he relearns his own tribal place when he hears Francisco telling the story of the organic Jemez ceremonial calendar embedded in the land.[144] The presence of this Mountain Chant story in the novel suggests that evil powers are at large in the world (bear, snake, owl, famine, witchcraft, and illness), but that humans can control them through symbolic acts such as making a petroglyph, ritual bathing and blessing with pollen, singing, and storytelling. All of these activities have medicine power and contribute toward making a "male child" like Abel or like Owl Boy, left alone by his mother, strong.

Momaday has based Ben's grandfather's bear stories on stories told by Sandoval and Sam Ahkeah, recorded in *The Dîné: Origin Myths of the Navaho Indians*.[145] The old man Sandoval told the stories of the Calendar Stone and Changing Bear Maiden. His nephew Sam Ahkeah told "The Story of the Mountain Top Chant, or the Story of the Maiden and the Bear."[146] Momaday in writing the novel has condensed and compressed these stories, connecting them associationally, thematically, and symbolically. Examining the words of the Navajo informants to the ethnographer Aileen O'Bryan who wrote them down "without interpolation," and comparing portions of this text to Momaday's, provides a fuller understanding of the artistic process of composition of "The Night Chanter" part of the novel.[147]

Sandoval, Hastin Tlo' tsi hee (Old Man Buffalo Grass), said in Navajo translated into English by his interpreter nephew Sam Ahkeah:

After these things happened many people planned to leave the mesas. They were afraid of the Woman who became a bear. They buried the Calendar Stone; they wrapped their dead; and leaving their belongings, they went away. But before they left they drew pictures on the rocks of all the things that trouble came from.[148]

Ben's grandfather in *House Made of Dawn* tells it like this:

And after those things happened, the people came down from the mesas. And they were afraid of *Esdzá shash nadle*. They buried the Calendar Stone and wrapped blankets made of feathers around their dead; they ran away, leaving their possessions. And there on the rock where they lived, they left the likeness of a bear.[149]

The two texts are essentially the same, but Momaday has written Changing Bear Maiden's name in Navajo, added the detail that the dead were wrapped in blankets made of feathers (probably turkey feathers), and specifically named the people's nemesis— the bear. Later, in chapter 4, we will return to this image of making a petroglyph as a parallel image to constructing *House Made of Dawn* itself. The substitution of the Navajo name for "Changing Bear Maiden" makes the text seem at once authentically traditional and obscure to a non-Navajo speaking audience. And, of course, the bear figure on the rock emphasizes the relentless power of the bear-human connection in the novel.

Most of Ben's grandfather's "Mountain Top Chant" referred to as "Dzil quigi" in the novel is paraphrased slightly from the Ahkeah version.[150] Focusing on the scene when Elder Sister arrives at the Yeíbichai's home, the subtle differences in texts become apparent. Ahkeah narrates:

From there the elder sister and the chipmunk went into the big kiva of the Yeí bichai. Four men and four women in ceremonial robes came forward to meet her. The women took her aside and bathed her; they rubbed her first with cornmeal and then with pollen and she was beautiful. They dressed her in ceremonial robes and led her into a room lined with fur. And there her little baby girl was born. The child had little tufts of hair back of its ears and downy hair on its arms and legs.

After the child was born the Yei instructed the people to give the Mountain Chant. . . . The old Mountain Woman and the Elder Sister, or the Bear Maiden as she was now called, traveled together.[151]

House Made of Dawn says:

The elder sister came at last to the great kiva of the Yeí bichai. Four holy men and four holy women came out to greet her. The women bathed and anointed her; they touched her with corn meal and pollen, and she was beautiful. She bore a female child. There were tufts of hair in back of its ears and down on its arms and legs. And then the Yei told the people to sing the Mountain Chant, and from that time on the elder sister was called the Bear Maiden.[152]

Momaday as storyteller has changed some of the details, leaving out the chipmunk spiritual helper and the description of the "bear den" where Elder Sister gives birth. He has emphasized the holiness of the woman's transformation (the helpers are "holy"), and reminded the reader of the bear girl's father Bear Man by describing the baby's parts with the not-quite-human word "its." Furthermore, the use of the word "anointed" suggests a Christian reference in the passage, linking Bear Maiden symbolically to Angela, a Catholic.

In order to demonstrate how closely Momaday has reworked the Ahkeah story, it is illuminating to contrast these two texts with yet another version of the story, this one given by Hasteen Klah:

The older maiden met a chipmunk who took pity on her and brought her into a cave, and Hashje-altye (the Talking

God of the Yehbechai) met her there and he led her, sprinkling corn meal, past various guards such as Bears, Lightning, until they came to a great holy room where four
Nohokah dinneh ("of the First Earth" people) met them
showing much sorrow at the suffering of the maiden, and
two women took her into a room made of fir and bathed
and dressed her and she stayed with these "First Earth"
people a long time, and there her female baby was born.
She had fur on all her limbs, breast and back of her ears,
and a white face.[153]

The Klah version of the story, which also would have been available to Momaday as a model, deemphasizes the blessing ritual
by not mentioning the sacred substances—corn meal and pollen—being used to symbolically cleanse and restore her body.
Perhaps the child's "white face" was too obvious a parallel to
Angela's child. It seems that the formality of the Ahkeah version
(with the four men and the four women greeters, for example)
likely appealed to Momaday, who heightened the formality further by changing "elder sister . . . went into the big kiva of the
Yeí bichai" to "elder sister . . . came at last to the great kiva of
the Yeí bichai."[154] This formality (changing "big" to "great," for
instance) increases the grandeur and dignity of Momaday's version. The most important point here, not to be lost sight of, is
that Momaday has included the bear material in the novel, because these are stories of illness, transformation, and renewed
health, as evidenced by recitation connected to chantway performance and by the detailed story patterns themselves, which
reveal the stages in illness and recovery that will be discussed
more fully in chapter 4.

    It is, of course, no secret that Momaday carefully selected
excerpts from the ethnographic record to use as part of the un-
dergirding of his novel. Floyd Watkins says that Momaday "has
no reluctance to admit his use of sources." Yet, Watkins himself
has some difficulty tracking them down.[155] In the case of the Bear
Maiden story, we can attribute the prototype version to a particular

storyteller, Ahkeah, which makes the story's transference to Momaday somewhat personal.

I think of the whole narrative of *House Made of Dawn* as an expansive multicultural matrix and the compressed partial narratives from Nightway and Mountainway within it as storysherds rather than fragments from oral tradition. Like a potsherd that tells part of a story of design, composition, and relationship, suggesting a remembered whole, the storysherds in *House Made of Dawn* are those brief stories from oral tradition that symbolically represent a world that is larger than themselves. The Pueblos recycle broken pottery or potsherds into the matrix that they mix with fresh clay to make a new creation, a new pot. Ground down and refined into powder, the ancient clay is mixed with the new.[156] So, too, in this analogy from material to literary culture, do contemporary Native American writer-storytellers like Momaday incorporate the beauty, design and vitality of old stories into new work.[157] This is one cultural adaptation that helps ensure that surviving stories from oral tradition remain viable for generations to come.

When Aileen O'Bryan recorded her informants' stories for the written record, she necessarily decontextualized them. By writing them down, she seemed to "freeze them in time and space," thereby divorcing them from their performative dimensions. Consequently, their range of associations and meanings was to some extent narrowed. Yet the new context for the telling, the printed page of a Bureau of American Ethnology report, gave them another different kind of life. O'Bryan's publication ensured that these versions of the Navajo stories survived publicly. It remained for a native scholar-storyteller like Momaday to come along, read them, and retell them in slightly altered fashion in a novel.

It is not unusual that these storysherds were not rerecorded in a form identical to the "originals." After all there are always variations in the story among traditional storytellers. Stories in oral tradition always have multiple versions, as individual as the narrators. Mountainway and Nightway are still sung in slightly different versions on the Navajo reservation. They are among the extant on-going chantways. But Sandoval, as described in

O'Bryan's Preface, was concerned that the stories and old ways might nevertheless some day die out. In 1928 Sandoval said:

> "You look at me," he said, "and you see only an ugly old man, but within I am filled with great beauty. I sit as on a mountaintop and I look into the future. I see my people and your people living together. In time to come my people will have forgotten their early way of life unless they learn it from white men's books. So you must write down all that I will tell you; and you must have it made into a book that coming generations may know this truth."[158]

Sandoval indicates that O'Bryan's ethnographic publication of his stories will ensure one form of their survival, and that the stories will have their truth value intact. O'Bryan adds,

> During the 17 days of his [Sandoval's] stay with us . . . he would often stop and chant a short prayer, and sprinkle the manuscript, Sam, and myself with corn pollen.
> He believed the Mesa Verde to be the center of the old cultures, and he said that it was fitting that the stories should be reborn, written down, in "the Place of the Ancients."[159]

This blessed manuscript was lying dormant until Momaday revitalized some of these stories by recontextualizing them. By working them into the context of his fiction, he gave them new life because Abel, Angela, and Ben act in accordance with the heroic patterns of development in them. On one level, it may seem that all that has occurred between these texts is the transference of a certain story from the pages of one book to another, but this view misses the dynamism of the storytelling process. Momaday structures *House Made of Dawn* so his characters *enact* the stories and this action renews them culturally, historically, and spiritually. The stories are "reborn," in Sandoval's words. One way that the meaning is changed when the stories are recontextualized in the novel is that the land or "setting" of the stories must be imagined by the characters when they tell them or hear them in Los Angeles. (Ordinarily these stories would be heard in a hogan on the Navajo reservation near the locale of the events in the stories.) And it is precisely this powerful reimagining of landscape that is appropriate and requisite for healing to take place. These are stories about healing, and whether they are told in the Southwestern desert, in a Los Angeles hospital, or on a nearby hilltop in the city, they function as stories for strength.

Strictly speaking, then, multiple storytelling voices emerge in the novel. Not only is Ben's "dialect" voice in Part 3 distinct from that of the formal third person narrator of the other parts, and not only do we find Francisco, Milly, and Tosamah, for example, as storytellers telling their personal stories within the story, but we also faintly hear echoes of older traditional storytellers—Sandoval, Sam Ahkeah, and Hatáli Natlói, among others—who ancestrally in the storytelling chain of transmission helped to create a portion of *House Made of Dawn*. The presence of these multiple voices telling a collective story contributes to the novel's healing power. A communally composed story, it orients its readers, especially its Indian audience, to traditional tribal values. This integration of person and story is healing. Being non-Navajo himself, Momaday learned traditional Navajo literature largely through books. The miracle of the novel lies in Momaday's ability to understand the spirit of the old narratives so well that he could comfortably manipulate them and evoke their healing power in much the same way that a medicine man might recite them to stimulate a healing response in one-sung-over.[160] The survival of the patient depends on the survival of the story.

Francisco's Bear Story

The fourth bear story in the novel is the one that Francisco tells on his deathbed. The story recalls his coming of age as a Jemez hunter and his symbolic initiation into Jemez manhood. Many critics have commented on this story's import, falling as it does near the close of the novel, but no one has probed its relationship to medicine power. It becomes evident that Francisco's slaying of the bear precipitates the development of his personal healing power, power that he rallies in the last day of his life to help Abel continue his spiritual transformation.

Briefly, grandfather Francisco recalls the autumn incident in his youth when he went alone into the mountains, probably the Redondo Peak area north of the pueblo, in order to kill a bear. He enters a cave and experiences the presence of dead ancestors by listening to the wind that sounds *"like ancient voices"* and by looking at their old pots, some of them broken into potsherds.[161] Francisco also experiences a surge of eagle power as an eagle swoops down and kills a rodent on the cliff nearby. This event dramatizes contact between hunter and hunted and foreshadows the bear's death to come. After tracking the young black bear for a long time and reaching an agreement with him (*"the hunter's offering of death and the sad watch of the hunted . . . brooding around at last to forgiveness and consent"*), Francisco closes in on him.[162] He notices *"the scored earth where the bear had left the rock and gone sliding down."* This image parallels that of the "scored . . . bark" in the Kiowa story about Devil's Tower and unites the bear material in the novel.[163] After Francisco shoots the animal, he blesses the bear by streaking yellow pollen above its eyes, and then eats the bear's liver. In a note to this hunting story published separately as "The Bear and the Colt," Momaday writes that Francisco eats the liver "to acquire the animal's strength."[164] Then he smears the young colt's nose with bear flesh, initiating that animal into the hunt, too. They ride into town with the old hunting horse and are cheered by the people for having hunted magnificently.

The critical literature on the novel recognizes this meaningful incident in Francisco's life, but scantily interprets the event. Nora Baker Barry says:

> . . . Francisco, Abel's grandfather, has a dream memory of his own initiation hunt for a bear. This version contains the tracking motifs . . . There is a waterfall and a cave . . .

Francisco continues to track the bear, kills it, and becomes a man in the eyes of his village.[165]

Marion Willard Hylton mentions that Francisco's

ritual killing of the bear to symbolize the coming of age, the marks of pollen made above the eyes of the bear . . . and the healing powers he later acquires as a result of his growing 'understanding' [are among] the important events of his life.[166]

Yet Hylton says little more than what is evident from the facts of the text itself. Carole Oleson says: "In the second memory, the story of Francisco's (and the colt's and half-grown bear's) coming of age illustrates the sacredness of man's proper relationship to earth creatures."[167] Harold McAllister sees the scene from a Catholic-Christian perspective, as well as from a "native" one. He develops a more thorough interpretation of this event. McAllister says:

In a deathbed dream, Francisco recalls the sacramental killing of a bear in his youth, his initiation into manhood, and the rite is in a sense Abel's initiation, the sacrament of Abel's atonement. After this rite, Abel can truly be the bear and feel its medicinal power. As Francisco and the bear act out their drama, they demonstrate that death is natural and not to be feared; Francisco sees death in a sacred manner. . . .[168]

McAllister is on the right track here, suggesting that grandfather Francisco's experiences are transferred to Abel and that Abel receives bear power for healing, but McAllister does not note why these transformations occur and clouds the issue by introducing the Christian considerations of "sacrament" and "atonement." McAllister should have pursued his discussion of Abel's "atonement" or reconciliation with Francisco in order to clarify these points. When McAllister says: "After this rite, Abel can truly be the bear," he must mean "after hearing this story of this rite" since Abel could not have been born when Francisco went on this hunt.

Before further developing my own interpretation of this hunting scene, it is crucial to cite the ethnographic sources that Momaday used, or in some cases may have consulted, to construct this powerful section of the novel. A. Irving Hallowell's classic study "Bear Ceremonialism in the Northern Hemisphere" provides pertinent information, particularly about bear hunting in the Southwest compared to hunting in other geographic regions. Following Elsie Clews Parsons, Hallowell says: "There is an association of the bear with medicine in most of the Pueblos (Hopi and Taos excepted). The animal 'is the doctor *par excellence.*'"[169] He adds: "At Jemez there is a dance for a dead bear and also a ritual to convert the dead enemy into a friend."[170] In a footnote, Hallowell quotes a long paragraph from the Parsons manuscript that was soon to become her study, *The Pueblo of Jemez.*[171] The Parsons description of returning from the bear hunt begins:

> The slayer of a bear is expected on his return to town to stop about a mile out, and to shout as in war. All the men go out with rifle to meet him, each receiving a piece of bear meat which he wraps around the barrel of his rifle. They all ride into town, the slayer in their midst, across his horse the bear. The women come out, armed with pokers with which they strike at the bear. . . .[172]

House Made of Dawn reads:

> *He shouted, and the men came out to meet him. They came with rifles, and he gave them strips of the bear's flesh, which they wrapped around the barrels of their guns. And soon the women came with switches, and they spoke to the bear and laid the switches to its hide . . .*[173]

The novel's closely rendered narrative, following Parsons' account, "deletes" subsequent Parsons information about the extended bear ritual that lasts for days.[174] And the novelist adds the detail that the women *"spoke to the bear,"* a custom that reflects the Jemez concept of Bear as person and Momaday's recognition in *House Made of Dawn* that speaking and storytelling are linking mechanisms between humans and the natural world.[175] When this link is well made, healing or renewal may occur.

The novelist devotes far more description to the process of the hunt than to description of the actual death of the bear. Hunting in itself becomes a way for Francisco to realize his relationship with other living beings in the land. Not only is Francisco's personal life contextualized by the expansiveness of the landscape that he rides through—*"across the river and beyond the white cliffs and the plain, beyond the hills and the mesas, the canyons and the caves"*—but his life is also contextualized in relationship with the animals he encounters—deer, eagle, wolves, mountain lions, and coyotes.[176] The silence and slowness of the journey underscore Francisco's attention to detail—

> *Twice he had seen deer, motionless, watching, standing away in easy range, blended with light and shadow, fading away into the leaves and the land. He let them be, but remembered where they were and how they stood. . . .*[177]

—and the inevitability of the bear's death to come. When he gets close to the bear, Francisco realizes that the bear is *"certain of where it was and where he was."*[178] This knowledge of his place in the landscape in relationship to everything else is what Francisco learns from the bear. His experience as a young man parallels Ben's childhood experience. Ben recalled:

> *And that night your grandfather hammered the strips of silver and told you stories in the firelight. And you were little and right there in the center of everything, the sacred mountains, the snow-covered mountains and the hills, the gullies and the flats, the sundown and the night, everything—where you were little, where you were and had to be.*[179]

For Ben, these stories internalized the land within him, made him feel at home, and for Francisco the act of tracking the bear was an experience of perfection that was becoming a story. For both of them a hierophany or manifestation of the sacred occurs, and they receive power from being situated in the symbolic center of the world. Ben and Francisco's experiences empower them largely because at these moments they are connected to their ancestors, whose presence is radiated through traditional stories and *"the wind among the crags* [sounding] *like ancient voices."*[180] As Francisco hunts as his elders did, his ancestors' presence is made available to him in the form of energy to finish the hunt in beauty. Before the death scene, the bears honor Francisco by visiting his campsite. He sees *"the gray heads bidding only welcome and wild good will."*[181] Francisco's contact with the bears is direct and personal. After the hunt, Francisco is still in the "center of the world." *"He made camp that night far down in the peneplain and saw the stars and heard the coyotes away by the river."*[182] His return home at dawn the next day signifies the village's communal regeneration, realized through his manhood and the gift of black bear's life.

In a related deathbed memory, Francisco recalls the time when he emerged as a young man from the squash clan's kiva to join the drummers in the dance plaza. The old men were watching him closely like the bears had watched him in the clearing by firelight. The end of the passage describes the conclusion of the dance:

> *It was perfect. And when it was over, the women of the town came out with baskets of food. They went among the singers and the crowd, throwing out the food in celebration of his perfect act. And from then on he had a voice in the clan, and the next year he healed a child who had been sick from birth.*[183]

Lawrence Evers says that "Abel . . . participates in Francisco's memories of his initiation as a runner . . . as a dancer (from which he gained the power to heal, pp. l86–7) as a man . . . and as a hunter. . . ."[184] Certainly this personal/tribal knowledge is transmitted to Abel, but this passage in the novel indicates that Francisco is a drummer not a dancer on this particular occasion, and his *"perfect act"* that gives him *"a voice in the clan"* and the power of healing is killing the bear. Once he had come of age through the hunt, he was given the privilege and responsibility of becoming a drummer. The narrator mentions that *"It was late in the autumn"* the morning that Francisco closed in on the bear.[185] And the opening description of the squash clan dance says: *"It was November."*[186] Although there are two intervening memories, it seems that Francisco's story of the dance is a continuation of his story of the hunt. Through hunting, Francisco has acquired medicine power.

In the Pueblos, illness is thought to be caused largely by object intrusion or the presence of alien objects injected by witches into the sick one's body. Sometimes it is thought that the witches have removed a "patient's" heart. In order to dislodge these foreign objects and restore the heart, medicine men use power from strong animals. Hamilton Tyler quotes Leslie White as saying:

> But the medicine man could not cure illness nor oppose witches in hand-to-hand fighting without receiving 'power' from certain spirits, and without the aid of their paraphernalia. My informant stated that power was received from bears, mountain lions, and eagles.[187]

At Jemez bear legs are worn on the medicine men's arms during curing rituals.[188] Referring to Jemez practices, Tyler says that "There the Flint and Fire societies are collectively known as the Bear group because, 'bear calls and leg skins are used in cures in symbolic imitation of their tutelary deity.'"[189] Blanche Harper apparently witnessed a curing ceremony at Jemez in the 1920s. She writes: "All the men sing. Two men rise, dip the bear paws in the medicine bowl, and splash the room and all persons and objects in the room with the medicine." Later ashes are gathered. Then "Two men rise, dip the bear paws in the ashes and go around the room making motions with them."[190] Afterwards foreign objects are removed from the patient's body; the witch is identified and chased. Father Noël Dumarest noted in his monograph on Cochiti Pueblo that one version of the Cochiti origin story says that the Mother of All creator gave her children the ability

> to enter the body of lion or bear or wolf to conquer and destroy the witches. It is to frighten witches that *chiani* [medicine men] draw over their hand a bear's paw, or . . . wear a necklace of eagle talons or of bear or lion claws. . . ."[191]

Dumarest says that bear and mountain lion are "witch destroyers."[192] So the medicine men then, like Francisco, clearly are symbolically identified with bear (*köide*).[193] Frank Hibben, who hunted bears with the Jemez guide Tony Chenana, learned:

> To the Jemez Indians . . . bears are different from other animals. The black bruins of the Jemez mountains contain such powerful spirit medicine that they may not be hunted by ordinary men nor killed in an ordinary manner.[194]

Against this background of bear lore, Francisco appears as a person consciously carrying his bear medicine. He uses his medicine powers both against witches and for healing. These ritual events of witch-chasing and healing are connected processes. If the disruptive powers of witchery are held at bay, then healing or restoration to wholeness can take place.

Francisco and Abel are virtually indistinguishable in Part 4 of the novel, *The Dawn Runner*. As Abel takes care of his dying grandfather, Francisco imparts his stories to his grandson. The memories revolve around men's responsibilities to the village—knowing the turn of seasons according to the ceremonial calendar, clearing the ditches, running ceremonially, and coping with the presence of witches. The longest story of this cluster of memories, the bear hunting episode, is the central event of the story sequence. These stories are told in late February, the time of year when bears emerge from hibernation into new life. The "year's renewal [is] determined by the bear's emergence"; a "cosmic awakening" occurs.[195] Also noting this seasonal pattern of rebirth, Karl Luckert, in *The Navajo Hunter Tradition*, advances a "*submergence-reemergence* theory of disease and healing" that could apply to Abel.[196] Luckert says that "'submergence' and 'reemergence' are concepts which represent the Pueblo Indian influence in Navajo medical thinking."[197] He also says that "It is rather obvious here that the state of being ill corresponds to being in the underworld . . . healing is the process of reemergence and rebirth."[198] The bear, then, as a symbol of reemergence is connected to other such symbols in the text: the fence/ladder that Abel attempts to climb at the beach, and the rising sun at dawn.[199] Collectively, these are strong symbols of transformation. The process of emergence also parallels the initiation journey of a boy into manhood. "The bear ritual points to integration of the new personality following a period of dissociation."[200] The bear is "a spiritual and physical being who 'dies' and is renewed; hence it is the ideal model for the new birth into tribal participation." Since the bear is "the animal of beginnings, [and] also of re-beginnings," he is the appropriate model for both Abel, who is rejoining the village after being sick unto death, and for Francisco, who is moving into a new life through death.[201]

There is another level of bear presence in *House Made of Dawn* that significantly affects Abel's healing. This dimension of Bear is associated with the "feminine principle of birth, growth, death, decay, and rebirth" (that "lies at the heart of the veneration of the bear") and the masculine principle of empowerment through aggressive strength.[202] Paul Shepard says: "The bear is both mother and father, a whole and an association of parts . . ."[203] The bear figure, then, is a model of integration, a synthesis of the interdependent powers of creation and destruction that are associated with female and male being. The life of the bear shifts between these attributes and the process of moving from one self to another makes the bear at times a healer and at other times an enemy. When Peter Beidler says that Angela's "association of Abel with bear triggers in Abel much later an awareness of his own bear nature," he is right because Abel learns that he can be his own worst enemy, or he can activate his powers for self-healing.[204]

So Francisco functions as Abel's guide to the healing process in the closing scenes of the novel. The cumulative effect of bear stories leads to a sense of urgency and a compression of bear consciousness for Abel. Francisco's bear hunting story symbolically serves to bring bear power to Abel. Leslie White remarks about Pueblo concepts of healing:

> Medicine societies are able to cure sickness and drive out witches because they secure supernatural power from the 'real medicinemen'; they do not possess power in and of themselves. The 'real medicine men' are the bear, badger, eagle, wolf, and possibly the snake and the shrew. . . . The bear is regarded as the most powerful.[205]

When Abel prepares to run with the other men at dawn, as the novel circles back to its beginning, he rubs his upper body with ashes. This ritual action is connected to bear healing ritual, for ashes purify and ward off witches whether they are sprinkled from a bear paw or dusted onto a person's flesh.[206]

> His body was numb and ached with cold, and he knelt at the mouth of the oven. He reached inside and placed his hands in the frozen crust and rubbed his arms and chest with ashes. And he got up and went on hurriedly to the road and south on the wagon road in the darkness.[207]

The image of the oven laden with ashes recalls the sweet smoke that wafts out of it and also connects with an earlier description of the "runners after evil": "their white leggings holding in motion like smoke above the ground."[208] And these images are associated with Abel's wish years before, when he stood on a hilltop and tried to sing a creation song, that he had brought along "a crust of oven bread, heavy and moist, pitted with cinders and ash, or a blue cornmeal cake full of grit and sweet smoke."[209] His longing for transformation (healing) is linked to the life-generating powers of sweet smoke. And this smoke smells like the sweet smoke that prompted the sisters' transformations in Ben's Mountainway story.

> They [Bear and Snake] smoked pipes, and the smoke was sweet, and it rolled down the mountain. The sisters came upon the trail of sweet smoke and were enchanted . . . [210]

This Bear Maiden story is a female model for healing, just as Francisco's bear hunting story is essentially a male model of growth into wholeness. These two stories come together or "touch" in the character of Abel who is woodcutter and builder of fires, bear, and ashen dawn runner.[211] Abel imagined as Bear Man, then, embodies his own potential for surviving, "for the bear is the supreme model—and therefore the guiding spirit—of the theme of renewal."[212] Just as Francisco leads Abel back to a symbolic reunification with his "twin" brother Vidal through storytelling, so too he leads Abel into the inner landscape of bear country "*filled with sweet clover and paintbrush and sage,*" so that he may come to know himself.[213]

Story Made of Dawn

The world of the novel *House Made of Dawn* is created by a Navajo linguistic overlay on Pueblo space and land beyond. This "Navajo overlay" extends horizontally on a broad belt from the prairie of Oklahoma to the ocean that rolls into Southern California.[1] The phrase "House Made of Dawn," which means "the earth" according to Momaday, comes from one of the healing songs in the Navajo Night Chant.[2] The title of the novel makes it clear that the world is conceived of in Navajo terms through exertion of language on place. Jemez Pueblo, the major tribal setting for the events of the story, can then be thought of not only in terms of its own world view, but also in relation to this concept of an extended Navajo universe. Numerous historical connections exist between Jemez Pueblo and Navajo people, as previously mentioned, and this unification of Navajo words and Pueblo events underscores this ancient relationship. Therefore Navajo principles of healing prevail in the sphere of the novel, as do Pueblo ones. This is also to say that events may be interpreted from Navajo perspectives, as well as from other cultural vantage points. After all the land is continuous, and a feature of Pueblo sacred space such as the Jemez Mountains may resound in Navajo story, as is the case when Big Snake Man tracks Younger Sister to the Jemez Mountain ridge in the origin myth to the healing ceremonial Beautyway.[3]

In this chapter I compare, by means of analogy, the process of Abel's healing to the composition of the novel as a whole by considering Abel's illness in relation to Navajo theories of disease and his restoration in light of both Navajo song texts and Navajo, Kiowa, and Pueblo ritual patterns. Then I focus on the problematics of the alleged fragmented structure of the novel, showing that Momaday's method of text-building, which is rooted in mythic structures and symbols, enables him to create a powerful, unified, composite story with multiple overlapping narrative dimensions. Lastly, I assert that Momaday's literary offerings are a means of reordering the world every time the novel is read.

There are many indications in the Los Angeles portion of the narrative that Abel is profoundly ill. His estrangement from self and home, his negative experiences in war and an urban prison, and his inarticulateness all contribute to a devastating identity crisis that nearly kills him. In a drunken fit Abel abuses his friend Ben by "saying the worst thing he could think of, over and over" as he [Abel] goes out "to get even with *culebra*."[4] Culebra (snake) is their nickname for the policeman, Martinez, who had previously injured Abel's hands with his nightstick for no reason except hatred.[5] Ben already knew that for Abel the second encounter with Martinez:

> wasn't going to turn out right, because it was too late; everything had gone too far with him, you know, and he was already sick inside. Maybe he was sick a long time, always, and nobody knew it. . . .[6]

As Ben tells it:

> He didn't come back for three days. . . . I didn't know what to do. Then, three nights later, I woke up and heard something down there on the stairs. I went out and turned on the light in the hall, and I could see him down there in the dark at the foot of the stairs, like he was dead. Old Carlozini's door was open just a crack, and she was looking at him. The light from her room made a line across him, and he was all twisted up and still. It was him, all right, and he was almost dead.[7]

Ben runs downstairs, and in the light from old Carlozini's room examines Abel.

> He was lying there on his stomach and I turned him over and I wanted to get sick and cry. He was all broken and torn and covered with blood. Most of the blood was dry; it had dried up on his clothes and in his hair. He had lost an awful lot of blood, and his skin was pale yellow in the light. His eyes were swollen shut and his nose was broken and his mouth was raw and bleeding. And his hands were broken; they were broken all over. That was all I could see, his head and his hands, and I didn't want to open his clothing. I had to look away. It was the worst beating I had ever seen.[8]

Abel's absence for three days symbolically indicates a sense of incompleteness, or existence in a disharmonized state, to say the least.[9] The actual event of Martinez beating Abel is a scene "deleted" from the prose of the novel, which takes place in the reader's imagination instead. One of the effects of this "deletion" is to draw attention away from the perpetrator of this brutality and to focus on Abel as victim. Abel suffers trauma from multiple fractures and loss of blood. The leaking blood represents a loss of vitality of the life force, unlike blood spent in sacrifice that rejuvenates life. In his physical degradation, Abel's outer self parallels his inner alienated state that made him susceptible to harm. He had been "good with his hands" working on the assembly line, and

> He had loved his body. It had been hard and quick and beautiful; it had been useful, quickly and surely responsive to his mind and will. . . . Once he could have run all day.[10]

Now his body was thoroughly broken. The four-fold repetition of "broken" in the previous passage where Ben describes Abel's injuries indicates how completely the man is shattered. Moreover, his eyes are "blinded." At this moment Abel is both blind Elder Brother and crippled Younger Brother of the Stricken Twins, as discussed in chapter 2. But here the pairing represents a negative convergence of selves whereby Abel is denied both the means to vision and knowledge, and the freedom of motion. Also his breath is nearly cut off, and his voice resides somewhere wounded beneath his maimed mouth.

Soon after this beating, Abel lay on the beach at night, nearly succumbing to death. This scene may well provide the novel with its negative climax, balanced, like the roll of a wave, by the positive climax later when Ben sings the "House Made of Dawn" prayer for Abel's return to health. These "twin climaxes" are united by the image of vision. Lawrence Evers says: "Yet it is by the sea that Abel gains the insight required to begin his own re-emergence. For the first time he asks himself 'where the trouble had begun, what the trouble was. . . .'"[11] The imagery of death and rebirth is overpowering in this scene. The sea represents the tumult of Abel's inner world, churning beneath consciousness. "He could not understand the sea; it was not of his world. It was an enchanted thing, too, for it lay under the spell of the moon."[12] Not only is the moon associated with water, one of Younger Brother's associations, too, but some accounts of the birth of the Twin War Gods say that Moon fathered Younger Brother.[13] In this scene, then, Abel attempts to deny all of his connections with the natural world: with water, the moon, and his father. But the power of nature conveyed both physically and through story persists in pushing him away from fear, toward awareness of the possibility of reordering a deranged existence. Abel thinks: "'Beautyway,' 'Bright Path,' 'Path of Pollen'—his friend Benally talked of these things. But Ben could not have been thinking of the moonlit sea."[14] Abel then finds that the "small silversided fishes spawned mindlessly in correlation to the phase of the moon and the rise and fall of the tides."[15] Actually Abel has it skewed. The spawning is an image of physical rhythmic order in the cosmos, an image that spawns his own recollection of Beautyway, a ceremonial that is used for healing "mental confusion, fear, or loss of consciousness."[16] Recalling the Beautyway stories about wandering and returning home directs Abel on the path back to Ben who will sing for him again. And the thought of pollen acts as a blessing on the ocean—the element that catalyzes Abel's rebirth.[17]

Matthias Schubnell comments on the beach scene in one of the best developed analyses in his book on Momaday. Based on his reading of Mircea Eliade, Schubnell theorizes that this scene represents "a rite of passage [for Abel] in which Abel progresses from lack of understanding to knowledge, from chaos through ritual death to rebirth."[18] I concur with this statement, and would add that Abel's journey toward acquisition of knowledge and healing conforms to part of the pattern of plot construction of the Navajo hero stories, such as the story of Beautyway and the story of the Stricken Twins in Nightway. The hero's predicament is resolved only through rescue by the supernaturals, the Holy People. In the novel the grunion seem to function in this way— as mediators between sea and land, and as arbitrators of Abel's vacillation between consciousness and unconsciousness, and life and death. Whereas Schubnell sees Abel's transformation very generally as part of a world-wide rite of passage, it can also be viewed more specifically in the Navajo cultural context that the author has carefully constructed.[19] Schubnell is particularly apt discussing the water/moon imagery in the beach scene. He sees the moon as a symbol of rebirth, "as a unifying and controlling force in the universe," and as a means of connecting "Abel's present and past experiences."[20] I would add that since the moon was made by Navajo Holy People First Man and First Woman out of a piece of rock crystal, it embodies the fusion of light and hard substance that remains a durable energy, continuous from the time of first creation. Abel receives this primordial energy from both moon and water.[21] It is not coincidental that the Stricken Twins' healing ceremony was held by the gods at the foot of Tsé' intyel or Broad Rock "near the place where two creeks join," "near the junction of Monument Creek with Chelly Creek in the Chelly Cañon."[22] This place was carefully selected by the Holy People as the place where the paired energies of two flowing bodies of water could function as a medicine substance to propel the boys' transformations. Abel, likewise, is deliberately placed on the beach where the dampness of the sea can seep into him, gradually floating him toward renewal.

In Navajo culture, illness is thought to be brought about through humans' disturbed or impaired spiritual relationships with the Holy People. Leland Wyman says:

> Improper contact with inherently dangerous powers—even though it be indirect, unintentional, or unconscious—or the breaching of traditional restrictions [taboos] may lead to illness, the price man pays for disturbance of the normal order, harmony, or balance among elements in the universe.[23]

Ritual must then be performed in order to control these "dangerous elements." Wyman describes part of the procedure.

> In a ceremonial, the Holy People, the supernatural beings involved, are the judges of the completeness and correctness of the ritual, and if satisfied they are compelled by the ethic of reciprocity to restore universal harmony and thus cure the patient.[24]

Diagnosis is directed toward the causes not the symptoms of illness; for, the physical symptoms of the one-sung-over are only the outward manifestation of inner imbalance. Furthermore in Navajo culture "illness is a shared phenomenon."[25] Illness is not a strictly personal matter, because it is seen to be part of the larger sociocultural environment. Mircea Eliade suggests that "suffering is perturbing only insofar as its cause remains undiscovered."[26] And Fritjof Capra says that "illness may be an opportunity for introspection."[27] Once "suffering becomes intelligible," in Eliade's words, it becomes "tolerable."[28] Ceremony, which ritually reorganizes the world and contextualizes sufferings in the cosmic patterning of events, makes the world meaningful, thus tolerable.

Abel is ill for many reasons. Not only has he lost his family, except for Francisco, but he had violated a tribal taboo by killing Eagle (a Holy Person), had been cursed by the old Bahkyush witch, had killed another witch, had been to war, had served time in prison, and had been relocated to Los Angeles, a foreign place. His personal existence has been isolated and fragmented, especially out of kilter for a "longhair" Pueblo man whose home culture stresses cooperation and kinship. Abel's world view through most of the novel reflects his separation from his people. He sees the world in terms of fragmentation and isolation. He is not even accepted by other Indians in the skid row bars of Los Angeles. Abel is ill because of his separateness; he has no social bonds. Like the Stricken Twins he is forced to wander because he has become alienated from his people. His isolation leads to ill health and a near-death experience. As Larry Dossey says "connection is a requirement for life."[29] And in the beach scene we see Abel groping toward introspection, toward connection. The "fog rolling in from the sea" parallels his own beclouded inner landscape.[30] "The pain was very great, and his body throbbed with it; his mind rattled and shook, wobbling now out of a spin, and he could not place the center of his pain."[31] Still he is trying to think through his existence and this attempt at introspection is his first step in making his suffering meaningful. Pain has brought insight.

Regarding some specific incidents in stories from Holyway ceremonials, Karl Luckert, in *The Navajo Hunter Tradition* says: "Disease in all of these mythical events is caused by Holy-people, generally by responding to man's trespassing of a sacred hunting rule."[32] From a Navajo standpoint, Abel may be psychically and physically fractured, because he has trespassed a "sacred hunting rule" in killing Eagle. Years later, little more than a month after the beating, Francisco, back at home, tells Abel his bear hunting story, teaching him that proper relations must always be maintained between hunter and game. It is possible that Abel's participation in his grandfather's story may make partial restitution to the offended eagle.

Karl Luckert maintains that the Navajo religious system contains five theories of disease and healing. One of these—submergence-reemergence—is discussed in chapter 3 in relation to

Abel as Bear Man reemerging into new life. The other theory that is appropriate for Abel's situation is "fragmentation and reassemblage."[33] Describing this theory, Luckert says:

> Whole people can be smashed into pieces and fragments. They can be scattered; and this, indeed, signifies illness. Healing, accordingly, requires gathering and reassembling.
>
> The healing rituals which match this ideational type are the ones which Navajo "medicine men" have classified as Lifeway. They are rituals performed for curing injuries that have resulted from accidents—sprains, strains, fractures, bruises, swellings, cuts, and burns.[34]

Abel's hands are swollen; his body is raw and broken. Yet there are no overt references to Lifeway myths or ceremonial procedures in the novel. But Luckert points out the close relationship between Lifeway and Holyway, citing a "similarity between Holyway and Lifeway ideology," and "the contention of Father Berard [Haile] that Lifeway rites should be classified with Holyway rites."[35] The most commonly performed Lifeway ceremonial—Flintway—is based on an origin story that tells of Gila Monster as singer (medicine man) who cuts up, scatters, and reassembles his own body before he ceremonially restores the obliterated body of a young hunter who had been shattered by White Thunder's lightning in retaliation for the hunter sleeping with this Holy Person's wife and slaying a holy mountain sheep.[36] Like the young hunter, Abel's body is smashed by an overwhelming force and requires the power and knowledge of a singer to be reassembled or made whole.

Ben Benally functions as Abel's singer by singing prayers over him which engage the powers of restoration or self-healing. Of course, Ben does not perform an entire nine-day ceremonial for Abel, as a mature singer might do back on the reservation. But Ben's prayers may symbolically be meant to represent a condensation of the entire performance and a distillation of the essence of the Navajo conception of hózhǫ́, as a world animated by beauty. Ben gives Abel two important models of healing—

songs from Blessingway and Nightway, and stories from Mountainway. The songs are models of the process of composition
and reassemblage, and the stories are models of redefining or
remaking one's place in the natural world. Ben's songs are "The
War God's Horse Song" and the "House Made of Dawn" prayer.
His stories, of course, are the bear myths from Mountainway,
discussed at length in chapter 3. Although the narrative sequence of "The Night Chanter" part of the novel is not chronological, it is clear that Ben told Abel the bear stories in the
hospital when he was recuperating from the beating, sang the
Horse Song in a story, and sang the "House Made of Dawn"
prayer on the night before Abel's departure on the train back to
New Mexico. Both the songs and the stories contain images and
ritual patterns that link Navajo and Pueblo worlds. Ben's bear
stories connect with Francisco's, his horse song connects with
the "red and blue and spotted horses" grazing in the Jemez plain,
and his "House Made of Dawn" prayer describes the dry, colored
terrain waiting for rain at Jemez as well as Canyon de Chelly.
At the same time, the Stricken Twins' song for restoration ("House
Made of Dawn") links the Pueblo Twins to Navajo pairs, and
Abel to Vidal. Although Ben does not tell twin stories per se, he
must know them as part of the context of his Nightway prayer,
and just as he saves his bear stories to bring Abel power after
the beating, he saves his twin-composed song to bind Abel's
fragmented selves together for the journey home.

Only one critic has ventured to comment at all extensively on
the nature of the Horse Song and its role in the novel. Yet that
critic, Floyd Watkins, has not only failed to identify it and analyze
it (beyond saying that it contains similes and metaphors), but
he has also wrongly contextualized it in an effort to determine
who the Turquoise Woman is.[37] Momaday undoubtedly "found"
this Horse Song in the anthology *American Indian Prose and Poetry*,
edited by Margot Astrov, where it appears "back to back" with
"A Prayer of the Night Chant."[38] Astrov's source for the Horse
Song is the Coolidges' *The Navajo Indians*.[39] And the Coolidges'
source for the song was the singer Tall Kia ah'ni, whose words
were interpreted by Louis Watchman. This version of the song

has been anthologized or reprinted ten times since it first appeared.

The ethnomusicologist David McAllester discusses the publication and scholarly history of the poem, as well as the Navajo components of the song, in "'The War God's Horse Song,' An Exegesis in Native American Humanities."[40] McAllester says that this horse song, like other horse songs from other Navajo singers, "is part of the Blessingway origin story, which, in turn, is a component of the Navajo Creation Story."[41] Later I will return to McAllester's points about the critical misinterpretations of this text based on printing it divorced from its mythic context. In the novel, Momaday imaginatively recontextualizes it by having Ben sing it as he rides along "on a black and beautiful horse." Later he tells Abel the story of the time he sang it early in the morning.[42] Although Momaday does not put the prayer in a ceremonial context, he does put it in the context of the land between Cornfields and Klagetoh, and he parallels the rhythmic movement of the words to the gait of Ben's horse "loping . . . into the slow morning air."[43]

It is evident that "The War God's Horse Song" is a sacred text because Ben begins singing it saying: *It was good going out like that, and it made you want to pray.*"[44] Ben sings:

I am the Turquoise Woman's son.
On top of Belted Mountain,
Beautiful horse—slim like a weasel.
My horse has a hoof like striped agate;
His fetlock is like a fine eagle plume;
His legs are like quick lightning.
My horse's body is like an eagle-plumed arrow;
My horse has a tail like a trailing black cloud.
I put flexible goods on my horse's back;
The Little Holy Wind blows through his hair.
His mane is made of short rainbows.
My horse's ears are made of round corn.
My horse's eyes are made of big stars.
My horse's head is made of mixed waters—

From the holy waters—he never knows thirst.
My horse's teeth are made of white shell.
The long rainbow is in his mouth for a bridle,
    and with it I guide him.
When my horse neighs, different-colored horses
    follow.
When my horse neighs, different-colored sheep
    follow.
I am wealthy, because of him.
Before me peaceful,
Behind me peaceful,
Under me peaceful,
Over me peaceful,
All around me peaceful—
Peaceful voice when he neighs.
I am Everlasting and Peaceful.
I stand for my horse.[45]

My discussion of the Holy People in chapter 1 comments on the striking imagery in this song, saying that:

> This horse is formed of sacred substances, reflecting a kinship of celestial phenomena, water, food and flesh. The singer's knowledge of these relationships empowers him toward wholeness.

This song is a model of the process of composition of a whole living being. It is a song about putting together, or the means of creation. Some stories say that Changing Woman created this beautiful mythical horse as a gift for the people.[46] Sam Gill says that "The horse is the primordial form, expressing the shape of the Navajo cosmos."[47] It is not intended here to try to cite all of the cultural allusions to place, substance, and story contained within this brief text. Instead mentioning one allusion may suggest the richness of the other images. "Belted Mountain," the geographical location of the song, is a shortened form of "Black-belted Mountain" the name for the easternmost sacred mountain to the Navajo, *Sis Naajiní*, commonly identified as Mt. Blanca in Southern Colorado. This is the home of White Shell Woman, who wears the black belt of evergreens, a sister to Turquoise Woman and Changing Woman. It is important for Abel to hear the song precisely because he needs to be reoriented to the constituent parts of the cosmos that are shaped into the horse's body. One could think of the waters, the white shell, the corn and the agate, for instance, that make up parts of the horse's body, as diversely located substances that have to be reassembled in the person Beautiful Horse. The phrase "is made of," repeated five times stresses the process of composition and links this phrase by linguistic parallel to the same phrase in the "House Made of Dawn" prayer.

Horses are associated with reproduction and the concept of increase in Navajo ceremonial literature.[48] The second to last line of the song: "I am Everlasting and Peaceful" is an expression of the process of internalizing two of the most fundamental related concepts in Navajo philosophy: *Sạ'a Naghái* [Everlasting or Long Life] and *Bik'e Hózhǫ́* [Peaceful or Happiness]. Said together, "sạ'a naghái bik'e hózhǫ́ is associated with rejuvenation, reanimation, and temporal punctuation."[49] "Sạ'a naghái bik'e hózhǫ́ is the vehicle for increase, reproduction, and sexuality."[50] "Sạ'a naghái bik'e hózhǫ́, then, is continuous generational animation."[51] Put simply, this complex term designates the life force or the means to life. It ". . . is completeness, but its source is the lack of completeness of the individual."[52] If a man or woman were "complete," there would be no need for change, life, or continuance; so the kind of "completeness" that Navajos see as a goal of ceremony is a completeness that periodically has to be reconstituted to adapt to a dynamic universe. Although Blessingway songs are not considered healing songs, they contain some similar imagery and promote well-being or completeness. Thus, Abel, hearing the horse song, is not only infused with beauty and blessed by the prayer, but he is also provided with a "model of healing" (reassemblage) and identified with the means of continuing life. And since "The War God's Horse Song" belongs to a Navajo Twin War God, the aggressive life-giving powers of these twins are invoked for Abel through Ben, his singer.

While "The War God's Horse Song" has gone unanalyzed by nearly every critic, most have commented in some fashion on the "House Made of Dawn" prayer. Not only is the text a more obvious model of healing than the horse song, since the language of the "House Made of Dawn" prayer speaks directly of restoration, but also the title of the novel which derives from this prayer emphasizes its central thematic significance. After a review of some of the critical comments made about the function of this prayer in the novel, an analysis of its function and positioning in the novel from the perspectives of its mythological context in the Night Chant, and its verbal performance as healing prayer act, will be developed. Momaday's version of the prayer had been recorded by Washington Matthews in virtually identical form in *Navajo Myths, Prayers, and Songs.*[53]

Alan Velie refers to Abel's early inarticulate years in a chapter on Momaday: "The song Abel is looking for is the Navajo hymn 'House Made of Dawn,' which he later learns from his friend Benally."[54] Velie not only uses an inappropriate Christian term ("hymn") to describe the prayer, but also neglects to probe into the religio-symbolic level of the text. Floyd Watkins cites the wrong Matthews manuscript as the source for the prayer and consequently assumes that Momaday changed the chant. Watkins says: "Ironically, for a traditional Navajo, Momaday's version is a sacrilege."[55] Charles Larson in a short-sighted and largely misinformed section on *House Made of Dawn* in *American Indian Fiction* sees only death where there is life. He says:

By the end of the novel even the title image of a house made of dawn is used negatively, as a reverse symbol, indicating death instead of life. (Momaday appears to be intentionally distorting the Navaho purification song. Ben sings it to Abel when they are drinking with other Indians on the hilltop, yet he perverts its function by being intoxicated and feeling embarrassed that his singing will prevent the others from having a good time. . . .)[56]

For my comments on the hilltop scene, see chapter 3. Lawrence

Evers, however, accurately assesses Ben's contribution to Abel's life. Evers says: "Benally is the Night Chanter, the singer who helps restore voice and harmony to Abel's life."[57] Evers explains:

> The songs from both the Beautyway and the Night Chant are designed to attract good and repel evil. They are both restorative and exorcising expressions of the very balance and design in the universe Abel perceived in the runners after evil. Ben's words from the Night Chant for Abel are particularly appropriate, since the purpose of the Night Chant is to cure patients of insanity and mental imbalance. The structure and diction of the song demonstrates the very harmony it seeks to evoke. Dawn is balanced by evening light, dark cloud and male rain by dark mist and female rain. All things are in balance and control, for in Navajo and Pueblo religion good is control. Further note that a journey metaphor is prominent in the song ("may I walk . . .") and that the restorative sequence culminates with "restore my voice for me." Restoration of voice is an outward sign of inner harmony. Finally, note that the song begins with a culturally significant geographic reference: *Tségihi*. One of its central messages is that ceremonial words are bound efficaciously to place.[58]

In this passage, Evers points out the broad thematic functions of the prayer in repulsing evil and attracting good, and taking the one-sung-over on an imaginary journey into a healthy state. He also points out how these functions are created and maintained semantically, through the controlled structures of balance, repetition, and parallel sequence in the diction and lines. Linda Hogan comments, like Evers, on the way that power is built through language in the prayer.[59] Hogan says:

> By multiplying, through speech, the number of visual images in the mind of the hearer, the ceremony builds momentum. Language takes on the power of generation. Various forms of verbal repetition intensify the rhythm, and as

description and rhythm build, words become a form of internal energy for the listener. . . . In this way, healing can occur as a result of the proper use of language—language as a vehicle for vision, as a means of imagination.[60]

Hogan also says: "In traditional oral literature as well as *House Made of Dawn*, speaking is healing," and recognizes that prayer can "reassemble the division of the self."[61] This vision of order that Ben's sung prayer achieves is healing.

Yet this internal analysis of the "House Made of Dawn" prayer is incomplete unless the elements of the prayer are related to specific details of the Stricken Twins origin myth to the Night Chant. It is essential to relate the prayer to the story of the Stricken Twins who sang it. I first present the prayer text as a place to begin. Ben sings:

Tségihi.
House made of dawn,
House made of evening light,
House made of dark cloud,
House made of male rain,
House made of dark mist,
House made of female rain,
House made of pollen,
House made of grasshoppers,
Dark cloud is at the door.
The trail out of it is dark cloud.
The zigzag lightning stands high upon it.
Male deity!
Your offering I make.
I have prepared a smoke for you.
Restore my feet for me,
Restore my legs for me,
Restore my body for me,
Restore my mind for me,
Restore my voice for me.
This very day take out your spell for me.

Your spell remove for me.
You have taken it away for me;
Far off it has gone.
Happily I recover.
Happily my interior becomes cool.
Happily I go forth.
My interior feeling cool, may I walk.
No longer sore, may I walk.
Impervious to pain, may I walk.
With lively feelings, may I walk.
As it used to be long ago, may I walk.
Happily may I walk.
Happily, with abundant dark clouds, may I walk.
Happily, with abundant showers, may I walk.
Happily, with abundant plants, may I walk.
Happily, on a trail of pollen, may I walk.
Happily may I walk.
Being as it used to be long ago, may I walk.
May it be beautiful before me,
May it be beautiful behind me,
May it be beautiful below me,
May it be beautiful above me,
May it be beautiful all around me.
In beauty it is finished.[62]

The story of the Stricken Twins (Myth of *To' nastsihégo Hatál*) has already been discussed at length in chapter 2. Here it is important to expand the discussion of the story by focusing on the musical dimension of the Twins' experience in the wilderness. When the singer Hatáli Natlói began telling this myth, he said first: "This is a story about songs . . ."[63] Yet it is a long time in the story before any songs are sung. When the poor suffering boys are almost cured of their afflictions by the Yéi, Elder Brother, followed by Younger Brother in turn, breaks the taboo against talking in the sweat house. Their elation about getting well vanishes along with the sweat house, and they are left "the one as blind, the other as lame as ever."[64] The angry Yéi send the boys off to pay for a cure by charging them to bring back beautiful sacred articles of the finest quality. In despair, because they are cast out, still ill and ill-equipped to procure the fine goods required, the twins wandered, for "they had no purpose."[65] The story continues:

> . . . they wept as they walked along and as they wept they began to sing. At first they sang only meaningless syllables; but after a while they found words to sing. They cried to music and turned their thoughts to song. The holy ones still stood grouped behind them, and, hearing the song, said one to another: "Why do they sing?" "I wonder what they are singing about?" . . . "Come back . . . what were you singing as you went along?" They answered: "We were not singing. We were crying." . . . The cripple spoke: "We began to cry, and then we sang; we turned our cry into a song. We never knew the song before. My blind brother made it up as we went along, and this is what we sang:
>
>> From the white plain where stands the water,
>>   From there we come,
>> Bereft of eyes, one bears another.
>>   From there we come.
>> Bereft of limbs, one bears another.
>>   From there we come.
>> Where healing herbs grow by the waters,
>>   From there we come.
>> With these your eyes you shall recover.
>>   From there we come.
>> With these your limbs you shall recover.
>>   From there we come . . .[66]

"When the yéi had heard the boys' song they counseled once more and at last they said: 'We must never turn our children out again, blind, crippled and helpless as they are . . .'"[67] This song so impresses the Holy People that it changes the course of events. The twins are given magical weapons to assist in acquiring the goods, and eventually these offerings are sufficient incentive for the gods to cure them. The "House Made of Dawn" prayer is another one of their impressive songs.[68]

The Stricken Twins are social outcasts, alienated and physically "fragmented" at first. Their painful cry is initially a "meaningless" sound, but gradually evolves into musical words or song. When they "turned their thoughts to song," they concentrated on the aesthetics or the *hózhǫ́* of the experience. They mobilize their own resources to make up the song, and it is precisely this process of composition that leads to their eligibility for healing. They are reassembled through song. To put it another way, the act of singing dissolves their separation, reconnecting them to the natural world, to the gods, and to the powers of rejuvenation or *Sąʼa Naghái Bikʼe Hózhǫ́*. When the Yéi finally perform the curing rites for The Twins, the Yéi sing several hundred songs for them over a nine day period.

Discussing symbolic patterns of healing, Donald Sandner makes the point that singing (vibratory chanting) provokes an inner stimulus that taps an energy source that lends to higher consciousness and healing for the singer.[69] I would like to suggest that in the case of the Stricken Twins that "energy source" is the Bear People and the other Holy People who reside in the landforms—the white plain, the water, and the healing herbs of their song.[70] The Stricken Twins, like medicine men, learn to manipulate their own power symbolically by creating oral images to contemplate, parallel to the visual images of the sandpaintings that become part of their cure later. Sandner says that a medicine man uses:

> symbolic procedures that will render him [the one-sung-over] vulnerable to intense inner forces. . . . The medicine man must lead, and the patient follow, into a confrontation with dangerous as well as curative imagery. The effect is expected to be forceful, impressive, and transforming.[71]

Sandner theorizes that:

a forceful presentation of vivid images causes a transformation in the pattern of psychic energy flow. This can cause
fear and sickness, as in witchcraft, or calmness and healing,
as in the Navaho ceremonials.[72]

The vivid images that the twins see are the natural features or
landmarks of the canyon country that they walk through.

Returning to the "House Made of Dawn" healing song, in the
context of its performance for Abel, it can be said that Abel's
pain peaks when he hears it. Although Abel has suffered on the
beach and survived, with some incentive to live, he is still profoundly shattered and depressed on the hilltop. Like the Stricken
Twins, Abel needs music as medicine, but unlike them, he is
incapable of singing. Jerome Frank says that "some healers serve
as a kind of conduit for a healing force in the universe, often
called the life-force."[73] Ben is this kind of healer. His stories and
songs provide the conceptual framework to make the world
meaningful for Abel and to "stir him emotionally."[74] Abel needs
to restore his "fractured" relationship with Ben that was violated
when he cursed in front of Ben before leaving to seek culebra.[75]
On the hilltop, we find Abel starting to listen to Ben again.

The predominant Navajo pattern of symbolic healing that
Sandner notes is: return to origins, management of evil, death
and rebirth, and restoration.[76] This ceremonial progression takes
place on several levels. It is the general pattern of symbolic activities that the chantways follow. It is the pattern of the "House
Made of Dawn" prayer where world-wide cosmic processes take
place in the microcosmic personal breath of the song. And it
could also be the pattern that Abel's life follows over the span
of the seven years of the novel. "Return to origins" puts the one-
sung-over at the source of creation in mythical time to experience
primordial energies. "Management of evil" turns the evil back
on the witch or source of illness through use of ritual knowledge.
"Death and rebirth" refers to the one-sung-over dying a symbolic
death after crisis and being reborn into a new self. "Restoration"
is the activity of "putting the parts of the entire Navaho universe
in correct relation to one another."[77] This narrative pattern is

analogous to the hero pattern discussed in the early portion of chapter 2.

In terms of the broadest outlines of Abel's life, Abel "manages" evil in the personages of witchsnake and culebra (another double or "twin pair"), experiences death and rebirth on the beach, and progresses through the delicate early stages of his restoration on the beach, on the hilltop, and back home at Jemez. Applying these same four elements of the symbolic healing pattern to the "House Made of Dawn" prayer, it can be seen that the opening image of "dawn" refers to the origin of life and the cyclical nature of existence. The male deity of the prayer, Thunderbird, although not evil, but, rather, an offended Holy Person, is beseeched to cooperate with the singer's request.[78] "This very day take out your spell for me./ Your spell remove for me."[79] Because the proper offering, a smoke, has already been made, the response is instantaneous. "You have taken it away for me;/ Far off it has gone."[80] The one-sung-over is reborn: "Happily I recover."[81] And the world is restored in beauty in all directions: "May it be beautiful before me . . ."[82] The plea for restoration of body, mind, and voice, before the spell is lifted, is parallel to the land asking for the rain from "dark cloud." Both person and land are restored simultaneously ("Happily, with abundant showers, may I walk."), so closely identified as they are.[83] Sam Gill says that "prayer acts are active forces which can render effects on the world."[84] He maintains that "it is due to the semantic structure of the prayer act, rather than to its magically compulsive character, that Navajos see it as an active agent in their world."[85] The "imperative to remake" (in this case: "Restore my voice for me./ This very day take out your spell for me./ Your spell remove for me.") modulates the situation, as these words are spoken, into a harmonious one.[86] The immediate change in verb tense to the past perfect ("You have taken it away for me;") indicates that the process of "removal and dispersion" has taken place.[87] Recovery will follow. Abel does not receive the full power and blessings of the song, however, until he sings it himself in the closing scene of the novel.

At this point up on the hilltop, Abel does receive "the healing power of . . . the . . . expectation of help."[88] And he seems to experience "emotional arousal," one of the prerequisites of breaking through to healing, when he talks over his "plans" with Ben.[89] Ben recalls:

> . . . So I started to talk about the way it was going to be. We had some plans about that. We were going to meet someplace, maybe in a year or two, maybe more. He was going home, and he was going to be all right again. And someday I was going home, too, and we were going to meet someplace out there on the reservation and get drunk together. It was going to be the last time, and it was something we had to do. We were going out into the hills on horses and alone. . . . we were going to sing the old songs. . . .[90]

Abel does not want to let go of this positive vision. Ben "made all of that up" for Abel, and accentuated their plans through repetition of word and image.[91] Once Abel believed in it, Ben did too. Language has created a new reality for them together. Commenting on the importance of confidence and hope in healing, Jerome Frank says: "The patient's expectations are aroused by the healer's personal attributes, by his culturally determined healing role, or, typically, by both."[92] Abel has confidence in Ben. The day after Ben had made up the plans, Ben recalls: "he asked me about it. I had to remember what it was. . . ."[93] Abel's imagination had been sparked that night on the hill under the stars. Ben sends Abel home, providing him with direction, insuring that Abel will make contact with the land and his grandfather, the two sources of meaning remaining for him. As Sandner says, for

> the restoration of a stable universe . . . the patient must be put squarely back into his own life as the Navaho patient in the prayer is brought back to his hogan, restored in mind and body, surrounded by his possessions and familiar cornfields.[94]

Like the one-sung-over who inhales the dawn, returning to the outside world after ceremony, Ben sees to it that Abel will reexperience "how the sun came up with a little wind and the light ran out upon the land."[95] Ben says: "He was going home, and I wanted to pray. Look out for me, I said; look out each day and listen for me."[96] They had some plans.

There is one more aspect of healing in the novel that needs to be considered in order to understand the complex multicultural dynamics of Abel's slow movement towards restoration. The Kiowa peyote ceremony that Tosamah conducts for the men at the Los Angeles Holiness Pan-Indian Rescue Mission on the same night that Abel is beaten up provides another means of understanding Abel's spiritual and physical crisis in relationship to mythic patterns and events in the natural world. Tosamah, physician and priest of the sun, performs a ritual that emanates upward and outward from the dank basement, where the men are gathered, into the universe where it touches Abel.

After a sermon on the importance of The Word, Tosamah begins the all-night ceremony. The peyote way is a means of seeking vision through ingesting the hallucinogen peyote under highly controlled ritual circumstances, guided by members of the pan-tribal organization, the Native American Church.[97] Ben participates in this ceremony, although Abel does not. Tosamah says that: "Daddy peyote is the vegetal representation of the sun."[98] The sun is a connecting symbol between the Kiowa, Pueblo, and Navajo cultures in the novel.[99] The paraphernalia or peyote outfit that Tosamah uses in prayer is a collection of objects that come from the natural world (pheasant feathers, sage, and cedar) or are manmade (beaded drumstick, cigarette papers) to bind singing and smoke back into nature. The gourd rattle full of seeds, imitating the sound of raindrops when shaken, brings rain onto the roof and the sound of the drum brings thunder to the hills surrounding the city.[100] After the men have ingested the peyote, as they stare at images of sun and moon emblazoned on the peyote altar, they feel

a sheer wave of exhilaration in the room. There was no center to it; it was everywhere at once. Everyone felt himself young and whole and powerful. No one was sick or weak or weary. Everyone wanted to run and jump and laugh and breathe deeply of the air. Everyone wanted to shout that he was hale and playful and everlastingly alive. . . .[101]

The wave of emotion subsides, fades into sadness, and the men think of death. The individual prayers after midnight, which speak of the interdependency of life and death, begin. Henry Yellowbull begins by invoking the spirits to join them. "Be with us tonight. Come to us now in bright colors and sweet smoke. . . ."[102] Soon thereafter Ben exclaims: "Look! Look! There are blue and purple horses . . . a house made of dawn. . . ."[103]

J. S. Slotkin in "The Peyote Way" says that whereas peyote ceremonies are not healing ceremonies per se, that "Physiologically, Peyote seems to have curative properties."[104] Most significantly, he says, "Peyote teaches . . . by means of a mystical experience," and he defines that mystical experience as "consist[ing] in the harmony of all immediate experience with whatever the individual conceives to be the highest good."[105] The healing properties of Tosamah's ceremony are literally being spiritually extended to the "outside world." For at the same time that the ceremony is taking place, Abel is bleeding on the beach, recognizing that "something was going on"; he felt a "tremor," a "faint vibration."[106] Then he experiences the old men, the runners after evil from home, running in the night ritually rebalancing the forces of witchcraft with good. He thinks: "Because of them, perspective, proportion, design in the universe. Meaning because of them."[107] This insight begins to restore him. At the same time, back across town, Tosamah leaves the meeting and walks outside into the night.

The Priest of the Sun arose and went out . . . Then in the agony of stasis they heard it, one shrill, piercing note and then another, and another, and another: four blasts of the eagle-bone whistle. In the four directions did the Priest of the Sun, standing painted in the street, serve notice that something holy was going on in the universe.[108]

Then the scene shifts back to Abel lying broken on the beach. The peyotists' prayers and the runners' prayers converge in an eruption of sacred power that checks evil.

Not only does peyote seem to function as "medicine" for the men in the meeting, since they do experience a healthy euphoria, but also its ingestion establishes a visionary pattern of weakness, need for spiritual fulfillment, and vision. Before the peyote meeting, during his sermon, Tosamah had been strangely afflicted.

> Just then a remarkable thing happened. The Priest of the Sun seemed stricken; he let go of his audience and withdrew into himself, into some strange potential of himself.[109]

Later he gets hold of himself and talks about John the Apostle's vision:

> Old John, see, he got up one morning and caught sight of the Truth. It must have been like a bolt of lightning, and the sight of it made him blind. And for a moment the vision burned on in back of his eyes, and he *knew* what it was. In that instant he saw something he had never seen before and would never see again. That was the instant of revelation, inspiration, Truth. . . . And he said, "In the beginning was the Word. . . ."[110]

Tosamah, like John, is stricken physically just before breaking through to vision. Tosamah even says that John's knowledge of the intrinsic power of the spoken word blinded him temporarily and then gave him new vision or revelation. Momaday opens the prologue of his memoir *The Names*, speaking of the Kiowas, with these words:

> They were stricken, surely, nearly blind in the keep of

some primordial darkness. And yet it was their time, and they came out into the light, one after another, until the way out was lost to them. Loss was in the order of things, then, from the beginning. Their emergence was a small thing in itself, and unfinished. But it gave them to know that they were and who they were. They could at last say to themselves, "We are, and our name is *Kwuda*."[111]

This text, based on the Kiowa emergence story, reveals a narrative mythic pattern that Momaday has incorporated into his fiction. The progression of the pattern is: being stricken blind or paralyzed, emerging, acquiring vision, knowledge, and identity.

The Kiowas were incapacitated, blind and crippled, and uncultured until they emerged into light in the natural world. Then they acquired language, a sense of order, and identity through naming. Tosamah is stricken too until he achieves vision and knowledge through ritual. The Biblical John, as understood by Tosamah, is blinded by the truth of the vision when he comes to know that sound, that language, created the universe. Momaday extends the sight/paralysis imagery to Abel who is a crippled lost man until he gets a sense of the order of the universe. Afterwards, he begins to rebuild his identity. And the Stricken Twins, notably, suffer and grow according to the development of this pattern. Momaday has intertwined Kiowa and Navajo patterns of religious experience in order to show that they are two parallel means of achieving vision. Just as the Kiowa emerged out of a hollow log into the land, and Tosamah emerges out of his underground church into the rainy street, Abel emerges out of the "shallow depression" on the beach filled with "weeds and small white stones and tufts of long gray grass" to make one more journey up to the hilltop.[112] From the hilltop, Ben says:

We could see all the lights down below, a million lights, I guess, and all the cars moving around, so small and slow and far away. We could see one whole side of the city, all the way to the water, but we couldn't hear anything down there. All we could hear was the drums and the singing.

> There were some stars, and it was like we were way out in
> the desert someplace and there was a squaw dance or a
> sing going on, and everybody was getting good and drunk
> and happy.[113]

This vision of order and beauty in the land is only possible for
Ben and Abel because they have emerged and been reassembled
together through the power of song, storytelling and reciprocal
care. Although Abel is still "all banged up" on the hilltop, he is
beginning to heal, insofar as he knows where he is "in relation
to the stars."[114] In this context, healing is a process facilitated by
singing that reconstitutes people's sense of the natural order.

It is possible to think of the structural composition of *House
Made of Dawn* as analogous to the process of Abel's healing,
because both are dependent on the slow process of accretion to
create meaning and wholeness. If we understand the process of
accretion as a culturally based process of organic growth, in-
creased by continuous development from within, then we can
see how Abel's healing builds slowly but surely, and how the
text itself relies on a replication of its own key symbols in order
to build accumulated power and significance. In oral tradition
the earmark elements of circular narrative structure, of development by parallelism and repetition, and of spoken language
as inherently creative and forceful combine to allow for wide
variations and stylistic differences among the stories that may
be told about any particular event or place. When the human
imagination is applied to the traditions, endless recombinations
of old story details and structures and new human situations
converge to create new stories that still have the ring of the
familiar. Moreover, oral traditions are characterized by an "elas-
ticity of genre," because of their propensity for adapting
storysherds from other traditions and incorporating them into
the home tribal matrix. This hybridization across genres, and
between cultures, makes it possible for oral traditions to change
and thrive, while maintaining continuity with the old ways—
often amidst outside threats of cultural genocide and assimila-
tion.[115]

Furthermore, there is a constellation or core of organic symbols in oral tradition that is invariant because it represents the fundamental patterns of life on earth. These timeless, yet eternally mysterious, symbols of the natural world are the sun, the moon, water, fire, earth, and air. In native cosmologies, each animal and plant has its own place and distinct significance based on its relationship with the rest of creation. The symbols of deer, bear, and eagle, for instance, are unique and multivalent although each culture emphasizes certain aspects of each animal over other aspects, and no one person knows all of their meanings. For example, Bear is conceived of, in Navajo culture, primarily as enemy, and then as healer. But bears are not hunted nor eaten in Navajo culture, so Navajo hunting stories center around other game.[116] The Northern Pueblos still hunt black bear in the mountains of Northern New Mexico, however, so their stories stress Bear as game but also as friend and healer in the gift of his body for food and spiritual sustenance for the people.[117] These varied roles of Bear naturally make for diverse knowledge and different stories about the animal. In *House Made of Dawn*, then, we get a composite image of Bear that is neither from a wholly Navajo nor a wholly Pueblo perspective. These multiple angles of vision create a new composite image of Bear that is Native American, certainly, and consistent with the patterns of native cultures but is also imagined through story as being "multicultural." Put another way, Momaday's fiction allows us to see many bears through different cultural lenses and to enter into a kind of collective story about bearness that we have come to know through the mixed materials in the novel but not through any one traditional tribal literature. This overarching, synthesizing way of putting a story together is just one of the ways that fiction allows for the extension of Native American oral traditions, while at the same time creating a striking new context for the old stories.

The Navajo chantway ceremonial system also develops and expands through the process of accretion. Father Berard Haile points out that a given chantway "may share specific ceremonies with other chantways," yet, at the same time, remain distinct "with its own songs and prayers."[118] He continues:

The very fact, however, that the same ceremonies and . . . even entire rituals may be shared in common by several chantways, indicates a very *liquid* type of chantway in the Navaho ceremonial system.[119]

Some chantways become extinct, while new ones are "added to the system."[120] "The stronger chantway increases its repertory of ceremonials so that, in time, it may readily take care of the repertory of a weaker chantway, gradually absorb the latter. . . ."[121] He sums up this observation of change and continuity in Navajo religion by saying: "The process, therefore, both of adoption and absorption may be expected in the "Navaho chantway system."[122] *House Made of Dawn*, then, like the chantways, and like the oral traditions in which both novel and ceremony are based, seems at times to have a "liquid structure," constantly changing through absorption, redigestion, and ultimately reformulation of all the story elements that it has ingested. This process of incorporation of eclectic realities is at once traditional in its thrust and contemporary in its tendency to permit "the slow whine of tires on the Cuba and Bloomfield road" to merge, in parallel fashion, with the sound of the tank approaching and the strange wail of the Bahkyush witch.[123] The ultimate model for these "resemblances" in literature is, of course, the natural world where the "moan of the wind" through a "partly concealed" hole in the rock portends imbalance, illness, and the threat of death.[124] Momaday builds the meaning of his narrative "sequences" like this, then, not through linear chronological development but rather through symbolic association and the process of accretion. In order to read a text like this, one must be willing and imaginative enough to plunge into its "liquidity" and surface looking for the concentric rings of relationship.

There is a petroglyph panel in Chaco Canyon that shows the process of accretion at work in the juxtaposition of Navajo images of old trucks adjacent to shield-bearing horseback riders at a Ute encampment.[125] Nearby on a Chaco overhang, there are "recent" bright pink Navajo handprints stamped onto a ceiling covered with faded orange Anasazi handprints.[126] These multi-century marvels of composition suggest that form, color, and pattern are continuing aesthetic concerns in Southwestern tribal art, and that imagination, as always, is the final determinant of the form of the creative process. I will return shortly to a consideration of petroglyphs as a model of text-building, but first I will examine the history of critical difficulties and misunderstandings about the novel, which have formed the bedrock of the hermeneutic problems that have caused me to undertake this study.

In spite of the fact that *House Made of Dawn* won the Pulitzer Prize for fiction in 1969, ever since its publication there have been some unfavorable reviews, wherein critics either disliked the novel or utterly failed to comprehend it, or both.[127] Yet there are dozens of other scholar/critics who have labored to comprehend the text, have been frequently baffled, but nevertheless still persist in wanting to rethink, reteach, or rewrite their views of it.[128] All of us together face the critical dilemma of needing to know more about the religious dimensions of the text in order to understand the unique literary qualities of the novel. The —— ritual patterns in the novel are based on mythological stories from oral tradition, and these stories are grounded in religious views of the universe (distinct within each tribe) wherein the land is the fundamental reality. Everything comes from, and returns to, the land. As critics, then, we must know what is going on in this essentially connected land-religion-literature spindle of the story, and we also have to know in some authentic verifiable sense what the images, symbols, and native structures are that provide the themes of the story. The problem of "not knowing" is compounded when one considers that: some obviously ritualistic events have no oral text in the novel to "explain" them (i.e., running after evil), that a good deal of this "religious material" is culturally sensitive and therefore not available to outsiders, and that semi-obscure old ethnographic records are one of the best ways to understand the text in context. Still, the novel stands unto itself as a whole complete work. Momaday has provided, within the text, sufficient context to understand the basic elements of the novel adequately. For example, we are told that the runners after evil maintain "perspective, proportion, design in the universe," so we can understand their function against witchcraft and disorder in the story.[129] Nevertheless, it is never a literary writer's aim to explain everything, per se, in a literal fashion but rather to do as Momaday does, and extend the beauty and mystery of life into the imaginations of his readers.

It is the literary critic's job to reveal the artistry of the work, the issues that it raises, and, at the same time, in the case of Native American Literature, to provide sufficient cultural context for the general reader to understand in depth the tribal knowledge conveyed in the work. Otherwise, without the efforts of the critic the cultural gap between reader and writer may remain wide, and the work may seem like a true hermeneutic puzzle instead of the "bridge piece" that it is meant to be. Many serious attempts have been made to achieve these goals, but the results have been uneven. For instance, Baine Kerr is obviously intrigued by the novel. He writes:

> Momaday's ambition . . . is attempting to transliterate Indian culture, myth, and sensibility into an alien art form, without loss. He may in fact be seeking to make the modern Anglo novel a vehicle for a sacred text.[130]

He recognizes the importance of the "clear explication of mythic and intellectual context" and healing in the novel.[131] He even goes so far as to say: "The book *is* a creation myth," but, at the same time he calls himself a "mystified Anglo" reader, and levels various charges at Momaday.[132] Kerr claims that it is his responsibility to "catalog Momaday's literary offenses," including: "repetition," "pretentious[ness]," "disconcerting" language, "mutilation of narrative," "interrupted narrative," "suppressed information," "turbid events," and various "confusions."[133] Perhaps Kerr's most telling comment is the statement that: "The series of myths, each variously imperfect, each with common corruptions and shared strengths, overlap, blend, and fuse as this novel."[134] His final statement is partially true—the myths do "overlap, blend, and fuse," but they are neither imperfect nor "corruptions" of an imaginary perfect myth, as shown in chapters 2 and 3. Kerr's main point about Momaday having created a sacred text is a bit overstated. Whereas Momaday has most definitely incorporated sacred texts into this novel, his work does not impart holiness in the way that a verbal performance by a Navajo singer of the "House Made of Dawn" prayer would. *House Made of Dawn* in itself is not a literary shrine or religious object but is a means, through story, of knowing how to recognize sacred events, such as Abel sprinkling corn meal for his grandfather, and of knowing how to live in a sacred manner, respectful of relationships with others.

Floyd Watkins who clearly respects the novel still says:

> Thus in the mysteries of unexplanation and untranslation begins one of the finest recent novels in America . . . but made almost incomprehensible by a profusion of elaborate cultural, mythical, and ritualistic detail.[135]

Many critics of the novel say that the book is inordinately complex, and a few critics like Marion Willard Hylton try to solve this problem by writing simplistic overviews of it or by making vague unsubstantial statements such as: "Hearing Angela and seeing how she has changed has at last made clear to him [Abel] just how and why he has lost his way."[136] Even one of the finer critics, Matthias Schubnell, who chastises others for their "unawareness of the symbolic and ritualistic patterns in *House Made of Dawn*," and who cites Eliade as an important authority on myth and sacred time, does not develop more than a cursory knowledge of the function of myth in the novel.[137] He concludes his chapter on *House Made of Dawn* with a discussion of Abel's dawn run. Schubnell says: "The novel's final scene is charged with mythological overtones. . . ."[138] Then he proceeds to retell a portion of an unidentified pueblo's emergence myth that says that as the people "entered their new environment they were blind. . . . And when its [the sun's] rays shone upon the eyes of the people, they were opened and they could see."[139] By including this storysherd in his chapter, Schubnell has an inkling of the blindness-vision-knowledge patterns that are operative in the novel. But Schubnell merely hints at "mythological over-tones" and presses no further.

As a partial response to the common frustration of seeing the novel as composed of a collection of fragments from oral tradition, I have developed the concept of storysherds and song-sherds to deemphasize the negative term "fragments" and stress instead their persistent nature. Storysherds can be thought of as "survivals." Impressive new theories are being developed that address the problematics of how to read a text such as this or the yet broader questions of how to evaluate "genre mixing in social science" and the humanities, and how to find "some way of synthesizing" various approaches.[140] Viewing much contemporary academic work, especially in the social sciences, as blurring the genres between disciplines, Clifford Geertz says that we need to focus on the "properties connecting texts" and see texts "relationally" in order "to accommodate a situation at once fluid, plural, uncentered, and ineradicably untidy."[141] This fluidity is reminiscent of Haile's word "liquid" to describe certain Navajo chantways. One of Geertz's main concerns is "the analysis of symbol systems . . . [in] relationship . . . to what goes on in the world. . . ."[142] The text and the world interpenetrate one another. Bearing these broad issues in mind, a look at how some critics of Native American humanities have responded to several of these same concerns is worthwhile.

In a special issue of *MELUS* devoted to Native American Literature, the editor Wayne Charles Miller makes the following comment:

> The cosmography of *House Made of Dawn* is different from the cosmography of *Absalom, Absalom!* Aesthetic and epistemological premises are very different as well. In order to approach that book or any other Native American work the reader must have some knowledge of the aesthetic, epistemological, and cosmographical premises upon which it is at least partially based.[143]

This cultural contextualizing that Miller calls for is absolutely necessary to understanding any tribal literature. David McAllester cites the "fatal opacities" of many misinformed scholars who have looked at texts as objects, outside of their cultural contexts.[144] McAllester says:

My contention is that if we are studying Native American Humanities, our effort must be to get as close as possible to the original meaning of the expressions of these humanities, rather than to reinterpret them in terms of the poetic intuitions of outside cultures, whether these be in Africa, ancient India, south Siberia, or the United States. In Native American Humanities it is an error to consider a text such as that of the "Horse Song" out of its cultural context, for the context is what gives it its Native American meaning. We must be prepared for the connotative excursion into the indigenous philosophy, mythology, art, music, religion, medicine—ethnography, in short—with every poem.[145]

And in regard to his model for the study of Native American Music McAllester says:

There should be copious notes explaining esoteric references and putting the song into its cultural context. This would include the relevant mythic material and all other explanations offered by the original singer.[146]

Whereas we may expect this kind of preparation for a study in ethnomusicology, few of us demand it for fiction, but this is precisely the point where Native American literary study parts ways with criticism of "mainstream" American Literature. The fundamental assumptions about the structure of the world that are reflected in texts are different for Native American Literatures than for other American Literature, as these statements by Miller and McAllester indicate. Basic attitudes about story and myth help to explain part of this difference. Momaday has said that

history plus imagination equals story, a statement that emphasizes that stories are means of understanding historical or racial
experience, and myths means of knowing the original sacred
relationships of things.[147] Yet, the conventional American notion
of story, even in the context of literary studies, is a tale told to
instruct and delight, but not necessarily to be taken very seri-
ously. For Native Americans, however, stories define the param-
eters and possibilities of life. So knowing the cultural constituents
or references in a story is the point of departure for analyzing
themes, symbols, and structures, as well as assessing the literary
style of the text.

Recognizing that there are "multiple narratives" in contemporary Native American fiction, James Ruppert has developed
the concept of mediation in order to explain the relationships
between the narratives, and between writer and multiple au-
diences.[148] Ruppert says that Native American and white cultural
patterns illuminate one another in fiction, and that "multiple
narratives force readers to acknowledge the multiplicity of the
realities around them."[149] Ruppert continues:

> . . . in many tribal traditions, meaning is multidimensional,
> associative and accretive. . . . An accretive, fragmented nar-
> rative structure presented through a series of sequences
> which merge time, consciousness, and point of view can
> be one effective way to express an associative, holistic ep-
> istemology.[150]

And Paula Gunn Allen sees an "accretive, associative, and mul-
tidimensional" structure to both *House Made of Dawn* and *Ceremony*.[151] She maintains that this structure actually clarifies the
"circular associative progression of events as they impinge on
the characters and interact with them."[152] Allen says: "As in tales
from the oral tradition, American Indian fiction shifts from real
to surreal readily, while the underlying unity of person, setting,
event and outcome is maintained."[153] Both Ruppert and Allen
then see that the narrative "fragments" or storysherds in the
novel actually bind the story together. Allen sees four stories in

House Made of Dawn: the sociological story (regarding Abel's struggle between white and Indian worlds), the psychological story (that tells of Abel's "growth into manhood"), the ceremonial story (which is largely Navajo and "whose resolution depends on the protagonist's success in learning certain things and returning to the people with that knowledge so that they might benefit and prosper"), and the "arcane tale of earth, sky, moon, sun and season" which is largely Pueblo in origin.[154] My own study focuses on what Allen calls the "ceremonial story" and to some degree on the "arcane story," which is more esoteric.[155] Allen sees all four stories interconnecting in the whole story that is the novel.

In one of the most often cited critical articles on *House Made of Dawn*, Carol Oleson declares her frustrations in trying to analyze "the difficult concept of a house made of dawn."[156] She says:

> The associations of each word would greatly increase our understanding of the symbolism, but that kind of analysis should be done by a Navajo scholar, or at least by a student of Navajo culture. There is, I believe, an entire level of the book that remains unseen by those of us who do not know the languages and legends of the people depicted. . . . We can find the symbols by the emphasis given them, but we cannot read all the levels of their meaning once we have found them.[157]

These "deeper levels of meaning" that she alludes to reside in the story structures and symbolic patterns from oral tradition. My work has been written in an effort to provide precisely the kind of ethnographic-literary background that Oleson is calling for, so the full range of symbolic imagery in *House Made of Dawn* can be approached from a solid multicultural context. I have, of course, focused on the mythic context of Navajo and Pueblo twin and bear stories as the central images that make the healing processes in the novel cohere. This symbolic webwork releases ". . . the ultimate curative or restorative effect which is the basic purpose of [this] book."[158] As Paula Gunn Allen recognizes: "*House Made of Dawn* is an act of the imagination designed to heal . . ." and it accomplishes this task through a dynamic interplay of closely related images.[159]

An analogy from Navajo and Pueblo material culture is a useful model for discussing Momaday's methods of textbuilding in *House Made of Dawn*.[160] It is possible to think of the composition of the novel as analogous to that of a petroglyph panel. Although both novel and petroglyph seem to have a "fixation of meaning" and a fixation of form in that they are created in "durable" substances—paper and rock—the images in both this novel and a petroglyph panel seem to spatially emerge and recede.[161] This sense of movement can be observed sometimes when looking at large groupings of images or multi-figure complexes on petroglyph panels.[162] Representational and abstract styles of rendering images are often combined in one area. Images of dancers, deer, and concentric circles, for instance, may appear adjacent to one another or even superimposed on one another, creating overlapping images. The different styles, subject matter, and age of the images collectively form a story about that particular place. This sacred rock art literally composes a story in the land, a story that may be difficult to "read" or interpret because it has been composed over a long time by a series of people passing by. There may or may not be any obvious connecting links between the images, but their story becomes apparent by looking at their positioning and relationship with one another. The overlapping, superimposition of images gives a sense that there are many ancestral stories peeking through. These panels grow through the process of accretion, too, like stories in oral tradition "grow" through being reimagined as they are being retold. Many of the symbols that appear in other art forms also appear in the panels incised into the rock. It is possible to see depictions of baskets, bows and arrows, and the sun, for instance—images that also occur in stories, sandpaintings, and ceremonies. Depending on which images are chosen out of a constellation of tribal symbols, how these images are executed (in form, color, and pattern), and how they are imaginatively recombined, different stories are told. One contemporary artist from Cochiti Pueblo, Joe Herrera, who understands this way of composing, studies old petro-glyphs and kiva murals to get ideas for his paintings. He says that his work "puts the color back in the old images."[163]

Momaday, like Herrera, puts the color back in the old stories by resituating them in a new context.[164] Momaday manipulates the old symbols and themes in a style that seems, at times, to be an "abstract" presentation of a complex pattern arrangement that is just as "difficult to read" as some of the petroglyph panels. When he retells the story of the bear petroglyph left by the people who came down from the mesas, for example, he does not de-code mysteries or explain them, but passes on the sense of awe that the people felt who knew that Bear could mean either risk of death or transformation and healing.[165] Like complex layered petroglyph panels, *House Made of Dawn* compels the observer to imagine the relationship between stories.[166] The novel forces the reader to think imaginatively, associatively, and holistically, and this push towards seeking relationships parallels the impetus for healing. Momaday's method of putting symbols together in a new mode, with modern additions and accommodations, is a process of artistic composition that is analogous to the "frag-mentation-reassemblage" theory of healing, because once the storysherds are reassembled in the story of Abel's life, and he recognizes that they are impinging on him, he begins to heal. Land, body, and spirit come together through story.

This study has focused on twin patterns and patterns of bear power as the two dominant models of achieving wholeness in *House Made of Dawn*.[167] Both the stories of the wandering twins and the wandering bears are healing because as they walk down into the canyons, over to the springs, and up onto the mesas and mountain ridges, they are paying attention to the features of landscape, as they eventually circle back home. This con-necting process of knowing the contours of the land intimately and voicing that knowledge in story is at the core of the healing experience. Abel heals because he is both Younger Brother and Bear Man.

William Thackeray suggests in "Animal Allies and Trans-formers of *Winter in the Blood*" that an "awareness of the myth-ological sources of these animal characters provides a richer and deeper understanding of the novel. . . ."[168] He also says that animals have an "original significance as allied presences in man's relationship to nature and the supernatural."[169] In the same issue of *MELUS* that Thackeray's article appears in, Momaday is interviewed and asked about his personal identification with the Kiowa legend of Devil's Tower.[170] Momaday says:

> I'm serious about the bear. I want to know what happened to him. And I identify with the bear because I'm intimately connected with that story. And so I have this bear power. I turn into a bear every so often. I feel myself becoming a bear, and that's a struggle I have to face now and then.[171]

When asked what the bear symbolism in the Kiowa story means, Momaday responds: "I suspect it is that part of man which is subhuman."[172] Noting that bears are "powerful" and "wonderful creatures," Momaday comments on the significance of the Kiowa bear boy.[173]

> Most people cannot recover nature. At one time, we lived in nature. But somewhere along the way, we were severed from nature. And we cannot any longer comprehend the creatures of nature. We don't know about them as we once did. But this boy is an exception. He turns into a bear; that means that he reconstructs that link with nature. You could talk about the bear as being the underside of his existence.[174]

This notion of the bear boy as "reconstruct[ing] that link with nature" is crucial to understanding the bedrock importance of the inclusion of bear material in the novel. For the boy's transformation into Bear is an outward sign of his complete integration into the natural world. And this thorough connection with the land is healing. The bear boy story, then, is a model for humans who, likewise, are trying to reconstruct the link, a link with wilderness necessary for balance and sanity.

Vital connections with nature can be maintained by internalizing stories and songs of places and creatures that have retained their integrity since the beginning of time. In a penetrating talk at the Navajo Studies Conference, David McAllester stated that he sees "The War God's Horse Song" as maintaining a "bridge function" between Navajos and Anglos, between nature and humans. He called the song "cultural property relocated," and said that it is an example of a text that emerged through the ethnographic record to unite cultures.[175] This song can be thought of as a cultural offering or gift from the Navajo people to the world at large.

In a collection of horse stories and songs recorded in the O'Bryan text, the old Navajo man Sandoval tells a story of a man who wanted to see horses. "The Sun told the man that he must offer a gift to the plant called ga'tso dan that he had seen in the East. . . ."[176] "After that [many gifts] he would see the horse." And when the man chanted, "horses were given to men."[177] This basic Navajo pattern of offerings, prayer, and restored vision is also evident in *House Made of Dawn*, where it is manifested in different contexts.

Francisco, like the Yéi in the Stricken Twins story, wished for turquoise. He wanted:

> a stone, a great oval spider web, like a robin's egg, to wear upon his hand. . . . Such a stone was medicine, they said; it could preserve the sight. It could restore an old man's vision. They sang about it. . . .[178]

The Yéi considered turquoise a high offering for a cure, an offering as fine as doeskins and furs.[179] The sweet smoke that Bear and Snake offer to the sisters in Ben's story from Mountainway is a gift, too, because it will transform them into women of vision and ritual knowledge.

The old gray gabardine coat that Ben gives Abel as Abel boards the train in Los Angeles to go home to New Mexico is a type of fabric offering that is reminiscent of the fabrics that the Stricken Twins offer to the Yéi.[180] Back at Jemez, Abel places this old gray coat on his dying grandfather. The old man "lay under three blankets and Abel's gray coat. . . ."[181] "Abel smoothed the coat and drew it up to his grandfather's throat."[182] The fact that Abel's gift of the coat makes *four* layers of bedding for Francisco indicates that Abel is gaining a sense of completeness and wholeness. He is learning how to responsibly care for another person. John Farella says that at the time of the creation of the Navajo world: "Life substances [were] covered with spreads of jewels or of the cardinal phenomena and then ritually altered."[183] He also says: "The stories are constantly describing the 'covering' of substances and/or beings with 'blankets' or 'sheets' of jewels or light, and 'new' beings always result."[184] By symbolic parallel then, it can be understood that Abel's gift of Ben's old coat contributes to Francisco's transformation into death or new life. And when Abel blesses his dead grandfather with pollen and corn meal and runs in the dawn, he completes the gesture of helping Francisco change worlds.[185]

Abel offers his broken body in the run, the gift of his life, to his people. Physical pain is partially transcended and no longer matters, but the survival of the Pueblo through cooperative behavior does.[186] Abel's suffering is made meaningful, like the Stricken Twins', through his contemplations of the origins of his imbalance and through singing the "House Made of Dawn" prayer. His running toward the dark hills confers dignity on him, for Abel was beginning "to see according to holiness" on that moist morning when "the murky, leaden swell of light upon the snow and the dunes and the black evergreen spires" broke out upon the land creating a "story made of dawn."[187]

Notes

Chapter 1

1. Rudolfo Anaya, lecture on Chicano Literature, Rocky Mountain Modern Language Association Convention, Santa Fe, New Mexico, October 1976.

2. Leland C. Wyman, *Beautyway: A Navaho Ceremonial.* Bollingen Series 53 (New York: Pantheon Books, 1957), p. 3.

3. N. Scott Momaday, *House Made of Dawn* (New York: Harper and Row, 1968). Throughout this study I cite the Perennial paperback edition for reasons of accessibility. N. Scott Momaday, *House Made of Dawn* (New York: Harper and Row, Perennial Library, 1977); Simon J. Ortiz, *Going For the Rain* (New York: Harper and Row, 1976); Leslie Marmon Silko, *Ceremony* (New York: Signet, 1978; New York: Penguin Books, 1986.) Citations refer to the Signet edition.

4. Richard Ohmann, lecture on recent American fiction, English Department Seminar, University of Colorado, Boulder, 1982. Ohmann went on to contrast these "narratives of illness" to the "wisdom literature" developing today in the writings of N. Scott Momaday and John Irving.

5. *House Made of Dawn* has received considerable critical attention since it was published. But in the last decade these critics have taken more comprehensive approaches to studying the work than did earlier scholars. See Paula Gunn Allen, "A Stranger in My Own Life: Alienation in American Indian Prose and Poetry," *MELUS* 7, No. 2 (Summer 1980): 3–19; Lawrence J. Evers, "Words and Place: A Reading of *House Made of Dawn*," *Western American Literature,* 11 (February 1977): 297–320, reprinted in *Critical Essays in Native American Literature,* ed. Andrew Wiget

(Boston: G. K. Hall, 1985), pp. 211–230; Linda Hogan, "Who Puts Together" in *Studies in American Indian Literature: Critical Essays and Course
Designs*, ed. Paula Gunn Allen (New York: The Modern Language Association of America, 1983),pp. 169–77; Elaine Jahner, "A Critical Approach to American Indian Literature" in *Studies in American Indian
Literature: Critical Essays and Course Designs*, ed. Paula Gunn Allen (New
York: The Modern Language Association of America, 1983), pp. 211–
24; Kenneth Lincoln, *Native American Renaissance* (Berkeley: University
of California Press, 1983), pp. 117–21. For a plot synopsis of *House Made
of Dawn*, see Andrew Wiget, *Native American Literature* (Boston: Twayne
Publishers, 1985), pp. 82–85.

6. See, for example, Charles R. Larson, *American Indian Fiction* (Al-
buquerque: University of New Mexico Press, 1978), pp. 78–96; Alan
Velie, *Four American Indian Literary Masters: N. Scott Momaday, James
Welch, Leslie Marmon Silko, and Gerald Vizenor* (Norman: University of
Oklahoma Press, 1982), pp. 52–64; Floyd C. Watkins, *In Time and Place:
Some Origins of American Fiction* (Athens: University of Georgia Press,
1977), chapter 7: "Culture Versus Anonymity in *House Made of Dawn*,"
pp. 133–71.

7. Matthias Schubnell, *N. Scott Momaday: The Cultural and Literary
Background* (Norman: University of Oklahoma Press, 1985).

8. Ibid. Schubnell discusses these literary figures in relation to Momaday in chapter 3: "The American Earth," pp. 63–92. His discussion of
the novel appears in chapter 4: "The Crisis of Identity: *House Made of
Dawn*," pp. 93–139.

9. Ibid. Schubnell discusses, for example, "Momaday's indebtedness
to Faulkner" in regard to "fragmented narrative perspective, the dis-
jointed time scheme, the connection of surface meaning to underlying
symbolic patterns, the use of different styles for different characters,"
p. 68. Schubnell also cites Lewis M. Dabney, *The Indians of Yoknapatawpha
County: A Study in Literature and History* (Baton Rouge: Louisiana State
University Press, 1974), p. 156, as an example of a good study that
shows that Francisco's bear hunting story "owes much to Faulkner's
story," "The Bear." See Schubnell, pp. 70, 271.

10. Schubnell, *N. Scott Momaday*, p. 3.

11. Ibid., p. 4. Schubnell uses the phrase "'Indian' qualities."

12. Ibid., p. 100.

13. Momaday, *House Made of Dawn*, p. 171. For the "With Beauty"
chant, see Aileen O'Bryan, *The Dîné: Origin Myths of the Navaho Indians*
(Washington: Smithsonian Institution, Bureau of American Ethnology
Bulletin No. 163, 1956), p. 137. Beauty spreads to the four directions.

14. Paula Gunn Allen, "Bringing Home the Fact: Tradition and Continuity in the Imagination" in *Recovering the Word: Essays on Native American Literature*, eds. Brian Swann and Arnold Krupat (Berkeley: University of California Press, 1987), p. 570.

15. Elsie Clews Parsons, *The Pueblo of Jemez*, Department of Archaeology, Phillips Academy (New Haven: Yale University Press, 1925), p. 137. Actually, the first recorded version of the Jemez emergence story appeared in: Albert B. Reagan, "The Jemez Indians," *El Palacio* (April 1917): 47–49.

16. Of course, it is not to be expected that over sixty years ago, when Parsons was doing her work, anthropologists had the same training or cultural sensitivity that they do now. One can wonder about Parsons's techniques of collection, her purposes in gathering the data, and the ethics of her profession in regard to revealing esoteric knowledge.

17. For an account of the problem, see Joe S. Sando, *Nee Hemish, A History of Jemez Pueblo* (Albuquerque: University of New Mexico Press, 1982), p. 216.

18. N. Scott Momaday, *The Names: A Memoir* (New York: Harper and Row, 1976). See especially pp. 121, 128, 134–35, and 144–46. This autobiographical work, Momaday's "memoir," contains considerable information that relates to *House Made of Dawn*.

19. Washington Matthews, *The Night Chant, A Navaho Ceremony*, Memoirs of the American Museum of Natural History, Whole Series 6, Anthropology Vol. 5, New York, 1902; Gladys A. Reichard, *Navaho Religion: A Study of Symbolism*, Bollingen Series 18 (Princeton: Princeton University Press, 1950), pp. 94–95.

20. Ibid. The Navajo Holy People are the deities who are the inner life forms of all of the elements in the natural world. They may cause illness in humans, but they also are associated with creation and the means to health.

21. Dane Coolidge and Mary Roberts Coolidge, *The Navajo Indians* (Boston: Houghton Mifflin Co., 1930), p. 186. Matthews was an Army surgeon on the Navajo reservation, 1880–1884 and 1890–1894. He was also a self-trained social scientist ethnographer. For biographical details of his life, see: The Wheelright Museum of the American Indian, *Guide to the Microfilm Edition of the Washington Matthews Papers* (Albuquerque: University of New Mexico Press, 1985).

22. I treat this issue in "With Zig-Zag Lightning: Precarious Tellings of Sacred Stories by Matthews and Miguelito," paper presented at the Modern Language Association Convention, New Orleans, 1988.

23. Momaday, *House Made of Dawn*, pp. 177–78, 134. Black Mesa is the site of renewal of the organic ceremonial calendar and Tségihi Canyon is the place where physical recovery occurs in the heart of the book.

24. Washington Matthews, *Navaho Myths, Prayers, and Songs*, ed. P. E. Goddard, University of California Publications in American Archaeology and Ethnology, 5, No. 2, 1907, pp. 54–55. The Navajo familiarly call Nightway or the Night Chant *Yeibichai*, meaning "Maternal Grandfather of the Gods," a reference to Talking God, one of the Yéi Holy People who is a key figure in the ceremony.

25. Momaday, *House Made of Dawn*, p. 7.

26. Sam D. Gill used this phrase speaking about oral traditions in a seminar: Native American Religions/Symbolism at the University of Colorado, Boulder, 1982.

27. Sam Gill defines the complex Navajo term *"hózhǫ́"* as "being surrounded by a pleasant environment . . . simply beautiful . . . an environment fitting the pristine beauty of creation. . . ." The Navajo one-sung-over (patient) achieves this state of beauty through prayer acts of a chantway healing ceremonial. See Sam D. Gill, "Prayer as Person: The Performative Force in Navajo Prayer Acts", in *History of Religions* 17, no. 2, University of Chicago Press (November 1977): 151.

28. Wyman, *Beautyway: A Navaho Ceremonial*; Leland C. Wyman, *The Mountainway of the Navajo* (Tucson: University of Arizona Press, 1975); Leland C. Wyman, *Blessingway: With Three Versions of the Myth Recorded and Translated from the Navajo by Father Berard Haile, OFM* (Tucson: University of Arizona Press, 1970); Father Berard Haile, *Origin Legend of the Navaho Enemy Way* (New Haven: Yale University Publications in Anthropology, No. 17, 1938).

29. Rock Point Community School, *Between Sacred Mountains: Navajo Stories and Lessons from the Land*, eds. Sam and Janet Bingham (Tucson: SunTracks and the University of Arizona Press, 1982), p. 1. This book is written by a collective of Navajo people.

30. Wyman, *Blessingway*, p. 201.

31. Sam D. Gill, *Sacred Words: A Study of Navajo Religion and Prayer* (Westport, Connecticut: Greenwood Press, 1981), p. 53.

32. James Kale McNeley, *Holy Wind in Navajo Philosophy* (Tucson: University of Arizona Press, 1981), p. 1.

33. Gill, *Sacred Words*, p. 172.

34. Clyde Benally, Andrew O. Wiget, John R. Alley, and Garry Blake, *Dinéjí Nákéé Nááhane': A Utah Navajo History* (Monticello, Utah: San Juan School District, 1982), p. 2. "These beings [Holy People] have both an

inner, or spirit, form and an outer, or physical form. The outer form may change from time to time as needed, but the inner form never changes."

35. For a good discussion of the ceremonial elements of chantways, see Leland C. Wyman, "Navajo Ceremonial System," in *Handbook of North American Indians, Southwest,* Vol. 10, ed. Alfonso Ortiz (Washington: Smithsonian Institution, 1983), pp. 537–57.

36. Susan Scarberry-García, "White Shell Woman's Song: Remaking the Literary Tradition," lecture presented at The Colorado College SIROW Seminars, Colorado Springs, December 1984.

37. John D. Farella, *The Main Stalk: A Synthesis of Navajo Philosophy* (Tucson: University of Arizona Press, 1984), p. 181.

38. Momaday, *House Made of Dawn,* pp. 134–35; Matthews, *Navaho Myths, Prayers, and Songs,* pp. 54–55; in 1885 James Stevenson witnessed a performance of the Night Chant and published a description of ritual acts but admitted that he did not know much about the ceremony. See James Stevenson, "Ceremonial of Hasjelti Dailjis and Mythical Sand Painting of the Navajo Indians." Eighth Annual Report of the Bureau of American Ethnology 1886–1887 (Washington, 1891), pp. 235–85. Stevenson did not publish the "House Made of Dawn" prayer text. In 1909 a very brief description of the Night Chant appeared by Alfred Marston Tozzer, "Notes on Religious Ceremonials of the Navaho," in Putnam Anniversary Volume, *Anthropological Essays* (New York: G. E. Stechert, 1909), pp. 299–343. Included is a comparison of events of the Night Chant witnessed by Washington Matthews and by Tozzer. For a listing of all seven of the recorded Night Chant texts (both published and unpublished), see James C. Faris, "Navajo Nightway Chant History: A Report." *Diné Be'iina': A Journal of Navajo Life* 1, no. 2 (Winter 1988): 112. Also see John Bierhorst, ed., *Four Masterworks of American Indian Literature: Quetzalcoatl/The Ritual of Condolence/Cuceb/The Night Chant* (New York: Farrar, Straus and Giroux, 1974), pp. 279–351 for a reprinting of Matthews's song and prayer texts from *The Night Chant,* and a condensation of the chantway's ritual elements.

39. Matthews, *The Night Chant,* p. 143.

40. Momaday, *House Made of Dawn,* p. 191.

41. Barry Lopez, "Story at Anaktuvuk Pass: At the Junction of Landscape and Narrative," *Harper's* (December 1984): 50; reprint "Landscape and Narrative (1984)" in *Crossing Open Ground* (New York: Charles Scribner's Sons, 1988), pp. 61–71. Citations refer to the *Harper's* article.

42. Ibid., p. 51.

43. Ibid.

44. Ibid.

45. Gill, *Sacred Words*, pp. 34–35. The Holy People are integrally connected with Navajo concepts of sickness and health, as will be discussed; Rock Point Community School, *Between Sacred Mountains*, p. 2. Some of the Holy People reside in the sacred mountains.

46. Gill, *Sacred Words*, pp. 112, 81, 83.

47. For example, Hopi runners sometimes carry gourds full of water to attract the distant rain clouds. In the process of the run, the runners become the clouds themselves. See Peter Nabokov, *Indian Running* (Santa Barbara: Capra Press, 1981), pp. 154–58. "Organic symbols" is Reyes García's term.

48. See, for example, Wyman, *Blessingway*, p. 148. This Blanca Peak song is from Version 1 told by Slim Curly.

49. Momaday, *House Made of Dawn*, p. 155. The Navajo culture heroes, the Twin War Gods, Monster Slayer (*Nayénĕzgani*), and Born for Water (*To'badzĭstsíni*), are two of the Holy People. This prayer can be found in Coolidge and Coolidge, *The Navajo Indians*, p. 2. Belted Mountain is Mount Blanca in Southern Colorado.

50. Momaday, *House Made of Dawn*, p. 155.

51. Lopez, "Story at Anaktuvuk Pass," p. 51.

52. Ibid.

53. Ibid., p. 52.

54. Paula Gunn Allen, *The Sacred Hoop: Recovering the Feminine in American Indian Traditions* (Boston: Beacon Press, 1986), p. 89. Allen also says here that "They [the Holy People] are most like themselves in the story Abel's white lover Angela tells to her son about the bear and the maiden."

55. The Stricken Twins are two young maimed Navajo culture heroes who regain their health in a variant origin story to the Night Chant. See Matthews, *The Night Chant*, pp. 212–65. These twins are discussed as archetypes for Vidal and Abel in chapter 2.

56. Rock Point Community School, *Between Sacred Mountains*, p. 89. This point about oral tradition is made in the section called "Stories": "If a 70-year-old elder teaches clan history to a 20-year-old student, the story passes down 50 years. Only twenty tellings carry the story 1000 years. Families may tell the story differently after twenty tellings, but the heart of the truth has probably survived as well as many records written in ink."

57. Matthews, *The Night Chant*, pp. 81, 311 n. 29, 313 n. 43.

58. As *House Made of Dawn* is one of the Holy People's homes, a

temporary residence where they make their presence known to the "Earth Surface People" (a Navajo phrase for human beings), so is the novel *Ceremony*, by the Laguna Pueblo writer Leslie Marmon Silko, home to the Holy People Pollen Boy, the Bear People, and Mountain Lion.

Both Abel and Tayo, *Ceremony's* protagonist, share the personal experience of being estranged from the Holy People, the land, and their communities. They suffer accordingly. Yet when these young men are recognizably thrust into the healing patterns of the Navajo chantways (vast, interconnected, sprawling webs of stories), they begin to heal. Abel as Bear Man and Tayo as Pollen Boy (*Ceremony*, p. 148) are identified through story with potent energies of the land that move them from crisis to renewal. As Paula Gunn Allen says about Tayo: "Tayo's illness is a result of separation from the ancient unity of person, ceremony, and land, and his healing is a result of his recognition of this unity." From "The Feminine Landscape of Leslie Marmon Silko's *Ceremony*," in *Studies in American Indian Literature: Critical Essays and Course Designs*, ed. Paula Gunn Allen (New York: The Modern Language Association of America, 1983), p. 128.

Notice that, as *House Made of Dawn* opens, Abel's grandfather wishes to encounter the Holy Person Bluebird, to acquire feathers for prayersticks to bless Abel's return (p. 10). Francisco is Jemez, but to the Navajo "The bluebird (dóli') is the bird of dawn, of promise, and of happiness. Talking God told the Visionary of the Night Chant that he would appear among the Navaho in the form of a bluebird." Reichard, *Navaho Religion*, p. 192.

59. Reichard, *Navaho Religion*, pp. 67–68.

60. Wyman, *Blessingway*, pp. 26–28. Another "Follower Pair" is Talking God and Calling God.

61. Reichard, *Navaho Religion*, pp. 54–55 and 67–68. Reared-in-the Earth is Monster Slayer's infant name. Its counterpart is Changing Grandchild, Born for Water's name. See Matthews, *The Night Chant*, pp. 19–20.

62. Joseph Campbell, *The Hero with a Thousand Faces*, Bollingen Series 17 (New York: Pantheon Books, 1949), pp. 30–40.

63. Mircea Eliade, *The Myth of the Eternal Return or, Cosmos and History*, Bollingen Series 46 (Princeton: Princeton University Press, 1954), pp. 20–22.

64. Concerning the possible span of symbolic associations for such a figure, Davíd Carrasco says that:

Religious symbols, however are never simple expressions, but always multivalent and complex. They have the capacity to express simultaneously a number of meanings that have hidden but vital correspondences.

David Carrasco, *Quetzalcoatl and the Irony of Empire: Myths and Prophecies in the Aztec Tradition* (Chicago: University of Chicago Press, 1982), p. 4.
   65. Matthews, *The Night Chant*, pp. 166, 226–27 and 239–40.
   66. Karl W. Luckert, *The Navajo Hunter Tradition* (Tucson: University of Arizona Press, 1975), pp. 155–56.

Chapter 2

   1. Momaday, *House Made of Dawn*, p. 16.
   2. Claude Leví-Strauss, "Harelips and Twins: The Splitting of a Myth" in *Myth and Meaning* (New York: Shocken, 1979), p. 28.
   3. Ibid., pp. 29–30.
   4. Victor Turner, *The Ritual Process, Structure and Anti-Structure* (Ithaca, New York: Cornell University Press, 1969), p. 45.
   5. Allen, "A Stranger in My Own Life," p. 12; A. LaVonne Brown Ruoff, "The Brothers Motif in *House Made of Dawn*," paper presented in "The Influence of Tradition in Modern Native American Literature" session of the Modern Language Association Convention, New York, 1978; Joseph E. DeFlyer, "Partition Theory: Patterns and Partitions of Consciousness in Selected Works of American and American Indian Authors," (Ph.D. diss. University of Nebraska, 1974). See especially p. 212; Evers, "Words and Place," p. 317.
   6. Benally, et al., *Dinéjí Nákéé' Nááhane', A Utah Navajo History*, p. 31; Matthews, *The Night Chant, a Navaho Ceremony*, pp. 143–45; Paula Gunn Allen says that in *House Made of Dawn* "Momaday has reformulated the overt elements of the narrative [Crippled Boy and Blind Boy]." See Paula Gunn Allen, "Whose Dream is This Anyway? Remythologizing and Self-Definition in Contemporary American Indian Fiction" in *The Sacred Hoop*, p. 89.
   7. Elsie Clews Parsons, *Pueblo Indian Religion*, Vol. 2 (Chicago: University of Chicago Press, 1939), p. 1043. Parsons here says that the myth of the War Gods is strongly developed in Navajo and Western Pueblo cultures, but among the Eastern Pueblo, "it peters out into nursery tales." I maintain that the existence of *House Made of Dawn* adjudicates against this naive statement and, on the contrary, proves

that the Jemez War Gods are continually being recreated. Also, the Coolidges claim that the Stricken Twins myth of the Navajo is the origin myth for Big God Way, a chantway related to the Night Chant. They say, too, that this story has a Zuni counterpart. See Coolidge and Coolidge, *The Navajo Indians,* pp. 147, 187. For Acoma and Cochiti Pueblo counterparts to the Navajo Stricken Twins story see: Leslie A. White, *The Acoma Indians,* Bureau of American Ethnology Report 47 (Washington, 1929–30), pp. 162–64, "The Blind Brother and the Crippled Brother"; and Ruth Benedict, *Tales of the Cochiti Indians,* Bureau of American Ethnology Bulletin 98 (Washington, 1931); reprint, Albuquerque: University of New Mexico Press, 1981), pp. 165–67, "The Blind One and the Lame One."

8. Parsons, *The Pueblo of Jemez,* p. 140. Little is published concerning Masewi and Uyuyewe's adventures. However, José Rey Toledo, an elder from Jemez Pueblo, mentioned in a lecture "Talk on Survival" that "the Warrior Twins were taught the rudiments of life by the bear. They went to the North to learn from Bear." Fort Lewis College, Durango, Colorado, October 13, 1988. Also, in *Ceremony* Silko symbolically recreates the Pueblo War Twins—Ma'see'wi and Ou'yu'ye'wi—in the "brothers" Rocky (Elder) and Tayo (Younger). See Silko, *Ceremony,* pp. 48–50, 75 and note that "Tayo sign[s] his name after Rocky" for the Army recruiter when Rocky acknowledges their brotherhood.

9. Wyman, *Blessingway,* pp. 195–98, 529–30.

10. Reichard, *Navaho Religion,* p. 67. Also see Leland C. Wyman, *Southwest Indian Drypainting.* School of American Research (Albuquerque: University of New Mexico Press, 1983), p. 86. "Mythologically, Holy Man and Boy are considered to be the counterparts of the Slayer Twins, and in Shootingway myth the Twins may be the heroes in the first part of the story, while Holy Man and Boy take over later."

11. See Katherine Spencer, *Mythology and Values: An Analysis of Navaho Chantway Myths* (Philadelphia: American Folklore Society 48, 1957), for succinct condensations of the origin myths to extant chantways.

12. Eliade, *The Myth of the Eternal Return,* pp. 35–40; Campbell, *The Hero With a Thousand Faces,* pp. 3–46.

13. Momaday, *House Made of Dawn,* p. 15.

14. Given by Jeff King, Text and Paintings Recorded by Maud Oakes, Commentary by Joseph Campbell, *Where the Two Came to Their Father: A Navaho War Ceremonial,* Bollingen Series 1 (New York: Pantheon Books, 1943; Princeton: Princeton University Press, 1969), p. 11.

15. The hero of Waterway does not teach the ceremony. See Spencer, *Mythology and Values,* p. 108.

16. Haile, *Origin Legend of the Navaho Enemy Way*, p. 111. Enemyway is a rite conducted to exorcise the ghosts of non-Navajos. Such Monsterway episodes are subsumed into Enemyway (p. 19).

17. Matthews, *The Night Chant*, p. 229. Although Abel does not literally meet one of the Bear People (*Sásdĭne*), he is symbolically unified with them through story. See p. 226 of *The Night Chant* where a bear appears.

18. Momaday, *House Made of Dawn*, p. 83.

19. Matthews, *The Night Chant*, p. 228.

20. In an interview with Lawrence Evers in *SunTracks* 2, no. 2, Tucson: University of Arizona (Spring 1976): 19, Momaday says about Abel:

He has been uprooted. He has been physically dislocated. He has lost his place in the world, and he's desperate, therefore, he's a man who's trying to fit himself back into his natural world. And he can't do it.

21. DeFlyer, "Partition Theory," chapter 5. "Indian and Christian: Momaday's Dual Structures of Consciousness in *House Made of Dawn*," pp. 127–235.

22. Ibid., pp. 205–11.

23. Ibid., p. 206.

24. Ibid.

25. Ibid., p. 231.

26. Ibid., p. 207. Also see Momaday, *House Made of Dawn*, p. 172.

27. Momaday, *House Made of Dawn*, pp. 14, 109–10. Abel follows Vidal. See Wyman, *Blessingway*, pp. 26–28.

28. Momaday, *House Made of Dawn*, p. 140.

29. Historically there has long been contact between these people.

There has been close kinship between the Navajos and the Jemez since that time [July 24, 1694]. Many Navajos of the *Ma'ii Deesh-giizhnii* Clan (Coyote Pass People, the Navajo name for Jemez) are descended from the Jemez who joined the Navajos after de Vargas burned their town.

Rock Point Community School, *Between Sacred Mountains*, p. 109. So just as it is possible that Abel's father was Navajo, so could Ben's parents be partially Jemez, thus, strengthening their tie through blood.

The novel speaks of an "old fellowship, Tanoan [Jemez] and Athapascan [Navajo]." See Momaday, *House Made of Dawn*, pp. 71–72.

30. Momaday, *House Made of Dawn*, pp. 133–35.

31. Donald Sandner, *Navaho Symbols of Healing* (New York: Harcourt Brace Jovanovich, 1979), p. 202.

32. Lopez, "Story at Anaktuvuk Pass," p. 50. Also recall that Lopez has said that a "profound sense of well-being . . . results from bringing the two [exterior and interior] landscapes together," p. 51.

33. Momaday, *House Made of Dawn*, p. 14.

34. Ibid. (Italics mine.)

35. Ibid. (Italics mine.)

36. Ibid.

37. Ibid., pp. 15–16.

38. Ibid., pp. 177–78 and 185–86.

39. Ibid., p. 185.

40. Ibid., p. 16; LaVonne Ruoff says: "After Vidal's death, Abel is cut off not only from a close companion but also from a part of himself. That Vidal's existence was necessary to Abel's feeling of wholeness is suggested by their names: Abel means 'breath' in Hebrew; and Vidal, derived from 'vid,' means 'life' in Spanish. Like his Biblical counterpart, Abel has been deprived of life by his brother." Ruoff also notes their relationship with Monster Slayer and Child-of-the-Water. A. LaVonne Brown Ruoff, "The Survival of Tradition: American Indian Oral and Written Narratives," *The Massachusetts Review* 27 (Summer 1986): 284, 283.

41. Momaday, *House Made of Dawn*, p. 109.

42. Ibid. Again, Vidal and Abel appear to be a "Follower Pair."

43. Momaday quoted the Danish author Isak Dinesen as saying this and added his own parallel observation in an address at the Modern Language Association Convention in New York, December 1978.

44. The other origin myth to the Night Chant is called "The Visionary," and tells the story of a young hero, one of many brothers who is wisked off by the gods for a visit to their homes when his brothers disbelieve his hunting stories. For a recording of the myth, see Matthews, *The Night Chant*, pp. 159–212. For a brief but comprehensive discussion of the myth in relationship to sandpainting, see Sam D. Gill, *Native American Traditions* (Belmont, California: Wadsworth, 1983), pp. 71–77. For another version of the myth commonly called "Yeibichai," see Mary C. Wheelwright, *Tleji or Yehbechai Myth*, Bulletin no. 1 (Santa Fe: Museum of Navajo Ceremonial Art, 1938).

45. Matthews, *The Night Chant*, pp. 212–65. These pages contain

"The Stricken Twins" story, the "Myth of *To'Nastsihégo Hatál*," part of the Night Chant, *Klédze Hatál*, commonly called Yeibichai. Father Berard Haile calls the Stricken Twins myth "txó ná·źí . . . across water branch" of Nightway. See Father Berard Haile, *Head and Face Masks in Navaho Ceremonialism* (St. Michaels, Arizona: St. Michael's Press, 1947; New York: AMS Press, 1978), pp. 13–14. It is obvious from the Matthews text that Elder Brother is dominant in most situations, although Younger Brother can assert himself, too. "'You must decide on the trail for to-day,' said the elder. 'No,' said the younger, 'you must decide for you are the older brother.'" Matthews, *The Night Chant*, p. 216. On occasion, the boys are virtually interchangeable. "When he [Talking God] had asked for the fourth time, one of the twins replied: 'We come from *Ĭndestsíhonia'*,'" p. 217.

46. Ibid., p. 215.

47. Ibid., p. 219.

48. For a synopsis of the Stricken Twins story, see: Spencer, *Mythology and Values*, pp. 162–64.

49. Matthews, *The Night Chant*, p. 256.

50. Ibid., p. 257.

51. Sandner, *Navaho Symbols of Healing*, pp. 168–69.

52. Wyman, *Blessingway*, pp. 539–50.

53. Momaday, *House Made of Dawn*, p. 25. When Abel was leaving home to go to fight in World War II, we learn: "It was time to go, and the old man was away in the fields. There was no one to wish him well or tell him how it would be . . ."

54. Ibid., p. 50.

55. Matthews, *The Night Chant*, p. 241.

56. Momaday, *House Made of Dawn*, p. 13.

57. Reichard, *Navaho Religion*, p. 138.

58. Matthews, *The Night Chant*, p. 220. Matthews translated *Hastséhogan* as "House God", but Wyman corrects this error and retranslates Talking God's companion's name as "Calling God". See Leland C. Wyman, *Southwest Indian Drypainting*, p. 105.

59. Matthews, *The Night Chant*, p. 215.

60. Momaday, *House Made of Dawn*, p. 110. Also see Matthews, *The Night Chant*, p. 230. Elder Brother says: ". . . for I can see nothing. You look around, younger brother, and tell me what you see."

61. Momaday, *House Made of Dawn*, p. 111.

62. Ibid., pp. 110–11. Also see Peter G. Beidler, "Animals and Human Development in the Contemporary American Indian Novel," *Western American Literature* 14, no. 2 (August 1979): 138. Here Beidler says: "The

theme of vision is central to *House Made of Dawn*, central to an understanding of Abel's development . . . Immediately after the beating Abel's physical blindness mirrors his mental blindness."

63. The Navajo word for ugliness or a state of disharmony is *hóchǫ́*, a contrast to *hózhǫ́*. See Gill, *Sacred Words*, p. 52.

64. George Mills, *Navajo Art and Culture* (Colorado Springs: The Taylor Museum, 1959), p. 190.

65. Farella, *The Main Stalk*, p. 175.

66. Benally et al., *Dinéjí Nákéé' Nááhane'*, p. 2.

67. Hamilton A. Tyler, *Pueblo Gods and Myths* (Norman: University of Oklahoma Press, 1964), pp. 209, 220.

68. H. K. Haeberlin, "The Idea of Fertilization in the Culture of the Pueblo Indians," Memoirs of the American Anthropological Association 3, no. 1 (January–March 1916): 34.

69. Momaday, *House Made of Dawn*, p. 91.

70. Benally et al., *Dinéjí Nákéé' Nááhane'*, p. 13.

71. Gladys A. Reichard, *Navajo Medicine Man* (New York: J. J. Augustin, 1939), p. 15.

72. Reichard, *Navaho Religion*, p. 54.

73. Ibid., p. 249.

74. Reichard, *Navajo Medicine Man*, p. 15; Reichard also says that "Pairing is an illustration of a cultural compulsion." See Reichard, *Navaho Religion*, p. 249. Speaking of spirit and matter as paired realities, Paula Gunn Allen says: ". . . the two are seen to be two expressions of the same reality—as though life had twin manifestations that are mutually interchangeable and, in many instances, virtually identical aspects of a reality . . ." quoted in Schubnell, *N. Scott Momaday*, p. 65.

75. Reichard, *Navajo Medicine Man*, p. 40.

76. Reichard, *Navaho Religion*, pp. 68–69.

77. Momaday, *House Made of Dawn*, pp. 63–64, 77–79.

78. Farella, *The Main Stalk*, p. 170. *Sǫ'a naghái bik'e hózhǫ́* is completeness. Additionally *sǫ'a naghái* is Thought and *bik e hózhǫ́* is Speech. See Charlotte J. Frisbie, *Navajo Medicine Bundles or Jish : Acquisition, Transmission, and Disposition in the Past and Present* (Albuquerque: University of New Mexico Press, 1987), p. 3.

79. Farella, *The Main Stalk*, p. 170.

80. Momaday, *House Made of Dawn*, p. 94.

81. Ibid., pp. 177–78. Unlike the Stricken Twins who are never separated from one another, Abel has suffered greatly from losing his brother. But Fransisco reminds Abel that as long as he remembers Vidal, Vidal is always with them.

82. Ibid., pp. 127, 189. Ben sings for Abel on the evening of February 19th.

83. Ibid., p. 64.

84. Ibid., p. 15.

85. Ibid., p. 16.

86. Ibid.

87. Matthews, *The Night Chant*, p. 229.

88. Ibid., pp. 237–38.

89. Ibid., p. 256.

90. Ibid., p. 257.

91. Farella, *The Main Stalk*, p. 174.

92. Matthews, *The Night Chant*, p. 254. Unwounded buckskins, requirements for certain ritual paraphernalia such as jish or medicine bundles, are obtained by running down deer on foot and smothering the deer with pollen, a blessing. See Frisbie, *Navajo Medicine Bundles or Jish:* pp. 13, 18–19.

93. Momaday, *House Made of Dawn*, p. 189.

94. Ibid., p. 93. When Vidal and Abel were little, after their mother died, Fat Josie took them in and comforted them with her immense love. It is obvious that the love between the boys and her was reciprocal: "And the children huddled against her and laid their heads on her great brown arms," p. 106. Many years later on the occasion of Abel's fall, however, Francisco's prayers and herbs had failed to help. Undoubtedly Francisco was a member of a Jemez curing society. See p. 187.

95. Matthews, *The Night Chant*, p. 262. Elder Sister and Younger Sister strengthened the Stricken Twins' bent backs and crooked limbs with black and blue plumed wands pressed to the boys' bodies.

96. Momaday, *House Made of Dawn*, p. 57.

97. Rising vertically, or coming up, is one of the primary ritual directions in the Southwest. In Navajo culture, the downward direction is associated with illness and the upward direction with healing power. See Karl W. Luckert's Introduction to Father Berard Haile, *Upward Moving and Emergence Way*, American Tribal Religions 7 (Lincoln: University of Nebraska Press, 1981), p. ix.

98. Matthews, *The Night Chant*, p. 239.

99. Ibid., George Mills says of the Holy People depicted in Navajo sandpaintings that "People 'follow one another' . . . actually circulate in the space they occupy." Gary Witherspoon quotes Mills in *Language and Art in the Navajo Universe* (Ann Arbor: University of Michigan Press, 1977), p. 170. The radial composition method of sandpainting visually

represents at least four Holy People whose bodies, from the feet up, radiate out from the center of the design, like spokes in a wheel. Susan Scarberry-García, "Myths and Multiple Selves: Images of Navajo Holy People in Sandpaintings from the Huckel Collection," lecture and unpublished MS. Colorado Springs Fine Arts Center, Taylor Museum Fiftieth Anniversary Lecture Series, June 1, 1986. See, for example, "Moisture in the Mountain," a sandpainting from Mountainway by Hosteen Bezody, Chinle, 1902.

100. *Diné*, meaning The People, is the term that the Navajo call themselves.

101. Momaday, *House Made of Dawn*, p. 72.

102. Farella, *The Main Stalk*, p. 24.

103. Witherspoon, *Language and Art in the Navajo Universe*, p. 21. Witherspoon states that there are thousands of forms of the Navajo verb *naagháii*, to go, indicating that Navajos greatly value all aspects of motion.

104. Momaday, *House Made of Dawn*, p. 175.

105. Ibid. p. 191. The four-fold repetition here of "He could see" accumulates power for his vision.

106. Ibid., p. 12. The ledger book functions as a native calendar depicting crucial seasonal events.

107. Ibid., p. 189.

Chapter 3

1. Ruth Benedict, *Tales of the Cochiti Indians* (Albuquerque: University of New Mexico Press, 1981), p. 17. This volume was originally published as Bureau of American Ethnology Bulletin 98, 1931.

2. Ibid., p. 209. This story points up the truth that ceremonies do not always work, among other reasons, because of the constant disruption of the world through the interplay of creative and destructive, or mysterious and unknown, forces. Although in the Cochiti story the dancers are not returned to human form, as a result of contact with animal powers Abel does return to a more distinctive human existence.

3. Richard J. Parmentier, "The Mythological Triangle: Poseyemu, Montezuma, and Jesus in the Pueblos" in *Handbook of North American Indians, Southwest*, Vol. 9, ed. Alfonso Ortiz (Washington: Smithsonian Institution, 1979), p. 614. Parmentier makes the point that Pueblo mythology is circular and contains a "high degree of internal reference."

4. Momaday, *House Made of Dawn*, pp. 54–56.

5. Ibid., p. 9. Momaday uses the Jemez people's own name for their town: Walatowa. Walatowa "Village of the Bear" is mentioned in Frederick Webb Hodge, ed., *Handbook of American Indians North of Mexico*, Bureau of American Ethnology Bulletin 30. Part 1 (Washington, 1907; New York: Rowman and Littlefield, 1971), p. 630. Also see Sando, *Nee Hemish*, p. 13. Momaday's legend closely follows the version recorded by White. See: Leslie A. White, "The Pueblo of Santa Ana, New Mexico," Memoirs of the American Anthropological Association, No. 60, *American Anthropologist* 44, No. 4, Part 2, 1942, p. 264.

6. Momaday, *House Made of Dawn*, pp. 39–40.

7. Mircea Eliade, *Patterns in Comparative Religion* (New York: Meridian Books, New American Library, 1958), p. 346. Eliade says: "A regeneration sacrifice is a ritual 'repetition' of the Creation. The myth of creation includes the ritual (that is, violent) death of a primeval giant, from whose body the worlds were made, and plants grew . . . *The ritual makes creation over again;* the force at work in plants is reborn by suspending time and returning to the first moment of the fullness of creation."

8. Vincent Scully, *Pueblo: Mountain, Village, Dance* (New York: The Viking Press, 1975), pp. 206–7 and 212. Scully describes the chicken pull at Santo Domingo Pueblo.

9. Momaday, *House Made of Dawn*, pp. 42–45.

10. Ibid., p. 43.

11. Erna Fergusson, *Dancing Gods: Indian Ceremonials of New Mexico and Arizona* (Albuquerque: University of New Mexico Press, 1931), pp. 61-65. Fergusson gives a detailed description of this event: "The Pecos Bull at Jemez." See Momaday, *House Made of Dawn*, pp. 73, 75–76. The sacred clowns appearing here during the dance are marvelous beings whose outrageous behavior ensures social control and conformity by humorous reverse example. See Alfonso Ortiz, "Ritual Drama and the Pueblo World View" in *New Perspectives on the Pueblos*, ed. Alfonso Ortiz, School of American Research (Albuquerque: University of New Mexico Press, 1972), pp. 145–53. For a good overview of clowns in North American Indian cultures, including a discussion of pueblo clowns' curing powers, see Barbara Tedlock, "The Clown's Way" in *Teachings from the American Earth*, eds. Dennis Tedlock and Barbara Tedlock (New York: Liveright, 1975), pp. 105–18.

12. René Girard, *Violence and the Sacred* (Baltimore: The Johns Hopkins University Press, 1972), p. 13. Paula Gunn Allen once said to me that the rooster slap is an impetus for Abel's process of transformation. Personal communication, 1980.

13. Momaday, *House Made of Dawn*, p. 77.

14. Ibid., pp. 26 and 77.

15. Ibid., p. 107.

16. Ibid., p. 64.

17. Ibid., p. 166. The albino's spirit is reembodied in Martinez. An anonymous Navajo friend once remarked to me that "Bad medicine can go as far as it wants." Personal communication, 1985.

18. Ibid., pp. 78–79.

19. Ibid., p. 96.

20. Ibid., p. 94.

21. Ibid., p. 95.

22. Ibid., p. 136.

23. Eliade, *Patterns in Comparative Religion*, p. 164.

24. Hamilton A. Tyler, *Pueblo Gods and Myths* (Norman: University of Oklahoma Press, 1964), p. 223.

25. Marc Simmons, *Witchcraft in the Southwest: Spanish and Indian Supernaturalism on the Rio Grande* (Flagstaff: Northland Press, 1974; Lincoln: University of Nebraska Press, 1981), p. 89.

26. Girard, *Violence and the Sacred*, p. 37. Girard carefully makes the distinction between beneficial violence and harmful violence.

27. Lawrence J. Evers, "The Killing of a New Mexican State Trooper: Ways of Telling an Historical Event" in *Wicazo Sa Review* 1, no. 1 (Spring 1985): 23. Evers's article compares the narratives of Momaday's *House Made of Dawn*, Ortiz's "The Killing of A State Cop," and Silko's "Tony's Story." For the short stories, see Simon J. Ortiz, "The Killing of a State Cop" and Leslie Marmon Silko, "Tony's Story" in Kenneth Rosen, ed. *The Man to Send Rain Clouds: Contemporary Stories by American Indians* (New York: Viking, 1974, pp. 101–8 (Ortiz), 69–78 (Silko).

28. Evers, "The Killing of a New Mexican State Trooper," p. 22.

29. Ibid., p. 21.

30. Allen, "A Stranger in My Own Life," p. 12.

31. Ibid.

32. Momaday, *House Made of Dawn*, pp. 18–25. See Momaday, *The Names*, p. 147 for a comment about an eagle kept in the village for ritual purposes. Eagles send messages from the people to the spirits.

33. Allen, "A Stranger in My Own Life," p. 12.

34. Paul Shepard and Barry Sanders, *The Sacred Paw: The Bear in Nature, Myth, and Literature* (New York: Viking, 1985), pp. xiii and xviii. The pairing of Elder Brother and Younger Brother discussed in chapter 2 reappears here in the persons of Bear and Badger.

35. For a description of the Navajo underworlds, see Ethelou Yazzie,

ed., *Navajo History,* Vol. 1 (Rough Rock, Arizona: Navajo Curriculum Center, Rough Rock Demonstration School, 1971), pp. 9–46; for a description of the Tewa Pueblo underworld see Alfonso Ortiz, *The Tewa World: Space, Time, Being, and Becoming in a Pueblo Society* (Chicago: University of Chicago Press, 1969), pp. 13–28.

36. Nora Baker Barry, "The Bear's Son Folk Tale in *When the Legends Die* and *House Made of Dawn,*" *Western American Literature* 12, no. 4 (February 1978): 281–82. Other critics who have commented pointedly on the bear elements in the novel include Beidler, Evers, McAllister, and Schubnell.

37. Albert B. Reagan, "The Jemez Indians" in *El Palacio* (April 1917): 70. "Four" carries ritual importance in Navajo and Kiowa cultures as well.

38. Paul Shepard, "The Ark of the Mind" in *Parabola: Myth and the Quest for Meaning* 7, no. 2, (Spring), Animals: 54.

39. Momaday, *House Made of Dawn,* pp. 117–25. Tosamah calls Rainy Mountain "an old landmark," p. 117.

40. Ibid., pp. 120–21. This story also appears in N. Scott Momaday, *The Way to Rainy Mountain* (Albuquerque: University of New Mexico Press, 1969), p. 8.

41. Momaday, *House Made of Dawn,* p. 120.

42. Susan Scarberry-García, "Beneath the Stars: Images of the Sacred" in *Approaches to Teaching Momaday's The Way to Rainy Mountain,* ed. Kenneth M. Roemer (New York: The Modern Language Association of America, 1988), pp. 92–93; Momaday, *House Made of Dawn,* p. 121.

43. There is a parallel in Jemez mythology where two brothers who escape the clutches of Bear are made into the morning star and the evening star. See Reagan, "Myth of the Mother Moon and the Great Bear" in "The Jemez Indians," pp. 46–47.

44. The scorings are perhaps symbolically parallel to the groove on Tosamah's peyote altar:

> There was a fine groove which ran the length of the altar; the groove symbolized the life of man from birth, ascending from the southern tip to the crest of power and wisdom at the center, and thence in descent through old age to death at the northern tip.

Momaday, *House Made of Dawn,* p. 102.

45. Ibid., p. 119. "According to their origin myth, they entered the world through a hollow log." For Momaday, Devil's Tower has a per-

sonal association, as well as a tribal one. His Kiowa name: *Tsoai talee* stands for the place. He is Rock Tree Boy. See Momaday, *The Names*, p. 42. Furthermore, in a letter to Matthias Schubnell, Momaday mentions that in his adult journey to retrace the path of his ancestors, he saw the place where the children were playing, but:

"There are no bears at the monument now, I am told. But, you know, . . . I am quite sure that a grizzly, an old thick animal, resides there somewhere in the Bear Lodge Mountains. He keeps an eye on Tsoai, surely. That is his trust. There is no Tsoai without the bear."

See Schubnell, *N. Scott Momaday*, pp. 176–77.

46. Schubnell, *N. Scott Momaday*, p. 177.

47. Ibid. Schubnell calls the bear Momaday's "guardian spirit." Although the bear protects Momaday, generally the Kiowas see the bear as dangerous. "The Kiowas regarded the bear as a powerful but sinister force." Maurice Boyd, *Kiowa Voices. Ceremonial Dance, Ritual and Song*, Vol. 1 (Fort Worth: Texas Christian University Press, 1981), p. 5.

48. Alice Marriott, *The Ten Grandmothers* (Norman: University of Oklahoma Press, 1945), p. 4. See especially "The Bear", pp. 3–14.

49. Momaday, *House Made of Dawn*, p. 169.

50. Ibid.

51. Ibid.

52. Gary Witherspoon, "Language and Reality in Navajo World View," in *Handbook of North American Indians. Southwest*, Vol. 10, ed. Alfonso Ortiz (Washington: Smithsonian Institution, 1983), pp. 572, 574. According to Navajo thought, as something is said it comes into being.

53. Momaday, *House Made of Dawn*, p. 170.

54. Ibid., pp. 133–34.

55. This "49" is an intertribal social sing and dance taking place in the hills north and east of downtown Los Angeles. Bernard Hirsch is inaccurate when he says that Benally "has divorced his religion from his everyday life," that he "hoards the old songs like treasure within his heart." See Bernard A. Hirsch, "Self-Hatred and Spiritual Corruption in *House Made of Dawn*," *Western American Literature* 17, no. 4 (Winter 1983): 319–20. Instead Ben takes care of Abel as if they were kin (honoring the Navajo value of reciprocity), and sings for his health, that he may live in the beauty way once again. It is interesting to note that Farella

in *The Main Stalk* says that witches characteristically hoard wealth and knowledge:

> He [a witch] refuses to transmit his knowledge. A witch could then be defined as one who passes on his programs neither genetically nor culturally. . . . Further, he refuses to (and cannot) pass on what he knows. He becomes an island.

See Farella, *The Main Stalk*, pp. 179–80. Even Hirsch who sees "Ben's honest, profound spirituality" in spite of his alleged "spiritual corruption" by white ways (see Hirsch, "Self-Hatred," pp. 314, 307) would probably never have described Ben as "hoard[ing] the old songs" if he (Hirsch) were more familiar with these Navajo distinctions.

56. Maria Leach, ed., *Standard Dictionary of Folklore, Mythology and Legend* (New York: Funk and Wagnalls, 1950), p. 127. There is also a variant wherein the natural father is a human or supernatural, and the step-father is a bear.

57. Ibid.

58. Evers, "Words and Place," p. 317; Floyd Watkins calls her story "a brief and inferior tale she has invented herself." He also says "In itself Angela's story has little background or significant meaning, but she hit upon the archetypal pattern for a Navajo legend . . ." Angela "apparently is engaged in an almost maddening search for meaning." Watkins, *In Time and Place*, p. 165.

59. Momaday, *House Made of Dawn*, pp. 34, 62.

60. Ibid., pp. 29–30, 34.

61. Ibid., p. 34.

62. Ibid., p. 62.

63. Beidler, "Animals and Human Development," pp. 136–37.

64. Schubnell, *N. Scott Momaday*, p. 91.

65. Parsons, *The Pueblo of Jemez*, p. 62.

66. Tyler, *Pueblo Animals and Myths*, pp. 4, 15, 17, 20. José Rey Toledo of Jemez Pueblo says: "For the Towa People, Badger is the legendary figure who brought the people up from the underworld." Lecture "What Indians are Responsible for and Threats," Fort Lewis College, Durango, Colorado, October 14, 1988.

67. Beidler, "Animals and Human Development," p. 137.

68. Schubnell, *N. Scott Momaday*, pp. 89, 91.

69. Ibid., pp. 90, 92, 89.

70. Momaday, *House Made of Dawn*, p. 34.

71. Ibid., p. 59.

72. Schubnell, *N. Scott Momaday*, pp. 91–92. Schubnell uses the Christian phrase "symbolic baptism" to describe Angela's transformation into calm and wholeness during a thunderstorm. See Momaday, *House Made of Dawn*, p. 70. It is this same storm, brought in during the Pecos Bull Dance and Corn Dance for rain, that provides blessings for the village in the form of growing crops, and that washes clean the knife that Abel uses to kill the snakewitch albino. See *House Made of Dawn*, p. 78. These three functions of the storm suggest that Angela's transformation is parallel to the village's, that she is a part of the larger pattern of human and natural events at Jemez that day, and that the pattern of events is purification, integration, and renewal.

73. Beidler, "Animals and Human Development," p. 137.

74. For a version of the "Myth of the Mother Moon and the Great Bear" see Reagan, "The Jemez Indians," pp. 46–47. For versions of Bispáli's (Elder Sister) encounters with Bear, see Wyman, *The Mountainway of the Navajo*, pp. 174–82, and for the Kiowa story, see Momaday, *House Made of Dawn*, pp. 120–21.

75. Barry, "The Bear's Son Folk Tale," pp. 281–87.

76. Ibid., pp. 276, 282–85.

77. Ibid., pp. 282, 287.

78. Ibid., p. 286.

79. Reagan, "The Jemez Indians," pp. 46–47; Floyd Watkins summarizes this story in *In Time and Place*, p. 149, but fails to interpret it.

80. Reagan, "The Jemez Indians," p. 47.

81. Momaday, *House Made of Dawn*, p. 170.

82. Ibid., p. 177. It seems from the text that Ben is recalling the story as he heard it from his grandfather when he was a little boy. When Ben retells it, he is indistinguishable from his grandfather storyteller.

83. O'Bryan, *The Dîné*, pp. 131–38.

84. Washington Matthews, *The Mountain Chant, A Navajo Ceremony*, Fifth Annual Report of the Bureau of American Ethnology 1883–1884 (Washington 1887), pp. 379–467; Coolidge and Coolidge, *The Navajo Indians*, pp. 201–21; Mary C. Wheelwright, *Myth of Mountain Chant and Beauty Chant* (Santa Fe: Museum of Navajo Ceremonial Art, Bulletin no. 5, 1951); Wyman, *The Mountainway of the Navajo*.

85. Wyman, *The Mountainway of the Navajo*, p. 142.

86. For a summary of plot structure in Mountaintop Way, see Spencer, *Mythology and Values*, pp. 126–34.

87. Momaday, *House Made of Dawn*, p. 170.

88. Paul G. Zolbrod, "Navajo Poetry in the Field and on the Printed

Page: A Working Paper on Textual Replication in Dinébakéyah," unpublished MS, p. 5. Zolbrod says:

> An important narrative does not necessarily have a fixed shape or length in preliterate cultures. It may begin where a particular storyteller wants it to for a particular storytelling occasion, end where it may seem appropriate to end at the time of recitation, and include details that might suit one immediate purpose but not another. Very often it is part of a larger issue, such as curing an illness or exorcising some negative force to restore harmony in the world. It points to a closer relationship between poetry and music or poetry and ritual than our conventional literatures usually indicate. Such a story—if it can really be called a single story— is actually an entire tradition residing in the minds of the people who hear it over a span of many generations.

89. Momaday, *House Made of Dawn*, p. 171.

90. O'Bryan says that "*Esdzá shash nadle*" is "the Woman who Became a Bear." She is more commonly known as Changing Bear Maiden, because she would change from human form to Bear and then back again to human form. See O'Bryan, *The Dîné*, p. 45. For a succinct discussion of the Changing Bear Maiden figure, see Father Berard Haile, *Navajo Coyote Tales: The Curly Tó Aheedlíinii Version*, American Tribal Religions 8, ed. Karl W. Luckert (Lincoln: University of Nebraska Press, 1984), pp. 22–24.

91. Mary C. Wheelwright and Father Berard Haile, *Emergence Myth, According to the Hanelthnayhe or Upward-Reaching Rite*, Navajo Religion Series, vol. 3 (Santa Fe: Museum of Navajo Ceremonial Art, 1949), p. 130, note. Eventually Changing Bear Maiden's body becomes transformed into sacred food for the people. Her nipples become piñon nuts. See Sandner, *Navaho Symbols of Healing*, p. 177.

92. Momaday, *House Made of Dawn*, p. 170.

93. Rock Point Community School, *Between Sacred Mountains: Navajo Stories and Lessons from the Land*, p. 85. "Some of our ancestors [Navajo] came down from the mesa and settled among the Anasazi people of *Kin Yaa'a*, the Towering House," says John Barbone, a Blessingway singer.

94. The story of Enemyway tells of the Pueblo war, then splits into two branches that form the origin myths to Mountainway and Beautyway. Mountainway is the story of Elder Sister and Beautyway is the

story of Younger Sister. See Wyman, *The Mountainway of the Navajo*, pp. 127–36.

95. Momaday, *House Made of Dawn*, p. 170.

96. A similar question "Where are you going?" is asked customarily at Jemez. See N. Scott Momaday, "The Morality of Indian Hating," *Ramparts* (Summer 1964): 30–40.

97. Owl is female. See O'Bryan, *The Dîné*, p. 136.

98. Momaday, *House Made of Dawn*, p. 171.

99. Harold S. McAllister, "Incarnate Grace and the Paths of Salvation in *House Made of Dawn*," *South Dakota Review* 12, No. 4 (Winter 1974): 118. Although McAllister is sharp in recognizing that Abel is the bear father, he uses the bear material to get at Christian points. He errs when he says that "Peter's white father is spiritually sterile like the sterile snake of the Navajo story." Actually Glishpah (Younger Sister) has two children by Snake according to the version of Beautyway recorded by O'Bryan. See O'Bryan, *The Dîné*, p. 131.

100. Momaday, *House Made of Dawn*, p. 137. See Ben's comment.

101. LaVerne Harrell Clark, *They Sang for Horses: The Impact of the Horse on Navajo and Apache Folklore* (Tucson: University of Arizona Press, 1966), pp. 93, 92. The first quotation is from W. W. Hill, "The Agricultural and Hunting Methods of the Navaho Indians," *Yale University Publications in Anthropology*, no. 18 (New Haven: Yale University Press, 1938), p. 158.

102. Reichard, *Navaho Religion*, p. 384.

103. Ibid.

104. Ibid., p. 385.

105. Clark, *They Sang for Horses*, pp. 95–99. The quotation is from Sandoval, O'Bryan's informant. See O'Bryan, *The Dîné*, p. 173 for a brief discussion of "Bear Chants."

106. Clark, *They Sang for Horses*, p. 93.

107. Ibid., p. 94.

108. Wyman, *The Mountainway of the Navajo*, pp. 140–41.

109. Beidler, "Animals and Human Development," p. 137.

110. Momaday, *House Made of Dawn*, p. 60. The narrator refers to "her distress."

111. Carole Oleson, "The Remembered Earth: Momaday's *House Made of Dawn*," *South Dakota Review* 11, no. 1 (Spring 1973): 63; Marion Willard Hylton, "On a Trail of Pollen: Momaday's *House Made of Dawn*," *Critique, Studies in Modern Fiction* 14, no. 2 (1972): 67; McAllister, "Incarnate Grace," pp. 117–20.

112. Evers, "Words and Place," p. 304.

113. Ibid.
114. Momaday, *House Made of Dawn*, pp. 33, 35.
115. Schubnell, *N. Scott Momaday*, p. 278, n.66. Schubnell says of Hylton and McAllister's work that their "articles are diametrically opposed in their view of Angela as a villain and a saint."
116. Momaday, *House Made of Dawn*, pp. 34, 62. Gladys Reichard says that Badger possessed strong sexual powers that drove women wild. Reichard says: "Badger went among the women when they were separated from the men and made them mad with sexual desire." Reichard, *Navaho Religion*, p. 382.
117. Sandner, *Navaho Symbols of Healing*, p. 176.
118. Sheila Moon, *Changing Woman and Her Sisters: Feminine Aspects of Selves and Deities* (San Francisco: Guild for Psychological Studies Publishing House, 1984), p. 77.
119. Ibid., p. 83.
120. Ibid., pp. 69, 87.
121. Ibid., p. 70.
122. Paul G. Zolbrod, *Diné bahane': The Navajo Creation Story* (Albuquerque: University of New Mexico Press, 1984), p. 166.
123. Farella, *The Main Stalk*, p. 176.
124. Sandner, *Navaho Symbols of Healing*, p. 238.
125. Ibid., p. 175.
126. Ibid.
127. Ibid., p. 176.
128. Momaday, *House Made of Dawn*, p. 171.
129. Ibid.
130. Reichard, *Navaho Religion*, p. 242.
131. Momaday, *House Made of Dawn*, p. 171. This is a description of Blessingway, a rite performed for a woman about to give birth. See Gill, *Sacred Words*, pp. 68–79.
132. See Wheelwright, *Myth of the Mountain Chant*, told by Hasteen Klah, p. 5, for a description of the bear child as also having a white face. Angela is repeatedly described as being very white. For a negative comment on Angela's whiteness, see Hylton, "On a Trail of Pollen," p. 67.
133. In addition to curing arthritis and swollen limbs, "the Mountain Chant is a preferred treatment for such manifestations of bear disease as mental uneasiness and nervousness, fainting, temporary loss of mind, delirium, violent irrationality, or insanity." Wyman, *The Mountainway of the Navajo*, pp. 19–20.
134. Momaday, *House Made of Dawn*, p. 171.

135. Wheelwright, *Myth of the Mountain Chant*, p. 6.
136. Ibid.
137. Ibid., p. 7.
138. Ibid., p. 7. Italics mine.
139. Wheelwright, *Beauty Chant*, pp. 20–21. Glishpah learns the sandpaintings to Beautyway and teaches the ceremony to her younger brother.
140. Momaday, *House Made of Dawn*, pp. 184–85, 46, 48, 51. The genealogy of Abel's family is cryptic, but it appears that the old priest Fray Nicholas and Nicholás *teah-whau* had three children: Viviano, Francisco, and Porcingula. Later, after a stillborn child was born to Francisco and Porcingula, Francisco fathered Abel's mother by another woman. Francisco is Younger Brother to Viviano.
141. O'Bryan, *The Dîné*, pp. 16, n.53, 35; Washington Matthews, *Navaho Legends*, Memoirs of the American Folklore Society, 5 (Boston, 1897), pp. 167, 195, 245 n.208.
142. O'Bryan, *The Dîné*, p. 35.
143. Ibid., p. 120.
144. Momaday, *House Made of Dawn*, pp. 177–78.
145. O'Bryan, *The Dîné*, p. vii.
146. Ibid., Sandoval: pp. 16, 17, 18, 35, 44–48, 120–21, and Ahkeah: pp. 131–38.
147. Ibid., p. vii.
148. Ibid., p. 47.
149. Momaday, *House Made of Dawn*, p. 170.
150. O'Bryan, *The Dîné*, p. 131.
151. Ibid., p. 135.
152. Momaday, *House Made of Dawn*, p. 171.
153. Wheelwright, *Myth of Mountain Chant*, p. 5. Note that Wheelwright probably understood "fur" to be "fir."
154. A kiva is an underground ceremonial chamber used for religious rituals, first by the Anasazi and then by their descendants the Pueblos. The reference here seems to be to a time in mythic history when the Navajos (Yeibichai) were related to the Anasazi. For a discussion of this possibility, see Rock Point Community School, *Between Sacred Mountains*, p. 83. Barney Mitchell says:

My grandfather, a well-known medicine man, used to say he didn't understand why people speak of the Anasazi as some foreign race. "We ourselves are Anasazi," he would say. He believed that pure Navajos once existed, but from time to time across the years they were joined by others who were refugees or had left their homes to find food. And surely some people always moved from place to place and did not settle in towns. In time they all came to speak Navajo and so called themselves Navajos. This can be seen in the stories of Navajo clans . . . So you can't point back in time and say, "Here the Anasazi ended and there the Navajos began."

155. Watkins, *In Time and Place*, pp. 152, 167.

156. Ruth L. Bunzel, *The Pueblo Potter: A Study of Creative Imagination in Primitive Art* (New York: Columbia University Press, 1929; New York: Dover Publications, 1972), p. 6.

157. Other contemporary Southwestern native writers who structure their narratives similarly are Simon J. Ortiz and Leslie Marmon Silko. See, for example, Old Man Faustin's dream about Flintwing Boy and Coyote in "Men On the Moon" in Simon J. Ortiz, *Fightin': New and Collected Stories* (New York: Thunder's Mouth Press, 1983), pp. 21–23. Also see the Laguna myth about the relations between the earth-surface world and the underworlds, mediated by Hummingbird and Fly, in Silko, *Ceremony*, pp. 55–56, 74, 86, 106, et cetera.

158. O'Bryan, *The Dîné*, p. vii.

159. Ibid.

160. Schubnell records that: "In a conversation Momaday mentioned a Navajo woman to whom he had given one of his books. She had read from it to an old man on the reservation, who said when she had ended: 'The man who wrote this is a Navajo.' Momaday takes great pride in the Navajo's compliment." Schubnell, *N. Scott Momaday*, p. 38. The one-sung-over (patient) receives healing power by being symbolically situated through story in the center of the world.

161. Momaday, *House Made of Dawn*, pp. 178–79.

162. Ibid., pp. 180–81.

163. Ibid., pp. 181, 121.

164. N. Scott Momaday, "The Bear and the Colt," in Natachee Scott Momaday, *American Indian Authors* (Boston: Houghton Mifflin, 1972), p. 123 n.4.

165. Barry, "The Bear's Son Folk Tale," p. 281.

166. Hylton, "On a Trail of Pollen," p. 61.

167. Oleson, "The Remembered Earth," p. 76.

168. McAllister, "Incarnate Grace," p. 123.

169. A. Irving Hallowell, "Bear Ceremonialism in the Northern Hemisphere," *American Anthropologist* 28, no. 1 (January–March 1926): 78.

170. Ibid., p. 77.

171. Ibid., pp. 77–78, n.314. This identical paragraph appears in Parsons, *The Pueblo of Jemez*, p. 62.

172. Parsons, *The Pueblo of Jemez*, p. 62.

173. Momaday, *House Made of Dawn*, pp. 183–84.

174. Parsons, *The Pueblo of Jemez*, p. 62.

175. Momaday, *House Made of Dawn*, p. 184. See Sam D. Gill, *Native American Religions* (Belmont, California: Wadsworth Publishing, 1982), p. 119: "It is widely reported that hunting peoples in this [Northern Salteaux] and other areas consider bears to be equal in intelligence to humans and capable of understanding everything that is said to them." Also see Tyler, *Pueblo Animals and Myths*, p. 184 for a Cochiti hunting story that concludes: ". . . bear was really a person. . . . he was only wearing a bearskin." Bear in his physical appearance, size, and omnivorous habits resembles human beings. Tyler also says that bears are "great talkers and bargainers." Ibid., p. 187.

176. Momaday, *House Made of Dawn*, pp. 178–84.

177. Ibid., p. 179. Parentheses mine.

178. Ibid., p. 180.

179. Ibid., p. 143.

180. Ibid., p. 178.

181. Ibid., p. 180.

182. Ibid., p. 183.

183. Ibid., p. 187.

184. Evers, "Words and Place," p. 319.

185. Momaday, *House Made of Dawn*, p. 181.

186. Ibid., p. 186.

187. Tyler, *Pueblo Animals and Myths*, p. 202. Tyler quotes Leslie White, "The Pueblo of San Felipe,"Memoirs of the American Anthropological Association 38, Menasha, 1932, pp. 42, 43, 45.

188. Tyler, *Pueblo Animals and Myths*, p. 192.

189. Ibid. The second point is made by Ellis. See Florence Hawley Ellis, "A Reconstruction of the Basic Jemez Pattern of Social Organization, with Comparisons to Other Tanoan Social Structures" University of New Mexico Publications in Anthropology, no. 11, 1964, p. 28.

190. Blanche Wurdack Harper, "Notes on the Documentary History, the Language and the Rituals and Customs of Jemez Pueblo," Master's thesis, University of New Mexico, 1929, pp. 12–13.

191. Father Noël Dumarest, "Notes on Cochiti, New Mexico," Memoirs of the American Anthropological Association 6, no. 3, Lancaster, 1919: 187.

192. Ibid., n.2.

193. *Köide* is the Jemez word for bear. See Elsie Clews Parsons, *Pueblo Indian Religion*, Vol. 1 (Chicago: University of Chicago Press, 1939), pp. 208–9, Table 2, "Spirits."

194. Frank C. Hibben, *Hunting American Bears* (Philadelphia: J. B. Lippincott, 1945), p. 93.

195. Shepard and Sanders, *The Sacred Paw*, p. 104.

196. Luckert, *The Navajo Hunter Tradition*, p. 157.

197. Ibid.

198. Ibid., p. 158.

199. Momaday, *House Made of Dawn*, pp. 92–93.

200. Shepard and Sanders, *The Sacred Paw*, p. 105. The authors quote J. L. Henderson as making this statement.

201. Ibid., pp. 105, 102. Shepard and Sanders make these statements.

202. Ibid., p. 106.

203. Ibid., p. 105.

204. Beidler, "Animals and Human Development," p. 137. I think that Abel's dawn run at the end of the novel exemplifies Abel's choice to recreate himself a whole man in spite of his serious injuries.

205. Leslie A. White, "The Pueblo of Santo Domingo, New Mexico," Memoirs of the American Anthropological Association no. 43, Menasha, 1935: 120–21.

206. Navajos also apply ashes in "blackening rites" to ensure that an enemy or ghost cannot recognize them. See Father Berard Haile, *Navaho War Dance: A Brief Narrative of its Meaning and Practice* (St. Michaels, Arizona: St. Michaels Press, 1946), p. 8. Haile says:

> . . . to get the blackening done. That means the ashes of charred herbs or charcoal of shrubs and trees are prepared and the patient is rubbed with them over his whole body to blacken him, so that even a ghost or ghost-like enemy has difficulty in recognizing him in this cover of darkness.

Abel here is running in the "race for good hunting and harvests." See Momaday, *House Made of Dawn*, pp. 11–12, 190–91; See Parmentier,

"The Mythological Triangle," p. 615 for a discussion of Ash Boy in Pueblo culture.

207. Momaday, *House Made of Dawn*, p. 190.

208. Ibid., p. 96.

209. Ibid., pp. 57–58. In conversation with Benny Shendo, Jr. of Jemez Pueblo, he said he thinks that this hill (mesa) that Abel climbs may be the place where the old men of the pueblo go at dawn every day to make offerings at a shrine. Personal communication, 1983. The creation song that Abel longed to sing would have made sacred the place where he stood by bringing the power of origins into the present moment. Simon Ortiz from Acoma Pueblo says that "song is part of the way you're supposed to recognize everything . . . It is basically a way to understand and appreciate your relationship to all things. The song as language is a way of touching." Simon Ortiz, *Song, Poetry and Language—Expression and Perception* (Tsaile: Navajo Community College Press, 1977), p. 9.

210. Ibid., p. 170; *House Made of Dawn* also contains this "twin" passage that speaks of the relationship of animals to men as mediated by sacred smoke:

Now and then, when the weather turns and food is scarce in the mountains, bear and deer wander down into the canyons. Once there were wolves in the mountains, and the old hunters of the town remember them. It is said that they were many, and they came to the hunters' fires at night and sat around in the dark timber like old men wanting to smoke. (p. 55)

211. Ibid., pp. 38, 190–91.

212. Shepard and Sanders, *The Sacred Paw*, p. 106.

213. Momaday, *House Made of Dawn*, p. 182. It would be a violation of cultural privacy and sanctity if Momaday had attempted to create an actual bear cult healing ceremony in the novel. Instead Francisco's stories symbolically achieve the same effect of infusing Abel with bear power.

Chapter 4

1. The scenes in Oklahoma take place in Tosamah's memories of his grandmother's Kiowa stories. The California scenes occur near the

Navajo deity Changing Woman's home in a mother of pearl hogan on an island in the western ocean. Changing Woman is a figure who embodies the cycle of seasons from youth in spring to old age in winter, hence her name. She is said to have gone to her island home after creating the ancestors of the Navajo. See Kay Bennett, "The Changing Woman Story" in *The Third Woman: Minority Women Writers of the United States*, ed. Dexter Fisher (Boston: Houghton Mifflin, 1980), pp. 44–48. This story also appears in Kay Bennett, *Kaibah: Recollections of a Navajo Girlhood* (Los Angeles: Western Lore Press, 1964).

2. In an interview with Floyd Watkins, Momaday says that "house made of dawn" is "the earth." See Watkins, *In Time and Place*, p. 169.

3. Wyman, *Beautyway: A Navaho Ceremonial*, pp. 132, 136. In the novel Ben Benally says: "'House made of dawn.' I used to tell him [Abel] about those old ways, the stories and the sings, Beautyway and Night Chant. I sang some of those things, and I told him what they meant, what I thought they were about." Momaday, *House Made of Dawn*, p. 133.

4. Ibid., p. 166.

5. Ibid., p. 159.

6. Ibid., p. 151.

7. Ibid., p. 167.

8. Ibid.

9. See Reichard, *Navaho Religion*, p. 244. She says that "blessing and divinity are represented by even numbers, evil and harm by odd."

10. Momaday, *House Made of Dawn*, pp. 138, 93.

11. Evers, "Words and Place," p. 311; the illumination or insight that Evers refers to tempers the negativity of the beach scene.

12. Momaday, *House Made of Dawn*, p. 91. Gladys Reichard notes that First Man and First Woman created the moon. "From a piece of rock crystal the First Pair made the moon, bordering it with whiteshell, forked lightning, and sacred waters. . . ." See Reichard, *Navaho Religion*, p. 17.

13. Clyde Benally, et al., *Dinéjí Nákéé Nááhane'* p. 13.

14. Momaday, *House Made of Dawn*, p. 91.

15. Ibid. These fish wash up in a "disordered" sprawl on the beach.

16. The moon, along with the sun, regulates the agricultural cycles and ceremonial calendars in the Pueblos. Abel seems to have temporarily forgotten this. See Tyler, *Pueblo Gods and Myths*, p. 161; for the Beautyway reference, see Sandner, *Navaho Symbols of Healing*, p. 45.

17. A Navajo friend of mine, Betty Reid, once told me that when her parents first saw the Pacific Ocean, off San Francisco Bay, they

sprinkled pinches of pollen from their leather pouches into it. Personal communication, 1978.

18. Schubnell, *N. Scott Momaday*, p. 125.

19. There are also faint echoes here of the episode in male Shoot-ingway where the hero Holy Boy (Younger Brother) falls into a pool and is "swallowed by a huge fish" in order that he may gain knowledge of the "water people." See Spencer, *Mythology and Values*, p. 121.

20. Schubnell, *N. Scott Momaday*, pp. 128, 130.

21. Davíd Carrasco, commenting on the religious dimensions of water symbolism, says:

> Underlying all the beliefs and attachment to sacred springs and water is the fundamental idea that life and the sacred come from one cosmic substance and water is that basic substance. . . . Water is a source of life, the potential energy of existence, the source of absolute reality. It is for this reason that in numerous cultures water is referred to as the Universal Mother. It gives birth to all things and is revered as a source of renewal. . . . Besides the general value placed on water as a fertility force, the history of religions shows that in some traditions, water is considered the supreme medicinal substance. It has the power to heal, restore youth and even ensure eternal life.

From Davíd Carrasco, "Sacred Space and Religious Vision in World Religions: A Context to Understand the Religious Claims of the Koo-tenai Indians," working paper for Native American Rights Fund, Boul-der, Colorado, 1980.

22. Matthews, *The Night Chant*, pp. 257, 311–12, n.32

23. Wyman, *The Mountainway of the Navajo*, p. 5.

24. Ibid.

25. Larry Dossey, M.D., *Space, Time and Medicine* (Boulder, Colorado: Shambhala, 1982), p. 66.

26. Eliade, *The Myth of the Eternal Return* , p. 98.

27. Fritjof Capra, *The Turning Point: Science, Society and the Rising Culture* (New York: Simon and Schuster, 1982), p. 331.

28. Eliade, *The Myth of the Eternal Return*, p. 98.

29. Dossey, *Space, Time and Medicine*, p. 76.

30. Momaday, *House Made of Dawn*, p. 92.

31. Ibid. Mircea Eliade has said that "illness is an occasion for

integration." "Waiting for the Dawn" lecture at the University of Colorado, Boulder, October 26, 1982.

32. Luckert, *The Navajo Hunter Tradition*, p. 153. Holyway is a classification of Navajo ceremonials that emphasize transformation and renewed blessings. Nightway, Mountainway, and Beautyway are included in this group.

33. Ibid., pp. 155–56. For discussions of the contrasts between Navajo and Western medical beliefs and practices, see John Adair and Kurt W. Deuschle, *The People's Health: Medicine and Anthropology in a Navajo Community* (New York: Appleton-Century-Crofts, 1970; Albuquerque: University of New Mexico Press, 1988) and Stephen J. Kunitz, *Disease, Change and the Role of Medicine: The Navajo Experience* (Berkeley: University of California Press, 1983).

34. Luckert, *The Navajo Hunter Tradition*, p. 155.

35. Ibid., p. 156.

36. Ibid., p. 155. Also see Gill, *Native American Religions*, pp. 24, 50–55 for a discussion of the symbolism of the Flintway ceremonial. For the original transcription, see Father Berard Haile, *Origin Legend of the Navaho Flintway* (Chicago: University of Chicago Press, 1943).

37. Watkins, *In Time and Place*, pp. 166–67. Speaking of the Horse Song Watkins states, "I have found numerous parallels to Benally's song in Navajo poetry but no close source." Trying to identify the mythological mother of the singer, he looked at Washington Matthews' *Navaho Legends*, Memoirs of the American Folklore Society, vol. 5, (Boston: Houghton Mifflin, 1897), pp. 104–5 and erroneously determined that the "small turquoise image of a woman" who becomes "*Estsánatlehi*" or the woman of rejuvenation is the Bear Maiden. Rather, Estsánatlehi should be correctly identified as Changing Woman, one of the sisters or other manifested selves of Turquoise Woman. Watkins attempts to cover up the confusion by stating that "the mystery of Turquoise Woman seems to be too difficult to translate into English." Concerning Turquoise Woman, Matthews says that one version of the Navajo Origin Legend says that "she was created from a small turquoise image into which life was infused by an elaborate ceremonial act of the gods . . ." Matthews, *The Night Chant*, pp. 31–32, 31 n.3, 307 n.3.

38. Margot Astrov, ed., *American Indian Prose and Poetry* (New York: Capricorn Books, 1962), pp. 183–86. This book originally appeared under the title *The Winged Serpent*, 1946.

39. Coolidge and Coolidge, *The Navajo Indians*, p. 2.

40. David P. McAllester, "'The War God's Horse Song,' An Exegesis in Native American Humanities" in *Selected Reports in Ethnomusicology*

3, no. 2, University of California at Los Angeles, 1980: 1–21. McAllester presented another version of this article as a paper entitled *"Ipsissima Verba:* The Loving Care of Navajo Texts" at the Navajo Studies Conference at the University of New Mexico, February 22, 1986.

41. Ibid., p. 6.
42. Momaday, *House Made of Dawn*, pp. 154–55.
43. Ibid.
44. Ibid., p. 155.
45. Ibid.
46. For a comparison with other horse creation texts, see Pliny Earle Goddard, *Navajo Texts*, Anthropological Papers of the American Museum of Natural History, 34, Part 1, New York, 1933, pp. 92–93, 164; O'Bryan, *The Dîné*, pp. 177–81.
47. Gill, *Native American Religions*, p. 140.
48. See Clark, *They Sang for Horses*, pp. 144–45; Matthews, *Navaho Myths, Prayers and Songs*, p. 35; O'Bryan, *The Dîné*, p. 179. There are some horse songs associated with the Night Chant.
49. Farella, *The Main Stalk*, p. 156.
50. Ibid., p. 186.
51. Ibid., p. 181. McAllester in "The War God's Horse Song," p. 4, says about "Everlasting" and "Peaceful" that:

> They are, in fact, an attempt to render the most potent phrases in the Navajo language, *Sǫ'ahnaaghéi, Bik' ehózhǫ́ǫ́*. The first means to live the perfect life into old age, again and again, as does Changing Woman herself. The second means that having achieved this ultimate goal of Navajo philosophy, one is accordingly in a state of transcendant peace, harmony, beauty, and blessedness.

McAllester cites Gary Witherspoon, "The Central Concepts of Navajo World View" (1) in *Linguistics* 119 (January 1974): 41–59, as the basis for this statement.

52. Farella, *The Main Stalk*, p. 181.
53. Matthews, *Navaho Myths, Prayers, and Songs*, pp. 54–55. For a longer version of this prayer, see Matthews, *The Night Chant*, p. 143–45, and Matthews, *Navaho Legends*, p. 273. The prayer text that Momaday uses is from the fourth day of the Night Chant ceremony.
54. Velie, *Four American Indian Literary Masters*, p. 61.
55. Watkins, *In Time and Place*, pp. 168–70.
56. Larson, *American Indian Fiction*, p. 92.

57. Evers, "Words and Place," p. 316. Also see Gladys Reichard's comment in *Navaho Religion*, pp. 33–34:

Closely related to breath and sound, in fact, a combination of the two, is voice, speech, or language. The 'word'—that is, the formulation of sounds into organized speech—is of great ritualistic value, and in order to be complete, man must control language. The better his control and the more extensive his knowledge, the greater his well-being. . . . In prayer, therefore, man requests, "My voice restore for me. . . ."

58. Evers, "Words and Place," pp. 316–17.
59. Linda Hogan, "Who Puts Together," pp. 169–77.
60. Ibid., pp. 169–70.
61. Ibid., p. 174.
62. Momaday, *House Made of Dawn*, pp. 134–35. Again, Momaday's source is Matthews's *Navajos Myths, Prayers, and Songs*, pp. 54–55.
63. Matthews, *The Night Chant*, p. 212.
64. Ibid., p. 244.
65. Ibid.
66. Ibid., pp. 244–45.
67. Ibid., p. 245. See Wyman, *Southwest Indian Drypainting*, p. 87. Wyman says: "The Ye'i are a group of supernatural beings who, after their creation, tried but failed to speak (Haile 1947a:3, 15). Hence, they are called by a term *hasch'ééh*, which could be rendered 'the Speechless Ones.' The Ripener Girl (Cornbeetle) gave them their calls, the only voice they have." No wonder the Yéi admire the Stricken Twins' singing ability. Also see Frisbie, *Navajo Medicine Bundles or Jish*, p. 1. Frisbie mentions the "Failed-to-Speak People."
68. The free translation of the "House Made of Dawn" prayer embodies a joint plea for restoration. Two lines are: "Oh, male divinity!/ With your moccasins of dark cloud, come to us." See Matthews, *The Night Chant*, p. 143.
69. Sandner, *Navaho Symbols of Healing*, pp. 246–47.
70. On two occasions I asked medicine men how they understood the relationship between singing and healing. Bear Heart Williams, a Muskogee, replied with a story that told of a woman's lament for a husband gone off to fight enemies. As she walked alone in the mountains, her wail became a song that helped her deal with her anguish. Kéetoowah, a Cherokee crystal gazer, told me yet another story. He

said that friends of his, some Northern California medicine men, on occasion walk out to a large boulder standing alone in a field, cup their hands around their mouths and sing into the cracks in the rock. "If that big rock can move by singing," he said, "then surely singing can heal." Personal communication, Boulder, Colorado, 1982.

71. Donald F. Sandner, "Navaho Indian Medicine and Medicine Men," in *Ways of Health, Holistic Approaches to Ancient and Contemporary Medicine,* ed. David S. Sobel (New York: Harcourt Brace Jovanovich, 1979), p. 125.

72. Ibid., p. 142.

73. Jerome D. Frank, "Nonmedical Healing: Religious and Secular," in *Ways of Health: Holistic Approaches to Ancient and Contemporary Medicine,* ed. David S. Sobel (New York: Harcourt Brace Jovanovich, 1979), p. 261.

74. Ibid., p. 252.

75. Momaday, *House Made of Dawn,* p. 166.

76. Sandner, "Navaho Indian Medicine and Medicine Men," pp. 134–40.

77. Ibid., p. 140.

78. Thunderbird or "the chief of pollen." See Matthews, *The Night Chant,* p. 143, and Sandner, "Navaho Indian Medicine and Medicine Men," p. 132. For Abel, Thunderbird may function as one of Eagle's manifestations or multiple selves. Thus, Ben and Abel make restitution to the spirit of Eagle whom Abel had offended when he was a young hunter. See Momaday, *House Made of Dawn,* pp. 18–25.

79. Momaday, *House Made of Dawn,* p. 134.

80. Ibid.

81. Ibid.

82. Ibid.

83. Ibid.

84. Gill, "Prayer as Person," p. 143.

85. Ibid., p. 144.

86. Ibid., pp. 149–50.

87. Ibid., p. 150.

88. Frank, "Nonmedical Healing," p. 244.

89. Ibid., p. 258.

90. Momaday, *House Made of Dawn,* p. 133.

91. Ibid.

92. Frank, "Nonmedical Healing," p. 262.

93. Momaday, *House Made of Dawn,* p. 133.

94. Sandner, "Navaho Indian Medicine and Medicine Men," p. 143.

95. Ibid., p. 134; Momaday, *House Made of Dawn*, p. 172. Ben thinks this when he remembers their plans.

96. Momaday, *House Made of Dawn*, p. 172.

97. Weston LaBarre, *The Peyote Cult* (New York: Schocken Books, 1969; reprint of Yale University Publications in Anthropology, no. 19, 1938). This is a classic study of the peyote way; also see David F. Aberle, *The Peyote Religion Among the Navaho* (Chicago: University of Chicago Press, 1966).

98. Momaday, *House Made of Dawn*, p. 101. James Mooney says that the buffalo is the counterpart or "animal symbol of the sun." See James Mooney, *Calendar History of the Kiowa Indians* (Washington: Smithsonian Institution Press, 1979; reprint of Seventeenth Annual Report of the Bureau of American Ethnology, 1895–96), p. 237.

99. Francisco talks about the sun's utter importance for the survival of Pueblo ways, and it is, of course, the progenitor of each dawn in the Navajo "House Made of Dawn" prayer. The sun's reappearance frames the novel, providing circular structure to the story, and an image of regeneration.

100. Momaday, *House Made of Dawn*, p. 104. The rainstorm shows that prayer affects the natural world. Nature persists even in the heart of downtown Los Angeles.

101. Ibid., p. 103.

102. Ibid., p. 104. The sweet smoke here is linked synesthesially to the bear's sweet smoke in Ben's Mountainway story. Smoke is an agent of transformation and blessing.

103. Momaday, *House Made of Dawn*, p. 105. This statement imaginatively compresses space by symbolically bringing Navajo land to Los Angeles or else taking Ben back home. The landmarks that Ben has known from boyhood have become internalized within his psyche. During this ceremony these places are renewed, like mountain shrines, in vision and prayer.

104. J. S. Slotkin, "The Peyote Way" in *Teachings From the American Earth: Indian Religion and Philosophy*, eds. Dennis Tedlock and Barbara Tedlock, (New York: Liveright, 1975), p. 103. He mentions that peyote "reduces fatigue," and testifies that he has "left a Peyote meeting permanently well again."

105. Ibid., p. 102.

106. Momaday, *House Made of Dawn*, p. 95.

107. Ibid., p. 96.

108. Ibid., pp. 105–6. The source or model for this passage in the novel can be found in La Barre, *The Peyote Cult*, p. 51. La Barre, in this

section on the Kiowa-Comanche rite, says that the whistle "imitate[s]" the water bird. This sound brings back memories of Vidal and Abel's geese. In Navajo culture ceremonial whistles blow sickness off of people. See Reichard, *Navaho Religion*, p. 258. One of my Navajo students, Donna Nez, has written about the peyote ceremony:

> The road man will go outside and talk with the gods and blow on the eagle bone. When he comes back in . . . they will be told that if they see any evil in the darkness, they shouldn't be afraid of it. If there is a vision that is given to them, they shouldn't be afraid of it too, because the peyote will protect them.

Donna Nez, "The Origin of Peyote," unpublished MS, 1988, p. 9.
109. Momaday, *House Made of Dawn*, p. 85.
110. Ibid., pp. 86–87.
111. Momaday, *The Names*, p. 1.
112. Momaday, *House Made of Dawn*, p. 92.
113. Ibid., p. 132.
114. In his essay, "The Man Made of Words" Momaday says:

> We have become disoriented, I believe; we have suffered a kind of psychic dislocation of ourselves in time and space. We may be perfectly sure of where we are in relation to the supermarket and the next coffee break, but I doubt that any of us knows where he is in relation to the stars and to the solstices. Our sense of the natural order has become dull and unreliable.

Momaday, "The Man Made of Words," in *Literature of the American Indians: Views and Interpretations*, ed. Abraham Chapman (New York: Meridian, New American Library, 1975), p. 101.
115. It is a matter of historic record that the cultural genocide against Native Americans that was so overt in the nineteenth century still continues in subtler forms. The old federal government policies of removal, relocation and termination, along with violation of religious, language, and land rights of native peoples, have largely given way to offers of cash settlement for stolen lands, programs of forced sterilization of Indian women, and incentives for rural people to voluntarily relocate in urban centers. See Simon J. Ortiz, "Fight Back: For the Sake of the People For the Sake of the Land,"*INAD Literary Journal*

1, no. 1 (Albuquerque: Native American Studies, University of New Mexico, 1980): 45–73. Here in the poem "It Will Come; It Will Come" and the story "No More Sacrifices" Ortiz discusses these issues in the contexts of the Southwest, the Tricentennial Anniversary of the Pueblo Revolt, and the spirit of resistance and endurance.

116. Some say that the Navajo brought the bear cult with them from the north when they travelled south as Athabaskan hunters. Subsequently, their hunting patterns changed. Andrew Wiget told me that he thinks that Bear from the north joins Snake from the south, for the sake of balance, in, for example, the Enemyway rite and the mythic stories of Beautyway and Mountainway. Personal communication, Chicago, December 1985.

117. As mentioned in chapter 3, not only is bear meat eaten, but also parts of the bear (i.e., paws, claws, legs and teeth) are used ritually as curative paraphernalia at Jemez.

118. Father Berard Haile, "Navajo Chantways and Ceremonials", *American Anthropologist*, n. s.40, no. 4, Part 1 (October–December 1938), p. 640. Haile uses the Windway and the Hand-Trembling Way as his examples.

119. Ibid., Italics mine.

120. Ibid.

121. Ibid.

122. Ibid.

123. Momaday, *House Made of Dawn*, pp. 12, 26, 16. Abel is observant when he first rides on a bus to go off to war: "There was a lot of speed and sound then, and he tried desperately to take it into account, to know what it meant," p. 25. Paying attention to sounds helps Abel protect himself from forces of ill will.

124. Ibid., p.16.

125. Polly Schaafsma, *Rock Art in New Mexico* (Albuquerque: University of New Mexico Press, 1975), pp. 55, 60.

126. Ibid., pp. 12–13, 55–56.

127. See Schubnell, *N. Scott Momaday*, pp. 98–99. He comments on some of the critically "misguided" reviews by Smith, Borg, Leonard, and others.

128. Some of these critics are: Paula Gunn Allen, Lawrence Evers, Linda Hogan, Elaine Jahner, Kenneth Lincoln, Kenneth Roemer, James Ruppert, LaVonne Ruoff, Andrew Wiget, and Paul Zolbrod, to name a few.

129. Momaday, *House Made of Dawn*, p. 96.

130. Baine Kerr, "The Novel as Sacred Text: N. Scott Momaday's Myth-Making Ethic," *Southwest Review* 63, no. 2 (Spring 1978): 173.

131. Ibid., pp. 176, 178.

132. Ibid., pp. 179, 176.

133. Ibid., pp. 173, 174, 175, and 177.

134. Ibid., p. 179.

135. Watkins, *In Time and Place*, p. 133. I contend that these same details, considered cumulatively, are the collective means for achieving healing in the novel.

136. Hylton, "On a Trail of Pollen," p. 68.

137. Schubnell, *N. Scott Momaday*, pp. 98, 56. Schubnell does, however, have a sense of the importance of some of the ritual patterns in the novel, such as running and eagle-catching. See pp. 138, 107.

138. Ibid., p. 138.

139. Ibid., Schubnell's source here, Richard Erdoes, *The Rain Dance People* (New York: Alfred A. Knopf, 1976), p. 2, is a nonscholarly work, as is the case with another one of Schubnell's written sources, Tom Bahti, *Southwestern Indian Tribes* (Las Vegas: KC Publications, 1972), that on p. 11 erroneously cites Leslie A. White (instead of Elsie Clews Parsons) as the author of *The Pueblo of Jemez*. See Schubnell's use of this source, p. 277 n.40. However, the vast majority of Schubnell's sources are sound.

140. Clifford Geertz, "Blurred Genres: The Refiguration of Social Thought," *American Scholar* (Spring 1980): 165, 174.

141. Ibid., p. 166.

142. Ibid., p. 179.

143. *MELUS*, Native American Literature Issue, ed. Wayne Charles Miller, 12, no. 1 (Spring 1985): 3.

144. McAllester, "The War God's Horse Song," p. 3.

145. Ibid.

146. Ibid., p. 6.

147. Momaday, "The Man Made of Words," p. 105. Momaday says, "Do you see what happens when the imagination is superimposed upon the historical event? It becomes a story. The whole piece becomes more deeply invested with meaning."

148. James Ruppert, "Mediation and Multiple Narrative in Contemporary Native American Fiction," *Texas Studies in Literature and Language* 28, no. 2 (Summer 1986): 209–25.

149. Ibid., pp. 209, 224.

150. Ibid., p. 224.

151. Paula Gunn Allen, "Chee Dostoyevsky Rides the Reservation,"

unpublished MS., p. 3; revised MS. published as "American Indian Fiction, 1968–1983" in *A Literary History of the American West*, The Western Literature Association (Fort Worth: Texas Christian University Press, 1987), pp. 1058–66.

152. Ibid., p. 5.

153. Ibid.

154. Ibid., pp. 2–3.

155. By esoteric, I mean that there is less ethnographic material available on Pueblo oral literature (than Navajo) to properly contextualize its study.

156. Oleson, "The Remembered Earth," p. 75.

157. Ibid.

158. Paula Gunn Allen, "Bringing Home the Fact: Tradition and Continuity in the Imagination," p. 570.

159. Ibid., p. 571.

160. Geertz says that: "theory, scientific or otherwise, moves mainly by analogy, a 'seeing-as' comprehension of the less intelligible by the more . . ." Geertz, "Blurred Genres," p. 168.

161. Ibid., p. 175. "Fixation of meaning" is Geertz's term.

162. Petroglyphs are rock carvings found often by rock shelters, springs, ruins or game trails in the sandstone country of the Southwest. See Polly Schaafsma, *Indian Rock Art of the Southwest*, School of American Research (Albuquerque: University of New Mexico Press, 1980).

163. Joe Herrera, Personal communication, Cochiti Pueblo, Christmas 1985.

164. Momaday is a widely exhibited painter as well as a writer. See Schubnell, *N. Scott Momaday*, p. 256, where it is mentioned that Momaday is a painter, and that "The protagonist of his novel in progress, Catlin Set, is a painter. . . . Set is the Kiowa word for bear."

165. Leslie Silko also creates an important she-elk pictograph who represents fecundity in *Ceremony*. See Silko, *Ceremony*, pp. 241–42.

166. In an interview, Momaday says: "In a way, history for the Indian is an account in shorthand; it is an image, a pictograph." From "A *MELUS* Interview: N. Scott Momaday—Literature and the Native Writer," Tom King interviewer, *MELUS* 10, no. 4 (Winter 1983): 68. I have used the term petroglyph (an image carved in stone) rather than pictograph (a painted image on rock), because petroglyphs are more numerous than pictographs in the Southwest.

167. The songs are the other central models of wholeness. Running as a ritual activity is yet another model for regaining health.

168. William W. Thackeray, "Animal Allies and Transformers of *Winter*

in the Blood," MELUS 12, no. 1 (Spring 1985): 37. Thackeray is referring to Blackfeet/Gros Ventre author James Welch's first novel *Winter in the Blood* (New York: Harper and Row, 1974; New York: Penguin, 1986).

169. Ibid., p. 39.

170. "A *MELUS* Interview: N. Scott Momaday—A Slant of Light," Bettye Givens, interviewer, *MELUS* 12, no. 1 (Spring 1985): 82. This interview appeared in print just after I had finished writing chapter 3, "Bears and Sweet Smoke."

171. Ibid. For another remarkable interview where Momaday discusses his bear power, see Charles L. Woodard, *Ancestral Voice: Conversations with N. Scott Momaday* (Lincoln: University of Nebraska Press, 1989), pp. xi, 13–18, 198, 207.

172. Givens, "A *MELUS* interview: N. Scott Momaday," p. 82.

173. Ibid.

174. Ibid.

175. David McAllester, *"Ipsissima Verba,"* Navajo Studies Conference, University of New Mexico, Albuquerque, February 22, 1986.

176. O'Bryan, *The Dîné,* p. 180.

177. Ibid., p. 181.

178. Momaday, *House Made of Dawn,* pp. 72–73. See my "Grandmother Spider's Lifeline" in *Studies in American Indian Literature: Critical Essays and Course Designs,* ed. Paula Gunn Allen (New York: The Modern Language Association of America, 1983), pp. 100–07, for a discussion of spider figures in contemporary Native American Literature. Also notice that a little spider tries to live in Abel's suitcase in Ben's room, and that they treat it well, pp. 161–62. Spider Woman is a creative deity and protector in Navajo and Pueblo cultures.

179. Matthews, *The Night Chant,* p. 254.

180. Momaday, *House Made of Dawn,* pp. 127–28; Matthews, *The Night Chant,* p. 254. In addition to the Stricken Twins' offerings of "doeskins, fawnskins, antelope skins and furs," they also had to give the Yéi "woven fabrics of all kinds."

181. Momaday, *House Made of Dawn,* p. 175.

182. Ibid., p. 176.

183. Farella, *The Main Stalk,* p. 86.

184. Ibid., p. 76.

185. Ward Yeppa, a student of mine from Jemez Pueblo, says:

When one dies we [Indians] believe he goes back to wherever he came from, like heaven maybe. From there we believe he is appointed a place somewhere, maybe in the mountains living as a Spirit helping the men with hunting or keeping them safe from all danger. Or it might be in the cropping fields so he can help with the crop growing that year. So we believe that when one dies he is still around us, but we just can't see him.

Ward Yeppa, "Symbols of Life and Death," unpublished MS. 1989, p. 3.

186. In the closing moments of the novel, Abel is "Impervious to pain" as the "House Made of Dawn" prayer asserts. Momaday, *House Made of Dawn*, p. 191, 134.

187. The phrase "to see according to holiness" is Navajo singer Natani Tso's translation of *sq a naghái bik'e hózhǫ́*. From Sanders, *Navaho Symbols of Healing*, p. 225. The description of dawn is from Momaday, *House Made of Dawn*, p. 190. The phrase "story made of dawn" comes from Dawn Boy's prayer in the Night Chant. Matthews says that Dawn Boy bears offerings to Kininaékai, White House, and that Dawn Boy's family lives on the edge of Tśe'gihi. See Matthews, *Navaho Myths, Prayers, and Songs*, pp. 29, 33. Dawn Boy's song beings: "In Kininaékai./ In the house made of dawn./ In the story made of dawn./ On the trail of dawn. O, Talking God!/ His feet, my feet, restore," p. 29. Larry Littlebird, from Laguna and Santo Domingo Pueblos, who played the part of Abel in the film *House Made of Dawn*, said, at the conference "American Indian Image on Film: The Southwest," that telling a story depends on sight, learning, and knowing how to see. Seeing, he said, means observing with all parts of being, not just with the senses. "Sight and real seeing is an act of creation, from the creator, an act of intuiting what creation is," concluded Littlebird. Lecture, University of New Mexico, February 12, 1982.

Bibliography

Aberle, David F. *The Peyote Religion Among the Navaho*. Chicago: University of Chicago Press, 1966.

Adair, John and Kurt W. Deuschle. *The People's Health: Medicine and Anthropology in a Navajo Community*. New York: Appleton-Century-Crofts, 1970. Reprint. Albuquerque: University of New Mexico Press, 1988.

Allen, Paula Gunn. "Bringing Home the Fact: Tradition and Continuity in the Imagination." In *Recovering the Word: Essays on Native American Literature*. Edited by Brian Swann and Arnold Krupat. Berkeley: University of California Press, 1987, pp. 563–79.

———. "Chee Dostoyevsky Rides the Reservation." Unpublished MS., pp. 2–3; revised MS. published as "American Indian Fiction, 1968–1983." In *A Literary History of the American West*. The Western Literature Association. Fort Worth: Texas Christian University Press, 1987, pp. 1058–66.

———. "The Feminine Landscape of Leslie Marmon Silko's *Ceremony*." In *Studies in American Indian Literature: Critical Essays and Course Designs*. Edited by Paula Gunn Allen. New York: The Modern Language Association of America, 1983, pp. 127–33.

———. *The Sacred Hoop: Recovering the Feminine in American Indian Traditions*. Boston: Beacon Press, 1986.

———. "A Stranger in My Own Life: Alienation in American Indian Prose and Poetry." *MELUS* 7, no. 2 (Summer 1980): 3–19.

Anaya, Rudolfo. Lecture on Chicano Literature. Rocky Mountain Modern Language Association Convention, Santa Fe. October 1976.

Astrov, Margot, ed. *The Winged Serpent, An Anthology of American Indian*

Prose and Poetry. New York: The John Day Co., 1946. Reprint. *American Indian Prose and Poetry.* New York: Capricorn Books, 1962.

Bahti, Tom. *Southwestern Indian Tribes.* Las Vegas: KC Publications, 1972.

Barry, Nora Baker. "The Bear's Son Folk Tale in *When the Legends Die* and *House Made of Dawn.*" *Western American Literature* 12, no. 4 (February 1978): 275–87.

Beidler, Peter G. "Animals and Human Development in the Contemporary American Indian Novel." *Western American Literature* 14, no. 2 (August 1979): 133–48.

Benally, Clyde, Andrew O. Wiget, John R. Alley, and Garry Blake. *Dinéjí Nákéé Nááhane': A Utah Navajo History.* Monticello, Utah: San Juan School District, 1982.

Benedict, Ruth. *Tales of the Cochiti Indians.* Bureau of American Ethnology Bulletin 98, 1931. Reprint. Albuquerque: University of New Mexico Press, 1981.

Bennett, Kay. *Kaibah: Recollections of a Navajo Girlhood.* Los Angeles: Western Lore Press, 1964.

Bierhorst, John, ed. *Four Masterworks of American Indian Literature: Quetzalcoatl/ The Ritual of Condolence/ Cuceb/ The Night Chant.* New York: Farrar, Straus and Giroux, 1974.

Boyd, Maurice. *Kiowa Voices. Ceremonial Dance, Ritual and Song,* Vol. 1. Fort Worth: Texas Christian University Press, 1981.

Bunzel, Ruth L. *The Pueblo Potter: A Study of Creative Imagination in Primitive Art.* New York: Columbia University Press, 1929. Reprint. New York: Dover Publications, 1972.

Campbell, Joseph. *The Hero with a Thousand Faces.* Bollingen Series 17. New York: Pantheon Books, 1949.

———. Commentary to *Where the Two Came to Their Father: A Navaho War Ceremonial.* Given by Jeff King, Text and Paintings Recorded by Maud Oakes. Bollingen Series 1. New York: Pantheon Books, 1943. Reprint. Princeton: Princeton University Press, 1969.

Capra, Fritjof. *The Turning Point: Science, Society and the Rising Culture.* New York: Simon and Schuster, 1982.

Carrasco, Davíd. "A Context to Understand the Religious Claims of the Kootenai Indians." Working Paper for Native American Rights Fund, Boulder, Colorado, 1980.

———. *Quetzalcoatl and the Irony of Empire: Myths and Prophecies in the Aztec Tradition.* Chicago: University of Chicago Press, 1982.

Clark, LaVerne Harrell. *They Sang for Horses: The Impact of the Horse on Navajo and Apache Folklore.* Tucson: University of Arizona Press, 1966.

Coolidge, Dane and Mary Roberts Coolidge. *The Navajo Indians.* Boston: Houghton Mifflin, 1930.

Dabney, Lewis M. *The Indians of Yoknapatawpha County: A Study in Literature and History.* Baton Rouge: Louisiana State University Press, 1974.

DeFlyer, Joseph E. "Partition Theory: Patterns and Partitions of Consciousness in Selected Works of American and American Indian Authors." Ph.D. diss. University of Nebraska, 1974.

Dossey, M.D., Larry. *Space, Time and Medicine.* Boulder, Colorado: Shambhala, 1982.

Dumarest, Father Noël. "Notes on Cochiti, New Mexico." Memoirs of the American Anthropological Association, vol. 6, no. 3, Lancaster, 1919.

Eliade, Mircea. *The Myth of the Eternal Return or, Cosmos and History.* Bollingen Series 46. Princeton: Princeton University Press, 1954.

———. *Patterns in Comparative Religion.* New York: Meridian Books, New American Library, 1958.

———. "Waiting for the Dawn." Lecture at the University of Colorado, Boulder, October 26, 1982.

Ellis, Florence Hawley. "A Reconstruction of the Basic Jemez Pattern of Social Organization, with Comparisons to Other Tanoan Social Structures." University of New Mexico Publications in Anthropology, no. 11, Albuquerque, 1964, pp. 7–69.

Erdoes, Richard. *The Rain Dance People.* New York: Alfred A. Knopf, 1976.

Evers, Lawrence J. "A Conversation with N. Scott Momaday." *SunTracks* 2, no. 2. Tucson: University of Arizona Press (Spring 1976): 18–21.

———. "The Killing of a New Mexican State Trooper: Ways of Telling an Historical Event." *Wicazso Sa Review* 1, no. 1 (Spring 1985): 17–25. Also in *Critical Essays on Native American Literature.* Edited by Andrew Wiget. Boston: G.K. Hall, 1985, pp. 246–61.

———. "Words and Place: A Reading of *House Made of Dawn.*" *Western American Literature* 11 (February 1977): 297–320. Reprint. *Critical Essays on Native American Literature.* Edited by Andrew Wiget. Boston: G.K. Hall, 1985, pp. 211–30.

Farella, John D. *The Main Stalk: A Synthesis of Navajo Philosophy.* Tucson: University of Arizona Press, 1984.

Faris, James C. "Navajo Nightway Chant History: A Report." *Diné Be'iina': A Journal of Navajo Life* 1, no. 2 (Winter 1988): 107–18.

Fergusson, Erna. *Dancing Gods: Indian Ceremonials of New Mexico and*

Arizona. Albuquerque: University of New Mexico Press, 1931. Reprint, with foreword by Tony Hillerman, 1988.

Fisher, Dexter, ed. *The Third Woman: Minority Women Writers of the United States.* Boston: Houghton Mifflin, 1980.

Frank, Jerome D. "Nonmedical Healing: Religious and Secular." In *Ways of Health, Holistic Approaches to Ancient and Contemporary Medicine.* Edited by David S. Sobel. New York: Harcourt Brace Jovanovich, 1979, pp. 231–66.

Frisbie, Charlotte. J. *Navajo Medicine Bundles or Jish: Acquisition, Transmission, and Disposition in the Past and Present.* Albuquerque: University of New Mexico Press, 1987.

Geertz, Clifford. "Blurred Genres: The Refiguration of Social Thought." *American Scholar* (Spring 1980): 165–79.

Gill, Sam D. "Prayer as Person: The Performative Force in Navajo Prayer Acts." *History of Religions* 17, no. 2. University of Chicago Press (November 1977): 143–57.

———. *Native American Religions: An Introduction.* Belmont, California: Wadsworth Publishing, 1982.

———. *Native American Traditions: Sources and Interpretations.* Belmont, California: Wadsworth Publishing, 1983.

———. *Sacred Words: A Study of Navajo Religion and Prayer.* Westport, Connecticut: Greenwood Press, 1981.

Girard, René. *Violence and the Sacred.* Baltimore: The Johns Hopkins University Press, 1972.

Givens, Bettye. "A *MELUS* Interview: N. Scott Momaday—A Slant of Light." *MELUS* 12, no. 1 (Spring 1985): 79–87.

Goddard, Pliny Earle. *Navajo Texts.* Anthropological Papers of the American Museum of Natural History, 34, Part 1, New York, 1933, pp. 1–179.

Haeberlin, H.K. "The Idea of Fertilization in the Culture of the Pueblo Indians." Memoirs of the American Anthropological Association, vol. 3, no. 1 (January–March 1916).

Haile, Father Berard. *Head and Face Masks in Navaho Ceremonialism.* St. Michaels, Arizona: St. Michaels Press, 1947. Reprint. New York: AMS Press, 1978.

———. "Navaho Chantways and Ceremonials." *American Anthropologist.* American Anthropological Association, n.s. 40, no. 4, Part 1 (October–December 1938), pp. 639–52.

———. *Navaho Coyote Tales: The Curly Tó Aheedlíinii Version.* American Tribal Religions 8. Edited by Karl W. Luckert. Lincoln: University of Nebraska Press, 1984.

————. *Navaho War Dance: A Brief Narrative of its Meaning and Practice.* St. Michaels, Arizona: St. Michaels Press, 1946.

————. *Origin Legend of the Navaho Enemy Way.* Yale University Publications in Anthropology, no. 17. New Haven: Yale University Press, 1938.

————. *Origin Legend of the Navaho Flintway.* Chicago: University of Chicago Press, 1943.

————. *Upward Moving and Emergence Way.* American Tribal Religions 7. Edited by Karl W. Luckert. Lincoln: University of Nebraska Press, 1981.

Hallowell, A. Irving. "Bear Ceremonialism in the Northern Hemisphere." *American Anthropologist* vol. 28, no. 1 (January–March 1926): 1–175.

Harper, Blanche Wurdack. "Notes on the Documentary History, the Language and the Rituals and Customs of Jemez Pueblo." Master's thesis. University of New Mexico, 1929.

Hibben, Frank C. *Hunting American Bears.* Philadelphia: J. B. Lippincott, 1945.

Hill, W. W. "The Agricultural and Hunting Methods of the Navaho Indians." Yale University Publications in Anthropology, no. 18. New Haven: Yale University Press, 1938.

Hirsch, Bernard A. "Self-Hatred and Spiritual Corruption in *House Made of Dawn.*" *Western American Literature* 17, no. 4 (Winter 1983): 307–20.

Hodge, Frederick Webb, ed. *Handbook of American Indians North of Mexico.* Bureau of American Ethnology Bulletin 30, Part 1, Washington, 1907. Reprint. New York: Rowman and Littlefield, 1971.

Hogan, Linda. "Who Puts Together." In *Studies in American Indian Literature: Critical Essays and Course Designs.* Edited by Paula Gunn Allen. New York: The Modern Language Association of America, 1983, pp. 169–77.

Hylton, Marion Willard. "On a Trail of Pollen: Momaday's *House Made of Dawn.*" *Critique, Studies in Modern Fiction* 14, no. 2 (1972): 60–69.

Jahner, Elaine. "A Critical Approach to American Indian Literature." In *Studies in American Indian Literature: Critical Essays and Course Designs.* Edited by Paula Gunn Allen. New York: The Modern Language Association of America, 1983, pp. 211–24.

Kerr, Baine. "The Novel as Sacred Text: N. Scott Momaday's Myth-Making Ethic." *Southwest Review* 63, no. 2 (Spring 1978): 172–79.

King, Jeff, and Maud Oakes. *Where the Two Came to Their Father: A Navaho War Ceremonial.* Given by Jeff King, Text and Paintings Recorded by Maud Oakes, Commentary by Joseph Campbell. Bollingen Series 1. New York: Pantheon Books, 1943. Reprint. Princeton: Princeton University Press, 1969.

King, Tom. "A *MELUS* Interview: N. Scott Momaday—Literature and the Native Writer." *MELUS* 10, no. 4 (Winter 1983): 66–72.

Kunitz, Stephen J. *Disease, Change and the Role of Medicine: The Navajo Experience*. Berkeley: University of California Press, 1983.

LaBarre, Weston. *The Peyote Cult*. Yale University Publications in Anthropology, no. 19. New Haven: Yale University Press, 1938. Reprint. New York: Schocken Books, 1969.

Larson, Charles R. *American Indian Fiction*. Albuquerque: University of New Mexico Press, 1978.

Leach, Maria, ed. *Standard Dictionary of Folklore, Mythology and Legend*. New York: Funk and Wagnalls, 1950.

Levi-Strauss, Claude. *Myth and Meaning*. New York: Schocken Books, 1979.

Lincoln, Kenneth. *Native American Renaissance*. Berkeley: University of California Press, 1983.

Littlebird, Larry. Lecture on the Film *House Made of Dawn*. "American Indian Image on Film: The Southwest" Conference. University of New Mexico, Albuquerque, February 1982.

Lopez, Barry. "Story at Anaktuvuk Pass: At the Junction of Landscape and Narrative." *Harper's* (December 1984): 49–52. Reprint. "Landscape and Narrative (1984)." In *Crossing Open Ground*. Barry Lopez. New York: Charles Scribner's Sons, 1988, pp. 61–71; New York: Vintage Books, 1989.

Luckert, Karl W. *The Navajo Hunter Tradition*. Tucson: University of Arizona Press, 1975.

Marriott, Alice. *The Ten Grandmothers*. Norman: University of Oklahoma Press, 1945.

Matthews, Washington. *The Mountain Chant, A Navajo Ceremony*. Fifth Annual Report of the Bureau of American Ethnology 1883–1884. Washington, 1887, pp. 379–467.

———. *Navaho Legends*. Memoirs of the American Folklore Society, vol. 5, Boston: Houghton Mifflin, 1897.

———. *Navaho Myths, Prayers, and Songs*. Edited by P. E. Goddard. University of California Publications in American Archaeology and Ethnology, vol. 5, no. 2, 1907, pp. 21–63.

———. *The Night Chant, A Navaho Ceremony*. Memoirs of the American Museum of Natural History, Whole Series vol. 6, Anthropology, vol. 5, New York, 1902.

McAllester, David P. "*Ipsissima Verba:* The Loving Care of Navajo Texts." Navajo Studies Conference, University of New Mexico, Albuquerque, February 22, 1986.

———. "'The War God's Horse Song.' An Exegesis in Native American Humanities." In *Selected Reports in Ethnomusicology* 3, no. 2., Ed. Charlotte Heth. Program in Ethnomusicology, Department of Music, University of California at Los Angeles, 1980: 1–21.

McAllister, Harold S. "Incarnate Grace and the Paths of Salvation in *House Made of Dawn.*" *South Dakota Review* 12, no. 4 (Winter 1974): 115–25.

McNeley, James Kale. *Holy Wind in Navajo Philosophy.* Tucson: University of Arizona Press, 1981.

Miller, Wayne Charles. "Editor's Column." *MELUS* Native American Literature Issue 12, no. 1 (Spring 1985): 1–4.

Mills, George. *Navajo Art and Culture.* Colorado Springs: The Taylor Museum, 1959.

Momaday, N. Scott. "The Bear and the Colt." In *American Indian Authors.* Edited by Natachee Scott Momaday. Boston: Houghton Mifflin, 1972, pp. 119–24.

———. *House Made of Dawn.* New York: Harper and Row, 1968. Reprint. New York: Signet, 1969; New York: Harper and Row, Perennial Library, 1977.

———. Lecture on Kiowa Oral Tradition. Modern Language Association Convention, New York, December 1978.

———. "The Man Made of Words." In *Literature of the American Indians: Views and Interpretations.* Edited by Abraham Chapman. New York: A Meridian Book, New American Library, 1975, pp. 96–110.

———. "The Morality of Indian Hating." *Ramparts* (Summer 1964): 29–40.

———. *The Names: A Memoir.* New York: Harper and Row, 1976.

———. *The Way to Rainy Mountain.* Albuquerque: University of New Mexico Press, 1969. Reprint. New York: Ballantine, 1969; University of New Mexico Press, 1976.

Moon, Sheila. *Changing Woman and Her Sisters: Feminine Aspects of Selves and Deities.* San Francisco: Guild for Psychological Studies Publishing House, 1984.

Mooney, James. *Calendar History of the Kiowa Indians.* Seventeenth Annual Report of the Bureau of American Ethnology, 1885–1886, Part 1. Washington, 1898. Reprint. Washington: Smithsonian Institution Press, 1979.

Nabakov, Peter. *Indian Running.* Santa Barbara: Capra Press, 1981.

Nez, Donna. "The Origin of Peyote." Unpublished MS., 1988, p. 9.

Ohmann, Richard. Lecture on Recent American Fiction, English Department Seminar, University of Colorado, Boulder, 1982.

O'Bryan, Aileen. *The Dîné: Origin Myths of the Navaho Indians.* Bureau of American Ethnology Bulletin 163. Washington, 1956.

Oleson, Carole. "The Remembered Earth: Momaday's *House Made of Dawn.*" *South Dakota Review* 11, no. 1 (Spring 1973): 59–78.

Ortiz, Alfonso. "Ritual Drama and the Pueblo World View." In *New Perspectives on the Pueblos.* Edited by Alfonso Ortiz. School of American Research. Albuquerque: University of New Mexico Press, 1972, pp. 135–61.

———. *The Tewa World: Space, Time, Being, and Becoming in a Pueblo Society.* Chicago: University of Chicago Press, 1969.

———, ed. *Handbook of North American Indians. Southwest,* Vol. 9. Washington: Smithsonian Institution, 1979.

———, ed. *Handbook of North American Indians. Southwest,* Vol. 10, Washington: Smithsonian Institution, 1983.

Ortiz, Simon J. *Fight Back: For the Sake of the People For the Sake of the Land. INAD Literary Journal* 1, no. 1, Albuquerque: Native American Studies, University of New Mexico, 1980.

———. *Fightin': New and Collected Stories.* New York: Thunder's Mouth Press, 1983.

———. *Going for the Rain.* New York: Harper and Row, 1976.

———. "The Killing of a State Cop." In *The Man to Send Rain Clouds: Contemporary Stories by American Indians.* Edited by Kenneth Rosen. New York: Viking, 1974, pp. 101–8.

———. *Song, Poetry and Language—Expression and Perception.* Tsaile: Navajo Community College Press, 1977.

Parmentier, Richard J. "The Mythological Triangle: Poseyemu, Montezuma, and Jesus in the Pueblos." In *Handbook of North American Indians. Southwest,* Vol. 9. Edited by Alfonso Ortiz. Washington: Smithsonian Institution, 1979, pp. 609–22.

Parsons, Elsie Clews. *Pueblo Indian Religion.* 2 vols. Chicago: University of Chicago Press, 1939.

———. *The Pueblo of Jemez.* Department of Archaeology, Phillips Academy. New Haven: Yale University Press, 1925.

Reagan, Albert B. "The Jemez Indians." *El Palacio* (April 1917): 24–70.

Reichard, Gladys A. *Navajo Medicine Man.* New York: J. J. Augustin, 1939. Reprint. *Navajo Medicine Man Sandpaintings.* New York: Dover Publications, 1977.

————. *Navaho Religion: A Study of Symbolism.* Bollingen Series 18. Princeton: Princeton University Press, 1950.

Rock Point Community School. *Between Sacred Mountains: Navajo Stories and Lessons from the Land.* Edited by Sam and Janet Bingham. Tucson: SunTracks and the University of Arizona Press, 1982.

Roemer, Kenneth M., ed. *Approaches to Teaching Momaday's The Way to Rainy Mountain.* New York: The Modern Language Association of America, 1988.

————. "Bear and Elk: The Nature(s) of Contemporary American Indian Poetry." In *Studies in American Indian Literature: Critical Essays and Course Designs.* Edited by Paula Gunn Allen. New York: The Modern Language Association of America, 1983, pp. 178–91.

Rosen, Kenneth, ed. *The Man to Send Rain Clouds: Contemporary Stories by American Indians.* New York: Viking, 1974.

Ruoff, A. LaVonne Brown. "The Brothers Motif in *House Made of Dawn.*" The Influence of Tradition in Modern Native American Literature session, Modern Language Association Convention, New York, December 1978.

————."The Survival of Tradition: American Indian Oral and Written Narratives." *The Massachusetts Review* 27 (Summer 1986): 274–93.

Ruppert, James. "Mediation and Multiple Narrative in Contemporary Native American Fiction." *Texas Studies in Literature and Language* 28, no. 2 (Summer 1986): 209–25.

Sandner, Donald. "Navaho Indian Medicine and Medicine Men. "In *Ways of Health, Holistic Approaches to Ancient and Contemporary Medicine.* Edited by David S. Sobel. New York: Harcourt Brace Jovanovich, 1979, pp. 117–46.

————. *Navaho Symbols of Healing.* New York: Harcourt Brace Jovanovich, 1979.

Sando, Joe S. *Nee Hemish, A History of Jemez Pueblo.* Albuquerque: University of New Mexico Press, 1982.

Sapir, Edward and Harry Hoijer. *Navaho Texts.* Iowa City: University of Iowa Linguistic Society of America, 1942.

Scarberry, Susan J. "Grandmother Spider's Lifeline."In *Studies in American Indian Literature: Critial Essays and Course Designs.* Edited by Paula Gunn Allen. New York: The Modern Language Association of America, 1983, pp. 100–7.

————. "Land Into Flesh: Images of Intimacy." *Frontiers* 6, no. 3, Native American Women Issue (Fall 1981): 24–28.

————. "Memory as Medicine: The Power of Recollection in *Ceremony.*" *American Indian Quarterly* 5, no. 1 (February 1979): 19–26.

Scarberry-García, Susan. "Beneath the Stars: Images of the Sacred." In *Approaches to Teaching Momaday's The Way to Rainy Mountain*. Edited by Kenneth M. Roemer. New York: The Modern Language Association of America, 1988, pp. 89–97.

———. "Myths and Multiple Selves: Images of Navajo Holy People in Sandpaintings from the Huckel Collection." Lecture and Unpublished MS. Colorado Springs Fine Arts Center, Taylor Museum Fiftieth Anniversary Lecture Series, June 1986.

———. "White Shell Woman's Song: Remaking the Literary Tradition." Lecture and Unpublished MS., The Colorado College SIROW Seminars, Colorado Springs, December 1984.

———. "With Zig-Zag Lightning: Precarious Tellings of Sacred Stories by Matthews and Miguelito." Paper presented at the Modern Language Association Convention, New Orleans, December 1988.

———. and Reyes García. "Bill Russ Lee: Into the Dawn." *ARTSPACE* 12, no. 3 (Summer 1988): 17–19.

Schaafsma, Polly. *Indian Rock Art of the Southwest*. School of American Research. Albuquerque: University of New Mexico Press, 1980.

———. *Rock Art in New Mexico*. Albuquerque: University of New Mexico Press, 1975.

Schubnell, Matthias. *N. Scott Momaday: The Cultural and Literary Background*. Norman: University of Oklahoma Press, 1985.

Scully, Vincent. *Pueblo: Mountain, Village, Dance*. New York: The Viking Press, 1975.

Shepard, Paul. "The Ark of the Mind." *Parabola: Myth and the Quest for Meaning* 7, no. 2 (Spring), Animals: 54–59.

———, and Barry Sanders. *The Sacred Paw: The Bear in Nature, Myth, and Literature*. New York: Viking, 1985.

Silko, Leslie Marmon. *Ceremony*. New York: Viking, 1977. Reprint. New York: Signet, 1978; New York: Penguin Books, 1986.

———. "Tony's Story." In *The Man to Send Rain Clouds: Contemporary Stories by American Indians*. Edited by Kenneth Rosen. New York: Viking, 1974, pp. 69–78.

Simmons, Marc. *Witchcraft in the Southwest: Spanish and Indian Supernaturalism on the Rio Grande*. Flagstaff: Northland Press, 1974. Reprint. Lincoln: University of Nebraska Press, 1981.

Slotkin, J.S. "The Peyote Way." In *Teachings from the American Earth: Indian Religion and Philosophy*. Edited by Dennis Tedlock and Barbara Tedlock. New York: Liveright, 1975, pp. 96–104.

Spencer, Katherine. *Mythology and Values: An Analysis of Navaho Chantway*

Myths. Memoirs of the American Folklore Society 48. Philadelphia, 1957.

Stevenson, James. "Ceremonial of Hasjelti Dailjis and Mythical Sand Painting of the Navajo Indians." Eighth Annual Report of the Bureau of American Ethnology 1886–1887. Washington, 1891, pp. 235–285.

Swann, Brian and Arnold Krupat, eds. *Recovering the Word: Essays on Native American Literature*. Berkeley: University of California Press, 1987.

Tedlock, Barbara. "The Clown's Way." In *Teachings from the American Earth: Indian Religion and Philosophy*. Edited by Dennis Tedlock and Barbara Tedlock. New York: Liveright, 1975, pp. 105–18.

Thackeray, William W. "Animal Allies and Transformers of *Winter in the Blood*." *MELUS* 12, no. 1 (Spring 1985): 37–64.

Toledo, José Rey. "Talk on Survival," Fort Lewis College, Durango, Colorado, October 13, 1988.

———. "What Indians Are Responsible For and Threats." Lecture at Fort Lewis College, Durango, Colorado, October 14, 1988.

Tozzer, Alfred Marston. "Notes on Religious Ceremonials of the Navaho." Putnam Anniversary Volume, *Anthropological Essays*. New York: G.E. Stechert, 1909, pp. 299–343.

Turner, Victor. *The Ritual Process, Structure and Anti-Structure*. Ithaca, New York: Cornell University Press, 1969.

Tyler, Hamilton A. *Pueblo Animals and Myths*. Norman: University of Oklahoma Press, 1975.

———. *Pueblo Gods and Myths*. Norman: University of Oklahoma Press, 1964.

Velie, Alan R. *Four American Indian Literary Masters: N. Scott Momaday, James Welch, Leslie Marmon Silko, and Gerald Vizenor*. Norman: University of Oklahoma Press, 1982.

Watkins, Floyd C. *In Time and Place: Some Origins of American Fiction*. Athens: University of Georgia Press, 1977.

Welch, James. *Winter in the Blood*. New York: Harper and Row, 1974. Reprint. New York: Penguin Books, 1986.

Wheelwright, Mary C. *Myth of Mountain Chant and Beauty Chant*. Santa Fe: Museum of Navajo Ceremonial Art, Bulletin no. 5, 1951.

———. *Tleji or Yehbechai Myth*. Santa Fe: Museum of Navajo Ceremonial Art, Bulletin no. 1, 1938.

———. and Father Berard Haile. *Emergence Myth, According to the Hanelthnayne or Upward-Reaching Rite*. Navajo Religion Series, vol. 3. Santa Fe: Museum of Navajo Ceremonial Art, 1949.

Wheelwright Museum of the American Indian. *Guide to the Microfilm Edition of the Washington Matthews Papers*. Albuquerque: University of New Mexico Press, 1985.

White, Leslie A. *The Acoma Indians*. 47th Annual Report of the Bureau of American Ethnology, 1929–1930. Washington, 1932.

———. "The Pueblo of San Felipe." Memoirs of the American Anthropological Association, no. 38. Menasha, Wisconsin, 1932.

———. "The Pueblo of Santa Ana, New Mexico." Memoirs of the American Anthropological Association, no. 60. *American Anthropologist* 44, no. 4, Part 2, 1942.

———. "The Pueblo of Santo Domingo, New Mexico." Memoirs of the American Anthropological Association, no. 43. Menasha, Wisconsin, 1935.

Wiget, Andrew. *Native American Literature*. Boston: Twayne, 1985.

———, ed. *Critical Essays on Native American Literature*. Boston: G.K. Hall, 1985.

———. with Clyde Benally, John R. Alley, and Garry Blake. *Dinéji Nákéé Nááhane': A Utah Navajo History*. Monticello, Utah: San Juan School District, 1982.

Witherspoon, Gary. "The Central Concepts of Navajo World View." (1) *Linguistics* 119 (January 1974): 41–59.

———. *Language and Art in the Navajo Universe*. Ann Arbor: University of Michigan Press, 1977.

———. "Language and Reality in Navajo World View." In *Handbook of North American Indians. Southwest*, Vol. 10. Edited by Alfonso Ortiz. Washington: Smithsonian Institution, 1983, pp. 570–78.

Woodard, Charles L. *Ancestral Voice: Conversations with N. Scott Momaday*. Lincoln: University of Nebraska Press, 1989.

Wyman, Leland C. *Beautyway: A Navaho Ceremonial*. Bollingen Series 53. New York: Pantheon Books, 1957.

———. *Blessingway: With Three Versions of the Myth Recorded and Translated from the Navajo by Father Berard Haile, O.F.M.* Tucson: University of Arizona Press, 1970.

———. *The Mountainway of the Navajo*. Tucson: University of Arizona Press, 1975.

———. "Navajo Ceremonial System." In *Handbook of North American Indians. Southwest*, Vol. 10. Edited by Alfonso Ortiz. Washington: Smithsonian Institution, 1983, pp. 536–57.

———. *Southwest Indian Drypainting*. School of American Research. Albuquerque: University of New Mexico Press, 1983.

Yazzie, Ethelou, ed. *Navajo History.* Vol. 1, Rough Rock, Arizona: Navajo Curriculum Center, Rough Rock Demonstration School, 1971.

Yeppa, Ward. "Symbols of Life and Death." Unpublished MS., 1989, p. 3.

Zolbrod, Paul G. *Diné bahane': The Navajo Creation Story.* Albuquerque: University of New Mexico Press, 1984.

————. "Navajo Poetry in the Field and on the Printed Page: A Working Paper on Textual Replication in Dinébakéyah." Unpublished MS.

Index

Abduction, as motif, 56–57
Abel, xii, 2, 10; as Bear, 52–54,
56–57, 61–62; as Bear Father,
55–56, 147n99; as Bear Man,
15, 56, 81–83, 121; as Bear
Son, 55 (*See also* Barry); as
Born for Water, 14–15;
childhood, 17, 23–24, 34,
135n40; as Elder Brother, 15,
21, 88; healing of, 10, 35, 38,
40, 62, 81, 83, 85, 91, 104–5,
153n213; identities, 14,
131n61, 31–33, 38, 88; illness,
17, 29–31, 36, 42, 45, 50, 56,
86–88, 90–91, 136–37n62; as
"inarticulate," 35–36; as
Monster Slayer, 21, 32;
multiple transgressions, 42,
45; as outsider, 19, 44–45; as
Owl Boy, 61; as pair of twins,
32; run at dawn, 10, 38, 124,
166nn186, 187; spiritual
journey of, 89; as symbolic
twin, 17; transformation of,
40, 74; and water, 31; as
Younger Brother, 21, 23, 27,
31, 33, 88, 121

Aberle, David F., 160n97
Accretion: and chantway
system, 111–12; and narrative
structure, 110, 112–14, 118–19;
and petroglyph making, 120
Adair, John and Kurt W.
Deuschle, 156n33
Adultery, as theme, 66
Aggression, warrior, 32
Ahkeah, Sam, 58, 67–69, 71–73
Air, as symbol, 111
Albino, Juan Reyes Fragua, as
source of evil, 14, 19–20, 32,
41–45, 141n17
Alcoholism, x, 23, 28, 42, 86, 91,
97, 105, 110
Alienation, 40; of Abel, xii, 34,
36, 42, 45, 87–88, 90–91,
131n58, 134n20; as fictional
starting point, ix; Stricken
Twins parallel, 35–37, 102;
from tribal life, x, 34, 45. *See
also* Outsiders
Allen, Paula Gunn, 1, 17,
127n14, 162n128, 163–64n151;
quoted, 4, 13, 45, 118–20,
130n54, 131n58, 132n6,

Faris, James C., 129n38
Fat Josie, 35, 138n94
Father Olguin, 41, 43
Faulkner, William, 3, 116, 126n9
Fear: healing of, 88; imagery of,
    23, 34, 42–43, 57
Feathers: bluebird, 131n58; eagle
    plume, 35, 94; life, 61;
    pheasant, 106; prayer, 38;
    turkey, 35, 68
Feminine principle, 63, 81
Fergusson, Erna, 140n11
Fertility: assurance of, 41;
    symbols of, 31, 43, 56, 155n21;
    and War Gods, 31
Fiesta of Porcingula, 42, 140n11
Fire, as symbol, 111
Fish, 20, 31, 43, 89, 155n19
First Man: and inner forms, 9;
    and First Woman create the
    moon, 89
Fisher, Dexter, 154n1
Flight, as motif, 60–61
Flintway, 92, 156n36
Follower Pair, 14, 21, 23, 27, 36,
    131n60, 134n27, 135n42
Four: significance of, 47, 64;
    layers, 124; ritual importance
    of, 107, 126n13, 139n105,
    142n37; sacred mountains, 11
"49," 51, 143n55
Fragmentation and
    reassemblage, 16, 91–93, 102,
    121. *See also* Integration;
    Reassemblage
Fragua, Juan Reyes. *See* Albino
Francisco, 19, 27; Abel's
    grandfather, 19, 24, 43, 74;
    Abel's guide to healing, 81–
    83; bear story of, 46, 73–83;
    blessed on his deathbed, 35,

38, 124; blessing on corn, 43;
    blessing dead bear, 74; as
    medicine man, 37, 61, 74, 78–
    80, 138n94; sunrise run
    recreated by Abel, 38, 124;
    teaches tribal knowledge to
    Abel, 78–79
Frank, Jerome D., quoted, 103,
    105, 159n73
Frisbie, Charlotte J., 137n78,
    138n92, 158n67
Fusion, of twins, 38

García, Reyes, xvii, 11, 130n47
Geertz, Clifford, quoted, 116,
    163n140, 164nn160, 161
Gender, 31–33, 81, 83; and
    branches of Mountainway, 58;
    relationships, represented by
    twins, 31
Genealogy: of Abel's family, 27,
    149n140; records of Jemez
    families, 5–6
Genocide, cultural, 110, 161n115
Genres, between disciplines,
    116; literary, 110
Geography: of Horse Song, 94–
    95; of sacred places, 7, 11, 58
Ghosts, 152n206; exorcism of,
    134n16
Gila Monster, 92
Gill, Sam D., 128nn26, 31, 33,
    130nn45, 46, 135n44, 137n63,
    148n131, 151n175, 156n36;
    quoted, 8, 95, 104, 128n27
Girard, René, 140n12, 141n26;
    quoted, 42
Givens, Bettye, 165nn170, 172
Glishpah, of Beautyway. *See*
    Younger Sister
Goddard, Pliny Earl, 157n46